Antosha & Levitasha

Antosha & Levitasha

THE SHARED LIVES
AND ART OF
ANTON CHEKHOV
AND **ISAAC LEVITAN**

Serge Gregory

NIU PRESS, DEKALB IL

Northern Illinois University Press, DeKalb 60115
© 2015 by Northern Illinois University Press

24 23 22 21 20 19 18 17 16 15   1 2 3 4 5

978-0-87580-731-7 (paper)
978-1-60909-190-3 (ebook)

Book and cover design by Yuni Dorr

Library of Congress Cataloging-in-Publication Data
Gregory, Serge Vladimir, 1948-
Antosha and Levitasha : the shared lives and art of Anton Chekhov and Isaac Levitan /
Serge Gregory.
     pages   cm
Includes bibliographical references and index.
ISBN 978-0-87580-731-7 (paperback) — ISBN 978-1-60909-190-3 (ebook)
1. Chekhov, Anton Pavlovich, 1860-1904—Friends and associates. 2. Levitan, Isaak
Il'ich, 1860-1900—Friends and associates. 3. Authors—Russia—19th century—
Biography. 4. Painters—Russia—19th century—Biography. I. Title.
PG3458.G67 2015
891.72'3—dc23
[B]
2015035459

CONTENTS

ACKNOWLEDGMENTS

The writing of *Antosha and Levitasha* had an unusually long gestation period. In 1990, the *Moscow: Treasures and Traditions* exhibition, jointly organized by the Smithsonian Institution and the Soviet Ministry of Culture, opened in Seattle. As I walked through the exhibition of more than 230 pieces, I was suddenly transfixed by a single painting: Isaac Levitan's *Moonlit Night. The Big Road* (1897). My experience was not unlike that of Yulia Sergeevna in Anton Chekhov's story "Three Years" as she stood before a Levitan-like painting at a Moscow Itinerant exhibition. Previously a lazy observer, she suddenly finds the landscape motif to be intimately familiar and deeply moving. As I took a long look at Levitan's painting, the shadows cast by the row of trees along the road on a bright moonlit night struck me as both uncanny and resonant.

Coincidentally, around the same time, I was asked by the Slavic Languages and Literature Department at the University Washington to teach a course on Chekhov in their evening degree program. In preparing for the course, I regularly came across Levitan's name in connection with both Chekhov's life and some of his stories and plays. Over the ensuing years, I would think from time to time about the significance of the relationship between Chekhov and Levitan in the context of late nineteenth-century Russian literature and art, and about how, surprisingly, no one outside of Russia had written about it in any detail. I did sporadic research, but it wasn't until 2011 that I had the time and opportunity to devote myself full-time to the project.

In writing this, my first book, I have felt the encouraging presence of a lifetime of teachers, some now deceased, looking over my shoulder: Sylvia Wilkinson and David Clay Jenkins at the College of William & Mary; Keith Salter and Peter Scorer at the University of Exeter, England; Barry Scherr, James West, and Willis Konick at the University of Washington; Hans and Claire Rogger at UCLA; and Grigory Byaly at Leningrad (now St. Petersburg) State University, who was my adviser during my doctoral IREX-Fulbright academic year fellowship.

I would not have been able to start this project without the existence of the University of Washington Libraries' extensive Slavic collection, including its Special Collections holdings. Galya Diment and Katarzyna Dziwirek of the UW Slavic Languages and Literature Department were kind enough to provide me with letters of introduction that were crucial to gaining access to three Moscow archives: the Moscow State Archive for Literature and Art, the Manuscript Division of the Russian State Library, and the Tretyakov Gallery Archives. I am grateful to the staff of all three archives for their generous assistance. While in Moscow, I enjoyed the warm hospitality of the historians Nikita Sokolov and Tatiana Safronova. At Melikhovo, I spent an afternoon touring the house and grounds with Kseniya Tchaikovskaya, the chief curator of the Chekhov museum, who was delighted to learn that I was the great-grandson of Vladimir Semenkovich, owner of the estate at Vaskino and Chekhov's closest neighbor.

I'm indebted to the writer and Russian historian Douglas Smith for his advice on archival research, for providing contacts in Moscow, and for inspiring me to have the confidence to write this book as an independent scholar. Steven Zipperstein at Stanford University offered early encouragement as well. Mariana Markova transcribed Levitan's virtually illegible handwriting; Marilyn Love translated several of Lidia Yavorskaya's letters from the French. Carol Tobin, Natasha Suter, and Karen Gorman read early chapters and offered helpful comments. J. Douglas Clayton of the University of Ottawa provided a detailed evaluation of the entire manuscript, including numerous corrections, for which I'm most grateful. Seattle cardiologist James Willems, MD, brought to my attention the clinical connection between aortic aneurysms and tertiary syphilis, although the conclusions I make regarding Levitan's medical condition are solely my own.

I would like to thank Amy Farranto at Northern Illinois University Press for her unwavering support in nurturing this book toward publication. The meticulous work of copy editor Judith Robey under the guidance of Nathan Holmes at NIU Press saved me from numerous errors, infelicities, and inconsistencies. Any mistakes that remain are my own.

When writing a book, it is a commonplace to acknowledge the long-suffering patience of a spouse. This, however, does not describe my wife, Rachel Ben-Shmuel. Her curiosity and enthusiasm have been unflagging; her excitement in seeing Levitan's paintings in Moscow and St. Petersburg was infectious. She has been my first reader, my first editor. Over the past three years, we have enjoyed long, lively dinner conversations on every permutation of the relationship between Chekhov and Levitan. So, it is with gratitude and deep love that I dedicate this book to her.

AUTHOR'S NOTE

I have used a simplified Library of Congress transliteration of Russian names and places, for the most part using the following modifications: ий and ый—"y," ю—"yu," я—"ya," ё—"yo." The soft sign (ь) has been omitted. I have preferred the most common English spellings (for example, "Isaac" rather than "Isaak") over consistency. The footnotes and bibliography revert to the standard Library of Congress system.

In quoted material, a three-point ellipsis ". . ." is used when suspension points appeared in the original text. I will use bracketed ellipses "[. . .]" to indicate any text that I have omitted from a quotation.

Dates are according to the Russian calendar, which in the nineteenth century was twelve days behind the Western calendar.

Since both Chekhov and Levitan lived off the earnings from their art, it is helpful to have a sense of the value of the ruble at the end of the nineteenth century. At the time, both Russia and the United States were on the gold standard, so it's possible to peg the ruble at roughly two dollars in 1900. It's more difficult to give a sense of the buying power of one ruble. A 1902 travel guide provided the following cost estimates for St. Petersburg: hotel rooms ranged from two to ten rubles a night; lunch at a restaurant cost two to three rubles; an orchestra seat at the Mariinsky Theater cost about six rubles. Donald Rayfield wrote that by the time Chekhov felt he had a substantial enough income in 1892 to buy a small estate, he was making 1,000 rubles a month. That same year Pavel Tretyakov bought Levitan's *Deep Waters* for the unusually high price of 3,000 rubles. Most of Levitan's paintings sold in the 300 to 500 ruble range.

INTRODUCTION

AMONG THOSE FAMILIAR WITH Anton Chekhov's biography, his life-long friendship with the painter Isaac Levitan is well known. Outside of Russia, however, little has been written about Levitan's life and art. This fact has made it difficult for those interested in late nineteenth-century Russian culture to appreciate the significance of their friendship. This book fills the gap for Western readers by providing both a detailed portrait of that relationship and the first biography in English of Levitan, Russia's greatest landscape painter. In Russia, where entire rooms in the Tretyakov Gallery in Moscow and the Russian Museum in St. Petersburg are devoted to Levitan's paintings, the lives of the famous writer and the equally famous artist have long been tied together.

To those who have seen Levitan's paintings and read Chekhov's works, it is evident that Levitan's "landscapes of mood" have much in common with the way that Chekhov's characters perceive nature as a reflection of their emotional states. Alexei Fyodorov-Davydov, the preeminent Soviet scholar of Levitan, understood that both Chekhov and Levitan, unlike realist writers and painters, presented nature in their art using "immediate and sensual effect rather than detailed description and depiction."[1] While Levitan in his later paintings started to use some of the optical techniques seen in French impressionism, his practice of imbuing his paintings with a lyrical or spiritual narrative stamped his impressionism as distinctly Russian. Chekhov and Levitan nevertheless shared an aesthetic that was moving toward the more subjective sensibility of early modernism. Their contemporaries recognized this affinity. For example, in November 1903, as Chekhov and Konstantin Stanislavsky traded notes between Yalta and Moscow in preparation for the premiere production of *The Cherry Orchard*, Stanislavsky sought to allay any concerns Chekhov might have had regarding plans for the play's décor by reassuring him that its "general tone is Levitan-like."[2]

The Chekhov-Levitan relationship is as significant as and similar to another friendship between a writer and a painter of the same era—Émile Zola and Paul Cézanne. Zola and Cézanne were friends from childhood. But when Zola's novel L'Oeuvre (The Masterpiece), interpreted as an attack on impressionists and impressionism, came out in 1885–1886, Cézanne was so offended by it that he never spoke to Zola again.[3] When Chekhov's story "The Grasshopper" was published in 1892, it was widely seen as a caricature of Levitan and his married mistress Sophia Kuvshinnikova. Chekhov and Levitan quarreled, and the two men refused to see each other for almost three years. Once reconciled, however, they remained friends for the rest of their lives.

Levitan had a much greater influence on Chekhov's writing than Chekhov had on Levitan's painting. Levitan the artist inspired Chekhov to use landscape as a metaphor for the emotional state of his characters. Levitan the man served as a persona that Chekhov reshaped into several fictional characters, most notably in "The Grasshopper" and The Seagull. In contrast, Chekhov's influence on Levitan was more social. He gave Levitan his friendship, such as it was. The writer Ignaty Potapenko, one of the few friends other than Levitan whom Chekhov addressed in the intimate form of "you," came to the conclusion that Chekhov was so strongly inclined to stand back and observe those around him that he was incapable of committing to a real friendship.

Chekhov and his siblings also gave the orphaned Levitan a lively, intelligent family that welcomed him and took his manic-depressive mood swings in stride. Chekhov's sister Maria refused Levitan's marriage proposal but continued to love him, after a fashion, for the rest of her life. Early in their friendship Levitan spent his summers with the Chekhov family at their dacha, and later he was a frequent guest at Melikhovo, the small estate Chekhov bought in 1892. Most importantly, Chekhov introduced Levitan to his circle of artistic friends, and to several women over whom they became romantic rivals.

Donald Rayfield's biography of Chekhov, which was translated into Russian in 2005, was the first to publish some of the previously censored portions of Levitan's letters to Chekhov. While prudish Soviet scholars may have excised these fragments for being merely salacious, taken together Levitan's uncensored letters present a frank and clearer picture of the intimacy of his friendship with Chekhov. Not only do the letters reveal that Levitan and Chekhov saw each other as sexual competitors (sometimes in jest, sometimes in earnest), they also reflect an anxiety about frequenting brothels that lends credence to the possibility that Levitan's fatal heart disease was the result of tertiary syphilis, a diagnosis that the reticent Dr. Chekhov may have kept hidden from his friend.

One major obstacle confronts any attempt to definitively characterize the Chekhov-Levitan relationship. Although Russian archives contain fifty-five letters from Levitan to Chekhov (almost one-third of all of Levitan's extant letters), no letters from Chekhov to Levitan exist. As he lay on his deathbed, Levitan instructed his brother Adolph to burn all his correspondence in his presence. Adolph dutifully carried out his request. Levitan had no desire for a record of a lifetime of romantic entanglements to live on after him. Fortunately, Chekhov was meticulous in preserving his correspondence, and Maria Chekhova devoted her life after her brother's death in 1904 to retrieving, organizing, and publishing his letters. Among the 4,468 letters published in 12 volumes of the 1974–1983 *Complete Collected Works and Letters* of Chekhov, there are numerous references to Levitan. Not surprisingly, Chekhov was sometimes blunter in expressing his opinion of Levitan in a letter to an acquaintance than he likely would have been writing directly to Levitan. Unpublished letters that mention Levitan, sent by mutual friends to Chekhov and to each other, provide additional details about the Chekhov-Levitan relationship.

There is a rich body of memoir literature devoted to Chekhov and Levitan. For Levitan it begins with the recollections of his classmates and teachers at the Moscow School of Painting, Sculpture, and Architecture. Several of these individuals belong to the pantheon of great Russian painters of the late nineteenth and early twentieth centuries, most notably Konstantin Korovin, Vladimir Polenov, and Mikhail Nesterov. Kuvshinnikova, a painter in her own right who accompanied Levitan during his summer excursions into the Russian countryside from 1887 to 1894, left a memoir in 1907, the year of her death, that is an invaluable record of his life and paintings during some of his most productive years. Several students who attended Levitan's landscape course, which he taught at the School of Painting toward the end of his life, recalled his classes and field trips, providing a rare insight into his aesthetics and painting techniques. Levitan himself never published any writings about his art other than indirectly, in a brief obituary for his own mentor at the School of Painting, Alexei Savrasov.

Recollections of their brother's friendship with Levitan and the interwoven lives of their mutual friends are found in the memoirs of Maria and Mikhail Chekhov, although both were careful to create a sanitized image of Anton. Among those friends the writer Tatiana Shchepkina-Kupernik left the most extensive memoir of the two men. She witnessed the reconciliation between Chekhov and Levitan and was present as a houseguest in the summer of 1894 when Levitan's long-standing affair with Kuvshinnikova came to a stormy end.

Soon after Levitan's death in 1900, Sergei Gloushev, a physician, art critic, and collector who knew the painter well, began preparing material for a biography. In 1913, together with the painter Igor Grabar, he published the first life of Levitan. In 1956 and 1966, Fyodorov-Davydov served as the general editor of two volumes of letters, memoirs, documents, a chronology, and a *catalogue raisonné* devoted to Levitan. He followed this up in 1976 with the handsomely printed and illustrated, large format *Isaac Ilich Levitan: His Life and Work, 1860–1900*. Recent works that build on Fyodorov-Davydov's foundational scholarship, without the ideological shackles he labored under in the Soviet era, include the catalogue produced by the Tretyakov Gallery to accompany its 2010 exhibition celebrating the 150th anniversary of Levitan's birth, and art historian Vladimir Kruglov's 2012 contribution on Levitan for the series "Russian Artists. Nineteenth Century" (produced by Golden Age Publishers of St. Petersburg).

During the Soviet period several popular biographies of Levitan were published, all with chapters on Chekhov, some annoyingly fictionalized. Among the most credible was Sophia Prorokova's *Levitan*, first published in 1960. Filled with revelatory anecdotes, it has an undogmatic tone free of the hagiography typical of Russian portraits of their cultural icons. Evgraf Konchin modeled his *Levitan Mysteries* (*Zagadochnyi Levitan*, Moscow, 2010) in the spirit of Prorokova's biography, although neither Konchin nor Prorokova adhered to scholarly standards. Konchin's work comprises a series of vignettes that result from years of investigating the provenance of Levitan's works and the fate of his missing paintings and sketches. Along the way, he offers lively portraits of those who knew Levitan and collected his art.

In 2011, Yulia Korolyova published in Moscow the first book devoted to the Chekhov-Levitan friendship: *Soprikosnovenie sudeb: A. P. Chekhov i I. I. Levitan* (Contiguous Fates: A. P. Chekhov and I. I. Levitan). Korolyova states in her introduction that she explicitly chose to focus only on the biographical connections between the two men:

> Many literary and art critics have observed that Chekhov and Levitan's friendship was a unique phenomenon. But at the same time, they have noted that this topic still awaits its researchers, that it is extremely broad, even overwhelming. The goal of this work is not so much a search for the answer to questions about the interrelationships of the writer and the artist, as much as an attempt to trace the parallels of their lives and creative journeys.[4]

In the pages that follow, I have taken a deeper look at those interrelationships.

The only book-length Western study of Levitan is Averil King's *Isaak Levitan: Lyrical Landscape*, which has been published in several editions. King is a sensitive interpreter of Levitan's paintings and, as an expert in nineteenth-century

European art, convincingly places Levitan's work in the context of his Russian and Western contemporaries. She devotes a chapter to Chekhov. However, King was unable to take advantage of Russian primary and secondary sources, relying mostly on works published in English.

I have touched on Chekhov's biography only to the extent necessary to elucidate his friendship with Levitan; Rayfield's biography is considered the definitive work on Chekhov's life. To redress an imbalance in what has been written about the Chekhov-Levitan relationship, I have chosen to focus on Levitan's life and work. Inescapably, to write about Chekhov and Levitan is also to offer a portrait of Moscow cultural life at the end of the nineteenth century. Together, the two men knew virtually every prominent writer, artist, actor, singer, musician, and impresario in the city. Yet, both men came from humble origins, a reflection of the opportunities that flowered for artists of all backgrounds in prerevolutionary Russia. Chekhov's father was born a serf; Levitan's father was the son of a rabbi confined to the Russian Pale of Settlement. Russia's own Gilded Age of wealthy patrons made it possible for them both to earn a living using their artistic talents and to achieve fame in their brief lifetimes.

1

1860–1885

MOSCOW SCHOOL OF PAINTING, SCULPTURE, AND ARCHITECTURE

ON MAY 6, 1885 ANTON CHEKHOV left Moscow with his mother and sister, Maria, for a rented dacha at Babkino, a country estate about forty miles away. The short journey turned out to be an ordeal. At the end of the rail line at Voskresensk, Chekhov hired two peasants with a cart who drove them along at an excruciatingly slow pace. He walked alongside the cart most of the way. By the time they reached the Istra River, night had fallen. Chekhov blindly stumbled into the water. He forded the river with the cart, while the women, shrieking in the dark, were carried across by boat. On the other side in the estate woods, a brake rod on the cart snapped. They sat and waited while the coachmen fixed it, and finally arrived at the dacha at one in the morning.

They unlocked the door and were pleasantly surprised at what unfolded before their eyes as they went about the house lighting the lamps: spacious rooms, comfortable furniture, and a cozy ambiance that far exceeded their expectations. Chekhov unpacked his suitcases, sat in front of the large square window in his room, had a shot of vodka and a bit to eat, and listened to the singing of a nightingale. In the morning he set out to place one of the fish traps he had brought from Moscow and carefully tied to the back of the cart. As he was lowering the trap into the river, he heard a voice shout out, "Crocodile!" He looked up and saw Isaac Levitan calling out to him from the other side of the river.[1]

~

Chekhov had first met Levitan several years earlier, soon after coming to Moscow in August 1879 to start medical school. Levitan and Chekhov's brother

Nikolai were fellow students at the Moscow School of Painting, Sculpture, and Architecture. Maria Chekhova, who also met Levitan through Nikolai, later recalled how strange it was that she knew nothing about the painter's early years: "Isaac Ilich never said anything about his family and his childhood. It appeared as if he never had a father or mother. At times it seemed to me that he wanted to completely forget about their existence. All he ever said was that he was very poor as a child."[2] What little we know about Levitan's childhood comes primarily from a 1908 interview with Levitan's sister Tereza after her brother's death. But even this account was rather thin—Levitan's mother remained unnamed and lost to memory.[3]

Isaac Levitan was born on August 30, 1860, in Kibarta, in what is now Lithuania. It was a railroad town near the Prussian border in the Pale of Settlement, within which Russian Jews were legally confined. His father, Ilya Levitan, came from a rabbinical family. However, after studying at a yeshiva, Ilya, influenced by the secularism of the Jewish Enlightenment, went on to master French and German. In Kovno (now Kaunas), he gave language lessons and then became a translator for a French firm contracted to build a railway bridge across the Neman River. This position did not last long and was followed by a succession of postings with the railway. He worked as a cashier at the Kovno station but soon was transferred to the Kibarta station sixty miles away, where Isaac was born. Ilya was sent back to Kovno, this time as the station comptroller. His family, now with two boys and two girls, had barely settled in before they had to move again.

At this point, in the early 1870s, Ilya made the fateful decision to quit his job, send his family back to Kovno, and go on to Moscow alone to seek better paying work more suited to his talents. He missed his children and soon brought the family to Moscow. But the only work he had found was giving lessons to wealthy Jewish households, and the pittance he earned was not enough to support his family.

There is no record of whether Ilya obtained any temporary legal right to live in Moscow. The reign of Alexander II was marked by policies permitting selective settlement of certain categories of Jews outside the Pale: merchants, bankers, distinguished veterans, and artisans. But Ilya belonged to none of those groups. He may possibly have bribed officials to register him as an artisan.[4]

Plunged into poverty and misery, the family lived in a small apartment on the fourth floor of a bleak merchant building on Solyanka Street. Ilya taught the children himself, but in 1871 he enrolled his oldest son, twelve-year-old Avel, in the Moscow School of Painting. The school was located in an imposing, three-story neoclassical building with a curved facade looking out onto Myasnitskaya Street. The ornate interior featured a grand staircase lined with classical sculptures

leading to hallways and classrooms that also served as exhibition spaces. Original paintings and copies of European masters hung on the walls.

The School was founded in 1833 as the Moscow Art Society, which offered
informal classes and exhibitions under the patronage of the city's governor
general Dmitri Golitsyn. In 1843 Nicholas I brought the Society under state
supervision (although it continued to be privately funded) by allowing it to
reorganize as a sanctioned school. His intent was to keep the School on an
inferior and subservient footing with respect to the St. Petersburg Imperial
Academy of Fine Arts. Catherine the Great had founded the Academy, taking
as her inspiration the French Academy of Fine Arts. Under Nicholas I, the
Academy became an instrument of his autocratic reign; its closely supervised
artists became civil servants trained to paint court-commissioned work. Even
after Nicholas's death and the reforms under Alexander II, the School was
refused an independent charter and remained under Academy supervision.[5]
However, in 1865 it was finally allowed to award the silver medal and the title
of classed artist to graduating students who passed their final examinations.
This honor provided the recipient with the benefits of a civil service rank and
the qualifications necessary to teach painting.

The School admitted students on the basis of a portfolio, without requiring
a secondary school diploma. To make up for their presumed deficiencies,
students were offered a general curriculum of not particularly rigorous courses
in Russian history, Russian language, anatomy, and mathematics in addition
to art classes. It also opened its doors to students regardless of their family
finances. Several times the School lent material support to Avel (who now
used the name Adolph) in view of his extreme poverty and artistic promise.
Vasily Perov, who taught the nature class starting in 1871 and was himself a
graduate of the School, recalled his first days as a student:

> We all came together, arriving virtually the same day, not only from the various
> corners and back alleys of Moscow, but without exaggeration, from all corners
> of our great and diverse Russia. Our students were from everywhere! They
> came from cold, distant Siberia, from the warm Crimea and Astrakhan, from
> Poland, the Don, from the Solovetsky Islands and Mount Athos, even from
> Constantinople. My God, what a rich and diverse crowd was gathered within
> the walls of the school![6]

Many of the faculty members had been among the founders of the Itinerants, a
secessionist group that broke away from the Academy in 1863. These fourteen
artists had refused to participate in the graduation gold medal competition,
rebelling against the long-held requirement of painting an assigned subject

(in this case, *The Entrance of Odin into Valhalla*) that had nothing to do with Russia or the present-day world. Their actions were inspired by the general impulse among educated Russians to throw off the remnants of Nicholas I's oppressive rule in the wake of Alexander II's emancipation of the serfs. In the spirit of the 1860s communes, the secessionists formed an artists' cooperative. Then in 1870 they founded the Association of Itinerant Art Exhibitions with the combined goals of promoting new art that was free from autocratic control and generating earnings from admission fees and the sale of paintings. Among the founding Itinerants at the School was Alexei Savrasov, who taught the landscape studio class.

The Itinerants were associated with the emergence of narrative paintings (the most famous of which is Ilya Repin's *The Volga Boatmen*) that cast a critical eye on Russian society. But from the beginning, the Itinerants also included among their ranks a substantial number of landscape painters. Almost half of the forty-six paintings at the first Itinerant exhibition in St. Petersburg in 1871 were landscapes, including Savrasov's masterpiece *The Rooks Have Come*. The landscapes did not always appeal to liberal critics, but they sold well and met the public's desire for paintings that found beauty in the Russian countryside.[7] The School's faculty reflected these two conflicting streams, with those advocating critical realism outnumbering those drawn to lyrical landscapes, but both camps in agreement on the School's implicit mission to champion a truly Russian national art that was distinctly Muscovite. The vast majority of students were there to learn to become genre painters and depict historical and religious subjects as well as scenes of everyday life. A significant contingent, mostly from poor families, went on to make a living painting church frescoes. Of the 179 students enrolled in 1872–1873, only twelve attended Savrasov's landscape class.[8]

In 1873 Isaac, at age thirteen, followed his brother and enrolled in the School, which had now grown to 228 students. He started in the "originals" class, where students painted copies of original works. The next year he transferred to the "head" class, where they drew from plaster classical heads and live models, and in the following year (1875) he began the "figures" class. Even in his first few years of school, his teachers and classmates recognized his unusual talent. It began with an award of paints and brushes from the teachers' union, but soon he was receiving periodic stipends and support from an anonymous donor. By the end of 1876, the School's governing body, the council of the Moscow Art Society, in response to a petition from the teachers' union, freed Levitan from paying his annual tuition "in view of his extreme poverty and in recognition of his great success in art."[9] The painter Mikhail Nesterov, who entered the School in 1877 and became a life-long friend, recalled that "all kinds of half-fantastic stories had traveled around" about Levitan's "great gifts and great needs."[10]

Levitan's mother died in 1875. In early 1877 both father and son came down with typhoid fever. Isaac was isolated from his father and admitted to a clinic. Only when he recovered did he learn that his father had died. Now the four children were orphaned and went their separate ways. Tereza married an unsuccessful merchant. The boys were homeless and depended on friends and strangers to put them up. Regularly after evening classes, Levitan would vanish unnoticed and hide in the top story of the School, waiting until the enormous building was empty and the night watchman Zemliankin made his final rounds, and then seeking out a warm spot where he could spend the night. Several times Zemliankin found him hiding, took pity on the young man, and made a bed for him across two sawhorses next to his room. Similarly, the Moiseivich family, who set up a food stand every day on a counter in front of the cloakroom, would extend credit to Levitan, whose diet often consisted of rye bread, sausage, and a glass of milk for both lunch and dinner.[11]

Among the eleven new students admitted to the School in August 1875 was Nikolai Chekhov. He had come to Moscow with his brother Alexander, who was enrolled in the university, while the rest of the family remained in Taganrog, a southern town on the Azov Sea. Nikolai's father, Pavel, who disapproved of his son's "scribblings," had initially insisted that he apply to the Academy, but since Nikolai had dropped out of the local gymnasium after completing only five of the eight classes, he could not meet the eligibility requirements. Pavel hoped that Nikolai would eventually transfer to the School's architecture department to pursue what he considered a more worthy profession.[12]

Nikolai Chekhov became acquainted with the Levitan brothers soon after starting classes at the School. He said little about the School or his fellow students in his letters home; he quickly became an indifferent student, often skipping classes, seduced by the bohemian attractions of Moscow taverns and brothels. In the fall of 1879, Isaac Levitan showed Nikolai a painting he had been working on: *Autumn Day. Sokolniki*. It depicted a wide path gently curving through Sokolniki Park, a favorite haunt for landscape art students on the outskirts of the city. Nikolai convinced Levitan that the painting was insufficiently expressive, that the path was waiting for someone to inhabit it. So Nikolai added a woman walking pensively in a black dress. Such collaborations were quite common especially between genre and landscape painters. In 1883 Nikolai asked Levitan to draw the sky in his painting *Messalina's Entry into Rome*.

Autumn Day. Sokolniki was one of four Levitan paintings included in the second annual student exhibition at the end of 1879. The Moscow Society of Art

Lovers awarded him a prize of eighty rubles. In January, when the exhibition closed, Pavel Tretyakov bought the painting for one hundred rubles, the first purchase of a Levitan painting by the wealthy merchant and art patron who would go on to buy twenty more Levitan paintings over his lifetime. Earlier in the century, private art collections were primarily the domain of St. Petersburg aristocrats who, influenced by the Hermitage collection, traveled abroad and returned with works by European masters. But by now industrialization had turned Moscow, a city with a population of one million, into a robust economic engine, enriching an entrepreneurial class, many of whom, like Tretyakov, came from Old Believer families. These déclassé philanthropists were steeped in Old Russian culture and values. While Tretyakov started his collection with works by Dutch masters, he soon turned his attention to acquiring the paintings of contemporary Russian painters. He publicly displayed the works in his house, which had to be renovated several times to contain his expanding collection. Tretyakov was amassing the largest private collection of national art in Russia, and in the process underwriting the success of the Itinerant movement.[13]

Given their radically different personalities, artistic interests, and levels of commitment to the School and its teachers, Nikolai Chekhov and Isaac Levitan were unlikely friends. No one at first glance could fail to notice Levitan's curly mane of hair and attractive, exotic features (including his large black eyes). Nesterov described him as an Italian beauty, handsome and graceful, "resembling those Italian boys with a scarlet flower in their curly hair who come out to greet the foreigners at Naples' old Santa Lucia or on the squares in Florence somewhere near Santa Maria Novella."[14] Another classmate, Alexander Golovin, described him as "an aristocrat from head to toe in the best sense of the word. Externally he didn't look to me like a Jew, but more like an Arab."[15] Levitan reveled in the ease with which he could cast a spell on women. His classmate Zakhar Pichugin recalled with irritation an incident when Levitan dropped by while he was quietly having tea with a model. Levitan began to flirt with her shamelessly. The woman became embarrassed and Pichugin protested to Levitan that this was not what friends do to each other. Levitan responded, "But I'm not a monk!"[16]

In contrast to the uniforms required at the Academy, the School had a tradition of scruffy attire (no ties or starched shirts) even among students who could afford to dress well. Levitan, on the other hand, self-conscious about being seen as a poor Jew in worn-out clothes, dressed as stylishly as he could manage. When he came to class one day wearing a white tie, the teacher, Sorokin, said to him, "What's that? Are you going to a wedding? Take it off, or you'll be in trouble."[17]

Equally striking were Levitan's natural talents and work ethic, which prompted as much attention (and envy) from his classmates as his good looks. Nesterov said that everything came easily to Levitan: "He came to our life class and painted a nude sketch not required for those taking the landscape class, painted it in his own way in two or three days although it wasn't due for a month. In general he quickly mastered that which took others a long time."[18] Once in Savrasov's studio class, Levitan went up to Sergei Korovin and, despite being younger than Korovin, started to lecture him on the importance of finding a dominant motif for his painting. Oblivious to the stern look that Korovin was giving him, Levitan resolutely continued his self-confident assertions.[19] But Levitan was just as demanding of himself as he was of others. He showed Vasily Baksheev a landscape that he was working on of a field covered in flowers under bright sunlight. "Here's what I can't figure out," he said to Baksheev. "It's bright sunshine but there are no shadows, and it's hard to convey sunlight without shadows." When Levitan came to the conclusion that he could not get the effect he wanted, he destroyed the painting. Another time Levitan showed Baksheev two canvases, both of which depicted the same landscape from exactly the same perspective. Working on both paintings at the same time, he transferred whatever effect worked on one to the other. This method allowed him to continuously improve his work without losing any of the discoveries he made along the way.[20]

Nikolai Chekhov made a totally different impression on people. His brothers called him "Crooked-Snout" and "Cross-Eyed Raisin" because of his lopsided features and tendency to screw up his eyes comically when focusing on something. Soon after arriving in Moscow, he wrote to his parents of his grandiose plans to attend both the School and Moscow University, while his brother Alexander complained that Nikolai had lost his way, was wasting his time, and drawing pictures only to throw them away unseen.[21] Desperately poor like Levitan, Nikolai scraped by with earnings from teaching calligraphy and drawing while also selling illustrations to periodicals, most successfully to the Moscow weekly *The Spectator*. At least until the early 1880s Levitan was wholly committed to the School, which recognized his promise through stipends, awards, and exhibitions. He stood proudly—handsome and long-haired—in the middle of a group photograph of young artists participating in the School's first student exhibition at the end of 1878. His exhibited painting, *View of the Simonov Monastery* (now lost), received favorable reviews in two Moscow newspapers. The School's opinion of Levitan as an artist and its financial support had a profound emotional impact on him. Nikolai's attitude toward the School was one of indifference. His poorly received *Prayer at the Grave* did hang at the third student exhibition in 1880, but by the end of 1883 he had turned his back on the School and exasperated his publishers by spending much of his time with other habitués of the seedy dives he frequented. He vanished for days on end, often leaving family and friends in the dark as to his whereabouts.

In St. Petersburg on April 2, 1879, Alexander Soloviev, a member of the radical group "Land and Freedom" (but acting without its approval), fired five shots at Alexander II while the tsar took his customary morning walk on the grounds of the Winter Palace. All five shots missed, but this was not the first attempt on the tsar's life, and government officials feared the rise of urban radicals. Soloviev was summarily tried and hanged on May 28. That same month, the assassination attempt prompted an order to expel all Jews from Moscow, although no Jews were implicated in the plot. Isaac and Adolph Levitan were forced to leave the city and move in with their sister Tereza and her husband, Pyotr Berchansky, at a dacha near the Saltykovka train stop, about ten miles outside of Moscow. The family struggled with poverty, and Levitan went about in a single old red shirt, worn-out pants, and shoes without socks.

Yet it was not entirely a curse for a landscape painter to spend the summer wandering the countryside, studying every lane and alley, sitting in a boat on a lake making sketches. Hiding from the rain on the empty station platform during a downpour, he was inspired to paint *Evening after a Rain* (now lost except for some preliminary sketches). The painting depicts a train approaching the platform at dusk, the steam engine throwing off shafts of light from its lanterns, the rails and platform glistening after the rain, and puddles reflecting the light. Levitan was so pleased with the piece that he sent his brother-in-law into Moscow to sell it for him. The painting fetched forty rubles.[22] By the end of September, Levitan was allowed to return to Moscow so that the office of the city's governor general, Prince Dolgorukov, could bestow upon him a stipend that he continued to receive until he left the School. Levitan used the money from the sale of the painting to rent a furnished apartment on Bolshaya Lubyanska Street.

While Levitan lived in exile outside of the city, Anton Chekhov arrived in Moscow from Taganrog with his younger brother Ivan on August 8, 1879, to begin his medical studies. By then the rest of the Chekhov family was already living in Moscow. Their father, bankrupt and trying to escape his creditors, had gone there in April 1876, and their mother and siblings Maria and Mikhail had followed. Soon after arriving in Moscow, Anton sought to help the family finances by submitting humorous sketches to the Moscow weeklies where Alexander and Nikolai already had established connections, particularly at *The Alarm Clock* and *The Spectator*. Initially he had little success in placing stories; Nikolai, despite his dissolute ways, was bringing in far more money for the family. But Anton soon joined Moscow's demimonde of hack writers. He began a relationship with Natalia Golden, whose sister Anna, *The Spectator's* secretary, became Nikolai's common-law wife. Through his collaborations with Nikolai on illustrated parodies of Moscow nightlife, Anton started to make a name for himself as the writer-satirist "Antosha Chekhonte." However much Nikolai's behavior annoyed him, Anton still respected his brother's native talents. In mid-1882 they worked together to prepare an illustrated edition of Anton's sketches called *Mischief*, but the book failed to get past the censors. The brothers made other kinds of mischief together as well and were no strangers to Moscow's brothel district. This underworld is reflected in Chekhov's story "The Seizure" (1888), the plot of which sounds like a joke told in a tavern: a medical student, an art student (from the School of Painting), and a law student decide to make a night of visiting the city's brothels. The art student shares some of Nikolai's characteristics—he is voluble and quick to get drunk. It is the law student who has the nervous breakdown of the story's title when he realizes that he cannot single-handedly save the fallen women of the world from their miserable fates.

Most likely Chekhov and Levitan met sometime in the early 1880s within a common circle of students and artists. Starting in 1882, the Chekhov and Levitan brothers all worked together for several short-lived illustrated magazines published by Ivan Klung, who previously had been a lithographer for *The Alarm Clock*. Levitan published twelve lithographs and Anton Chekhov published five stories that year in Klung's magazine *Moscow*.

In 1883 Levitan and Nikolai Chekhov found themselves living in the same squalid Eastern Apartments on Sadovaya-Spasskaya Street. This is where the twenty-year-old Maria Chekhova remembered dropping by Nikolai's apartment and seeing a handsome, dark-haired young man "with Eastern features and large, expressive eyes." Nikolai made the introductions. Acting surprised and with a characteristic flirtatious manner, Levitan held out both his hands and said, "My God, Marie! You are already a grown lady!" Maria was flattered by his attentions. She also noticed his peculiar speech, a typical "Jewish lisp," although she did not describe it as such: he gutturally swallowed the letter "r" in the French style and said "f" instead of "sh." When he came to know her well, he always called her "Mafa" instead of Masha.[23] Maria recalled that Levitan and Anton quickly became friends. The painter visited the Chekhovs often and grew close to the family. The journalist Vladimir Gilyarovsky, a mutual acquaintance, said that it was fortunate for Levitan that from a young age he was accepted into the Chekhov family: "Levitan was poor, but he tried as much as possible to dress nicely so as to fit into the Chekhov circle, which at that time was also poor, but also talented and jolly."[24]

Chekhov could see that Levitan, unlike many of his fellow students, actually spent most of his time painting. Nikolai's lack of focus and direction were a source of constant irritation for Anton and colored his general attitude toward art students. In 1882, in his humorous sketch of Nogtev in "A Nasty Story," Chekhov published his first satirical portrait of the kind of poseur he found among Nikolai's painter friends. Nogtev may have some of the external attributes of Levitan—he's a handsome, long-haired dandy with passionate Georgian eyes that rest on women with a devouring gaze—but with that the similarity ends: "He never paints anything, but he's an artist. [. . .] Sort of nice but dumb as a goose. He has a noble father and a noble mother as well, and a rich grandmother."[25]

By 1883 Anton was contributing both stories and a regular column on Moscow to the St. Petersburg weekly *Fragments*, having been taken under the wing of its demanding but supportive editor, Nikolai Leikin. For his September 24 "Fragments of Moscow Life" column, Chekhov wrote a sketch on the Moscow School of Painting on the occasion of its fiftieth anniversary. Hiding behind a pseudonym and the persona of a social satirist gave him the freedom to mock the faculty, including a chaste school inspector who in examining the classical sculptures arrayed in the hallways "became indignant at the Olympic gods because they didn't wear trousers and a jacket" and who "carried out a disgraceful operation on all the School's statues that wouldn't have occurred to even Savonarola himself." But Chekhov mostly chided the students themselves: "They draw, don't care about the sciences, sinfully love to drink schnapps, don't cut their hair, don't get any farther in anatomy than the neck bones . . . in general, they're nice folks. But they do have a specific feature that distinguishes them from other students: they quickly flower and quickly fade [. . .]. Not long ago everyone was talking about the creators of *Messalina, The Dnieper Rapids* and so forth, and where are these creators now? Where are Ellert, Yanov, Levitan *et tutti quanti*?"[26] He chastised the School's young artists with a broad brush and a lack of prescience. *Messalina* refers to his brother's *Messalina's Entry into Rome*. Nikolai Ellert became a landscape painter and a member of the Itinerant movement whose work is still collected today. Alexander Yanov became a stage designer who worked with Levitan on Savva Mamontov's private operas; Yanov and his sisters (whom Anton treated for typhus) became friends with the Chekhov family. Chekhov's portrait of the art students reflected the dismissive attitude of a medical student for those less grounded in science and the practical world.

By now Levitan was completely under the sway of Savrasov. Already in his late forties, Savrasov had evolved significantly as a landscape painter. Initially inspired by the pastoral romanticism of John Constable (Savrasov traveled to London and the Continent in 1862), he eventually developed a more realistic, often narrative, yet still poetic style that captured the simple, everyday beauty of the Russian countryside. The genre painting students talked of a mysterious aura emanating from Savrasov's studio classroom where "sacred ceremonies" were being performed. Levitan and Konstantin Korovin (Sergei's brother) were the "Don Quixotes" of the landscape group, setting out to do great work.[27] Levitan and Korovin were both recognized as preternaturally gifted, but there the similarity ended. Where Levitan was dark and earnest, Korovin was light and mischievous. Korovin struck Nesterov as a chameleon, sometimes diligent, sometimes lazy, sometimes charming, sometimes unbearable.[28] Levitan and Korovin became life-long rivals.

Savrasov was tall and powerfully built, but his face and brown eyes radiated warmth like that of a kindly doctor. He loved his students and they returned his affection. There was something otherworldly about him. In contrast to the other strict instructors in the School, who instilled fear, Savrasov told his students that they already understood everything they needed to know; it only remained for them to open their eyes and give expression to their feelings. With the coming of spring, he took his students out into the countryside and had them sketch the melting snow and budding trees. There was still something audacious about having students learn to paint *en plein air*, since only within the past two decades had it become acceptable to consider the Russian countryside as a suitable subject for landscape painting. At first even those landscapes tended to be conceived and executed in a studio, and romanticized in a way that lacked verisimilitude. The Academy, reflecting the patronage and tastes of the Russian court, continued to send painters to France, Italy, and Switzerland to capture the dramatic landscapes of the south of Europe. In comparison, the geography of northern Russia was generally considered far too unimpressive to be a worthy subject. Savrasov himself had spent five years painting the Swiss Alps. Yet many Russian painters, Savrasov included, eventually felt alienated by the foreign landscapes and longed to return home to find a way to paint their native Russia.[29] Among the European paintings that most helped guide Savrasov toward a Russian way of depicting landscapes were the gentle pastorals of the Barbizon School, especially the work of Jean-Baptiste Camille Corot.

Levitan learned about Corot from Savrasov and was especially inspired by the tonal qualities of his teacher's landscapes and by his ability to create a pensive mood in the subdued light of a late afternoon. Savrasov taught Levitan to look at nature with great concentration, with attention to detail, but also to bring his emotions into the work. Levitan, in turn, began to lecture his fellow students with the passion of an acolyte that a landscape painting needed to have not just a literal truth but a poetic truth as well—in its tone, its colors, and its mood. And for Levitan the mood evoked by a painting was often one of sadness. Korovin said that Levitan described the sadness emanating from nature as a kind of reproach, because the artist is transient and his work is imperfect. "No matter how you paint," Levitan told him, "nature will always do it better."[30] A "truthful" artistic representation conveyed a sense of inadequacy, even failure. It is tempting to exaggerate Levitan's lyrical gloom since his subjects often were autumnal or captured at twilight. But his early work also celebrated the radiance of natural light in other seasons or at other times of day, for example in *Sunny Day. Spring* (1876–1877), *Birch Grove* (1878), and most strikingly in *First Verdure. May* (1883).

Continuing to recognize Levitan's talents, the School in 1881 offered him funding to make a trip to the Volga region. But his sister Tereza came down with tuberculosis, and her doctors recommended that he find a place for her to live in the country. To repay her for supporting him when they were banished to Saltykovka, Levitan turned down the School's offer. Instead he rented a dacha for both of them in Ostankino, a village on the outskirts of Moscow where Korovin was spending the summer and where he would return the next two summers. Levitan's Ostankino paintings, with their black and rust colors, look very similar to Savrasov's landscapes.

When classes resumed in the fall of 1881, the students noticed that Savrasov was frequently absent from his studio. The School said he was ill. One day his students were gathered in his studio, showing each other the work that they had done in the summer. To their delight Savrasov appeared, but he was much changed. He had a troubled and bitter expression. He was thinner and grayer; his attire was strange: worn-out shoes that looked like filthy slippers, a black smock tied with a belt, a torn and dirty wide-brimmed hat. "Well, yes" he said, smiling strangely, "I haven't been here for a while, for a long time. I've been sick."[31]

Korovin found out from a soldier who regularly cleaned the studio that Savrasov had been drinking heavily over the summer. His wife had left him, taking their two daughters with her. Eventually he stopped coming to the studio. In March 1882, walking home from the School, Korovin bumped into Savrasov, who insisted that they go to a local coachmen's tavern. There his pitiful state became apparent. Everyone stared at Savrasov's threadbare clothes; his hand shook as he raised his vodka glass to his lips. Korovin, seeing the terror in his teacher's eyes, asked him to stop drinking, but Savrasov told him to shut up and went back toward the bar, falling before he got there.

Korovin helped him up. As they parted, Savrasov asked him not to be angry and promised to visit him when he felt better. "You need to understand that I have come to love sorrow, to love humiliation."[32] In the spring of 1882 Savrasov was dismissed from the School for chronic alcoholism. Korovin and Levitan were left without a mentor.

Levitan's dependence on the School was coming to an end. He spent more time painting *en plein air* outside the city and working with fierce concentration back in his apartment. In October 1882 Levitan requested permission to take his final exams in his general classes with the intention of applying in January to the Academy. With Savrasov gone, he felt that there was no one left at the School to study with. But he soon dropped this plan. Several factors led to his change of heart. First of all, Korovin returned disillusioned from taking a nature class at the Academy, where he had found the atmosphere of phony gravitas stultifying. Nesterov, too, had briefly transferred to the Academy only to return. Most significantly, in the fall the renowned Itinerant landscape painter Vasily Polenov took over Savrasov's classes at the School.[33] Polenov put his own unique stamp on the landscape classes he taught and talked about paints, coloring, impressionism, the Barbizon School, all that was new in Western art. "In a word," recalled Korovin, "everything we had heard little or nothing about." Polenov immediately started to pay a great deal of attention to Levitan and Korovin, but within a year Polenov had left on an extended trip to southern Europe and was unavailable to help Levitan complete his degree.

We know little about the nature or extent of Levitan's friendship with Chekhov in the early 1880s. Practically the only sources are Korovin's impressionistic sketches, first published in Parisian émigré newspapers in the 1930s. Gathered together, the sketches repeat certain events, observations, and descriptions like a set of musical themes and variations. He tells of one early encounter in the spring of 1883 when he accompanied Levitan to the latter's rooms at the Eastern Apartments. Levitan suggested to Korovin that they drop in on "Antosha," whom Korovin mistakenly recalled as also living in the same building. Actually, Nikolai Chekhov lived there, but Anton was known to stay there, especially when he needed to escape his hectoring father or, in this case, find a quiet place to study for his medical exams. Also in the room were several other medical students, talking heatedly, drinking tea and beer, and eating sausages.

The group decided to join Levitan and Korovin on a walk through Sokolniki Park. Along the way the medical students began to berate Chekhov for his lack of political engagement. One student asked, "You say you're a man without convictions. How is it possible to write a work without an idea? Are you without ideas?"

Chekhov answered, "No, neither ideas nor convictions."

Playing along, Levitan said that he too did not have any sort of ideas: "Is it possible for me to be an artist?"

"Impossible," said one of the students. "A man can't be without ideas."

"So, what should I do? Give it up?"

"Give it up."

Chekhov laughed, saying that Levitan would never be able to give up his painting.

Levitan asked what sort of an "idea" it is if he just wants to paint pines in the sun. The student taunted him, saying a pine tree was just a product. "Wood is the people's property. Nature creates it for the people."

Disgusted with the drift of the conversation, Levitan responded, "I can't think that way." Later, on the way back home, Chekhov made a very Levitan-like comment to Korovin: "There is some kind of sadness in spring. A deep sadness and unease. Everything is alive, but despite the life of nature, there is an incomprehensible sorrow in it." After they parted with the students, Chekhov turned to Levitan and Korovin: "These students will be fine doctors. They're good people. I envy them that their heads are filled with ideas."[34]

Writing about this encounter almost fifty years later, Korovin used creative license and descriptive shorthand in fleshing out the personalities of the two friends. But the passage gives us a sense of what attracted Chekhov and Levitan to each other. Both found themselves at odds with the prevailing notions of political engagement and didacticism in art. As critics began to take notice of Chekhov, they were "confounded by the absence of any kind of ideological freight in his work."[35] Levitan's refusal to consider making narrative paintings that expressed a political or social "idea" put him at odds with the dominant aesthetic of the Itinerant movement. Korovin said that the Itinerant teacher Pryanishnikov disdainfully called Levitan's *Autumn Day. Sokolniki* nothing but "colorful trousers."[36] However, in the early 1880s Chekhov, unlike Levitan, did not yet take himself seriously as an artist. He was a witty feuilletonist, who for eight kopecks a line gave the public what it wanted. He was sufficiently well-read to be able to parody a variety of writers and genres, but he did not think of himself as an artist seeking his place within a great tradition. The two men also had decidedly different personalities: Chekhov was always ironic and diffident, Levitan highly emotional and quick to take offense.

Yet there was a bond between them. In another of Korovin's anecdotes, he and Levitan went hunting outside of Moscow—Korovin claimed to have introduced his classmate to the sport, which became a passion for Levitan. They noticed a group of schoolboys taking an interest in them. Levitan said, "See. They are looking at us. Because we are hunters! If they knew that we were painters, they wouldn't want to know us." Korovin asked why this was so. "It's just the way it is. I'm telling you the truth. We're not needed. They don't understand us. I don't know what to say to them. When my sister says, 'Why do you paint a gray day or a muddy road?' I say nothing. But if a woman I loved said this, my woman, I would leave her right away." To Korovin's surprise, Levitan became very angry:

> He stopped, looking at me with his beautiful, serious eyes, agitated and said, "Yes, you dolt. You don't understand. But you just wait, you will. My sketch, this tone, this blue road, this sadness in the shaft of light beyond the forest, this is me, my spirit. It's in me. And if she doesn't see this, doesn't feel it, then who are we? Strangers. What will I talk to her about? Antosha understands this. He alone isn't falling in love all the time like you are."

Ever cheerful, Korovin admitted that he was currently infatuated with several women, including a certain Khrustaleva, who was auditing classes at the School. Levitan responded, "Granted Khrustaleva is very pretty ... but she says, 'It's boring to read poetry.' 'And what about Pushkin?' I asked her. 'Also boring.' Ask Antosha. He completely lost interest after he talked to her."[37]

Chekhov had already come to respect Levitan's talent, although, true to his nature, he chose to express it humorously. Gilyarovsky recalled a gathering at his place in 1884 that included Levitan, Chekhov, and his brother Nikolai. Anton decided to play the role of a philistine with great relish. Levitan and Nikolai sat at Gilyarovsky's table making pencil drawings in an album: Levitan drew a moonlit sea, Nikolai a woman's head. Chekhov watched them attentively for a long time and then said: "Is that how one draws? A head! Whose head? The sea! What sea? No. One needs to draw so that it's apparent to everyone what the artist wanted to express." With that Chekhov grabbed the album and drew a scene of a tourist in a hat descending a mountain on which there was a fort and a building with the sign "Tavern" on it; in fact he had labeled everything in the picture: sea, mountain, tourist, siskins. Chekhov handed the drawing back to Gilyarovsky and told him to save it: "It will be my one and only artistic work. I've never drawn before and I will never draw again so as not to steal any bread from Levitan's mouth."[38]

Meanwhile Levitan's relations with the School were deteriorating. In September 1883, Levitan submitted a painting, a landscape of a field with stacks of grain, in application for a major silver medal, which would qualify him for the title of classed artist. Levitan had shown the painting to Savrasov, now no longer at the School, who had approved of it and even wrote "major silver medal" on the back of the canvas. The School rejected the painting. Since Levitan had already passed his exams for the general class and received two minor silver medals in art, he considered himself done with the School and had stopped attending classes. The faculty expected that he would submit another, more appropriate work, but offended by the rejection, Levitan refused. On April 23, 1884, the School dismissed Levitan for failure to attend classes and recommended he receive the title of unclassed artist, which would qualify him to teach drawing and penmanship, but not painting.[39]

No one knows why the School snubbed one of its best students, whose paintings had already been recognized through exhibitions, purchases by collectors, and reproductions in Moscow journals. The absence of Polenov, his strongest supporter at the School, and the unwelcome intrusion of the disgraced Savrasov likely contributed to the rejection. Korovin cited gossip that anti-Semitism had a part in the decision, a conclusion repeated by the Soviet writer Konstantin Paustovsky, who wrote that some teachers felt that "a Jew shouldn't be painting Russian landscapes."[40] While these factors may have played a role, the most compelling explanation (offered by Korovin as well) was that, given the prominence of Itinerant genre painters on the faculty at the School (and especially with Polenov away), it was impossible for a landscape painting to be accepted for a first-class degree. Other students who had submitted landscapes also received second-class degrees, including Korovin. As he put it, the dominant thinking at the School was that a landscape painting was just a "tra-la-la," while a genre painting reflected deep thinking and political engagement. A painting worthy of the highest recognition could not just evoke a mood, it had to create a narrative.[41]

When Levitan received word of his dismissal he was outside of Moscow, living in the house of a Madame Gorbacheva at Savvin village near Zvenigorod. He had gone there to paint with a fellow student, Vasily Pereplyotchikov. Gorbacheva's house was very popular with Moscow landscape painters, including the Korovin brothers, who were attracted to the rural setting along the Storozhka and Moscow Rivers. This very productive summer for Levitan resulted in several paintings now found in the Tretyakov Gallery. Only toward the end of August did Levitan respond to his dismissal, requesting that the School reconsider and allow him to work toward a major silver medal. Nothing came of the request, and in what can only be considered as a final gesture of dismay, in 1885 Levitan petitioned the School to proceed with granting him the title of unclassed artist.

It was at this moment that Chekhov first mentioned Levitan in his letters. Their friendship had deepened. At the end of 1884, Levitan gave Chekhov one of his sketches, *Oak and Birch*, the first of several paintings that Chekhov received from Levitan and one that he kept for the rest of his life. It is now displayed at Chekhov's house-museum in Yalta. Soon after his arrival in

Babkino in early May 1885, Chekhov wrote to his publisher Leikin, "I wanted to set off with him [Levitan] over Holy Week to Vladimir province to give him some air (he's the one who insisted that I do it), but when I arrived at his place on the designated day of departure, I was told that he had left for the Caucasus . . . At the end of April he returned from somewhere, but not from the Caucasus . . . He had wanted to hang himself."

The final break with the School had triggered in Levitan an emotional breakdown. Chekhov, newly certified as a practicing physician, told Leikin, "Something is wrong with the poor fellow. Some kind of psychosis is starting."[42] He had felt that going off on a hunting trip with Levitan, enjoying his new-found passion a good one hundred miles away from Moscow, would lift his spirits. Having failed in this effort, Chekhov at the end of April invited Levitan to come stay in the vicinity of Babkino and spend the summer there painting. The young doctor had decided to take on responsibility for improving Levitan's well-being.

As he was setting his fish trap early on his first morning at Babkino, Chekhov immediately recognized that it was Levitan who had shouted "Crocodile!" from across the river. Both men enjoyed playing with the word, sometimes as an endearment, sometimes as a rebuke. Chekhov couldn't tell whether "Crocodile!" was directed at him or a fish in the river, since Levitan liked to embellish the truth by calling fish crocodiles. Vladimir Begichev—the former director of the Moscow Imperial Theaters whose daughter Maria Kiselyova and her husband, Alexei, owned Babkino—was charmed by Levitan.[43] Chekhov told Leikin that Begichev liked to call Levitan "Leviathan" and, as Chekhov put it, "sighs whenever the crocodile is not around."

After having coffee together, Chekhov and Levitan set off with the local huntsman Ivan Gavrilov: "We loafed around for three and a half hours, covered twelve miles and bumped off a hare," Chekhov wrote. "The hounds were no good." It was the "sharpshooter" Levitan who killed the hare. Levitan was staying about three miles from Babkino in the village of Maksimovka. He had rented a place from the local potter Vasily, an alcoholic with a perpetually pregnant wife, Pelegea. Chekhov hoped that inviting Levitan to spend time with his family at Babkino would lessen the painter's bouts of depression. "I have brought him with me to the dacha, and now we go for walks," he wrote Leikin, "It seems that things are getting better."

2

1885

FIRST BABKINO SUMMER

EVENINGS AT THE MAIN HOUSE at Babkino, or outside in the English park on warm nights, were given over to entertainments, recitals, and spontaneous merriment, often instigated by the Chekhov brothers. The house stood on a high bank above the Istra River. It had a small balcony, overgrown with convolvulus and wild grapes, overlooking the park. When guests walked through the park to the embankment, they could see a path on the other side of the river leading to the left into the Daraganov woods, where Chekhov and Maria Kiselyova engaged separately in covert and fiercely competitive mushroom hunts.[1] A rarely used church stood near the forest, a lonely spot that according to Mikhail Chekhov fascinated Anton and found its way into two of his stories: "The Witch" (1886) and "Evil Deed" (1887).

From the bank in front of the house, guests could see a village to their right with its huts and yards "looking tiny in the distance like little mushrooms scattered about the green glade."[2] On a clear day it was possible to make out the golden domes of the New Jerusalem monastery beyond the woods. Alexei Kiselyov had only recently fixed up the rather ramshackle main house, which had been boarded up for years, and the Chekhov family stayed in an outbuilding, which had been thrown as a plaything into the purchase price of the estate.

Everyone at Babkino woke up early. Chekhov was at work by seven in the morning, writing at his desk, which was actually a sewing machine table placed in front of a large square window with a magnificent view. Lunch was served around one in the afternoon, after which the Kiselyov family and their servants rested. Chekhov would go for a walk, fish, or hunt mushrooms, which he claimed made it easier to think up new stories. Tea was served at five, which was also reserved as the time of day that anyone attached to the estate or living in the village could visit and petition the Kiselyovs. Chekhov would go back to his writing table after tea and emerge for dinner and the gatherings in the main house.

For Mikhail these were "magical, unforgettable evenings." There would be long conversations about literature. Maria Chekhova recalled that Anton "did a lot of improvisations. He presented scenes, plots of stories, and sometimes even created almost complete literary miniatures." The actress Lily Markova remembered that one evening he told a humorous story about forgetting someone's name that later appeared in a slightly different version as "Horsey Name" in July in the *Petersburg Gazette*. On some evenings the children's governess would play pieces by Beethoven and Chopin. Sometimes a visiting tenor from the Bolshoi Theater would sing, as would Maria Kiselyova herself. These musical evenings made an unforgettable impression on the Chekhov brothers and on Levitan.[3] The lively, sometimes emotionally charged atmosphere of Babkino and the creative stimulation orchestrated by the Kiselyovs, representatives of an unpretentious and somewhat impoverished nobility, would later inspire the personalities and settings of Chekhov's major plays.

Levitan was quickly accepted into the Babkino circle. He embraced Anton's playfulness in particular, writing a note to "My dearest physician" from Maksimovka on May 19 and signing it as "the great artist Pavel Alexandrovich Medvedev." On a piece of scrap paper, he asked:

> Did you get the woodcock?
> Is everyone healthy?
> How's the fishing?
> How's the world outlook?
> How many lines [have you written]?
> And so I have the honor and so forth. I await your visit.

But these moments of levity, and the geniality he found in his visits to the Kiselyov house, failed to eliminate Levitan's depression. Maria Chekhova noticed that he would sometimes grab his rifle and his dog and disappear for days:

> These bouts of gloom had something sickly and abnormal about them. They happened suddenly for no reason without any cause. I could never figure out what lay at their root. There was a lot of self-dissatisfaction and wounded pride, but there was also something in addition that I could never determine. Levitan was damned proud of himself; he understood the power of his talent, but for him everything seemed inadequate. He wanted a lot more from himself. From

this sprang much of his depression, but this alone didn't explain everything. Anton Pavlovich saw something sickly in these moods, not arising externally but from inside the person.[4]

A psychiatrist would describe Levitan's condition as a form of bipolar disorder. Typically, onset occurs in the late teens or early adulthood and is characterized by mood swings that alternate between low self-esteem and grandiose overconfidence, between uninhibited people-seeking and introverted self-absorption, between apathy and sharpened creative thinking. The condition is also characterized by periods of hypersexuality.[5]

In mid-May a gloomy rain settled in at Babkino. Pelegea, the potter's wife, came to the estate to be treated for her ailments and mentioned that her renter, Levitan, had become sick. One wet night, in response to Levitan's note, Anton suggested to his brothers that they pay the painter a visit. Mikhail described what happened next:

> Anton, Ivan, and I put on tall boots, took a lamp, and walked into the darkness. We crossed the river, jumping from stone to stone, then splashed through a few soggy meadows and a swamp, and finally entered the thick and dark Daraganov forest. Our feeble lamp could barely light our way. The centuries-old firs and bushes grabbed at us in the dark, and we could feel thick torrents of water pouring through the branches. Finally, we reached Maksimovka. We were able to figure out which house was the potter's by the clay shards strewn around the yard. Without knocking or announcing ourselves, we broke into Levitan's room, and shone the light right into his eyes. Jumping from the bed, Levitan aimed his revolver at us until, squinting in the light, he finally recognized us and exclaimed, "Darn it! What fools! R-r-r-really stupid fools!" We all sat around laughing at Anton's prank, and our visit definitely raised Levitan's spirits.[6]

According to Maria Chekhova, when Anton spoke to Pelegea out of range of Levitan's hearing, she said that Levitan had attempted to shoot himself with a rifle but luckily had missed. Anton convinced Levitan to move to Babkino and stay with Mikhail in an abandoned chicken house on the estate. Levitan was again cheerful and full of energy. Maria recalled:

> [He] once again joked around with us, took part in our picnics, walks, fishing, etc. He very much loved to fish. Sometimes on non-working days we would sit for hours with fishing poles somewhere in the shadow of the shrubs along the shore [. . .]. Levitan put down his pole and began to declaim something from Tiutchev, Apukhtin, Nikitin, or Alexei Tolstoy. They were his favorite poets,

and he knew many of their beautiful poems by heart. These were wonderful moments! There was no fooling about. Something else arose from the depths of your soul. It was as if all of nature was revealing the secrets of its magical beauty, and everything became somehow inspirational.[7]

Levitan's stay in his Babkino chicken-house studio lasted several weeks. He painted *The River Istra* (1885), a mid-day view of a stretch of the river and the expansive fields around it, and gave it to Chekhov. He also painted *Twilight. River Istra* (1885), which has an almost identical composition (at the center is a wide bend in the river that flows diagonally to the bottom right of the canvas) but depicts another stretch of river with a darker palette and a distant forest forming a ridge in the background. Chekhov and Levitan continued their hunting excursions, primarily going after woodcock. Lily Markova, with whom Chekhov had a flirtatious relationship, joined them.[8] When a medical concern came up while she was at Babkino, Chekhov recommended that Markova visit his colleague Dr. Pavel Rozanov, in nearby Voskresensk. Chekhov treated her concerns lightly, writing to Rozanov, "I am sending Miss Markova for a medical examination of her vascular system, particularly her heart, on which she informed me your image is imprinted. I ask you to preserve that image in alcohol and send it to me."

In early June, Levitan left Babkino for Savva Mamontov's estate at Abramtsevo, accompanied by fellow painters Victor Vasnetsov and Ilya Ostroukhov. In 1870 the railroad baron and art patron Mamontov purchased Abramtsevo, located thirty-seven miles from Moscow near the St. Sergius–Trinity Monastery, and developed it into an artists' colony that for the next thirty years was at the center of the folk art and art nouveau movements that came to define Russia's Silver Age. As part of the informal Abramtsevo circle, painters applied their talents to media other than canvas, including theatrical scenery. Together, Mamontov and Tretyakov, who married Savva's sister, were the two men most responsible for turning Moscow into a cultural capital that now rivaled St. Petersburg. The abolition of the state monopoly on theaters in 1882 had opened up opportunities for Moscow entrepreneurs, and Mamontov, a trained pianist and singer, decided to become the impresario of his own private opera company. Polenov, seeking paying work for his favorite landscape students, introduced Levitan and Korovin to Mamontov, who was looking for artists to paint background sets for his productions.[9]

Using Vasnetsov's sketches, Levitan painted some of the scenes for the inaugural production of Dargomyzhsky's *Rusalka*, which premiered in Moscow on January 9, 1885. The scene paintings for the opera were a spectacular success. It was the practice of the Imperial State Opera to pay little attention to the set decoration and simply reuse sets and backgrounds from previous productions. Mamontov's approach was innovative: he hired artists rather than decorators, and they worked collaboratively as a team to create unique sets that were essential to the atmosphere of each production. In his memoirs, Polenov recalled the opening night of *Rusalka*: "When the curtain went up on the underwater kingdom (painted by Vasnetsov and Levitan), the public was first stunned into silence, then broke out into loud applause, calling for the author and the talented performer. Before them was an illusion of water and underwater flora; it was a beauty and a poetic truth not seen before. For the first time the set decorations, previously considered secondary, received applause."[10]

Chekhov, through his brother Nikolai, observed the preparatory work on Mamontov's operas. Victor Simov, who went on to become the set decorator for Chekhov's plays at the Moscow Art Theater, recalled that Chekhov made several visits in the fall of 1884 to the large, dingy studio on First Meshchanskaya Street where the scene paintings were progressing. He described one evening, already past ten o'clock, when Chekhov dropped by to find him, together with Levitan and Nikolai, standing on top of an enormous Russian-style stove in the middle of the studio. The stove offered the best vantage point to view the work below. The studio was lit with conical shades: "The light fell downward in broad beams turning the ceiling dark and invisible. The air was stuffy: it smelled of glue and the linen of new canvases. The entire floor was covered with scene curtains painted during the day that had just been sewn and primed." Chekhov climbed the stepladder to the top of the stove where his friends served him tea and sausages. Simov said that Chekhov "looked over the décor, actively took part in the exchange of opinions, made apt and very sound comments, not as a professional painter, but simply as a natural artist." Chekhov launched into a humorous anecdote told with a wry seriousness and a straight face. Levitan laughed hysterically, rolling on his stomach and kicking his legs.[11]

Chekhov made his opinion of Mamontov's ambitious launch of his private opera company evident in a series of review articles in his weekly "Fragments of Moscow Life" column following the premiere of *Rusalka*. His comments were far from flattering:

> The Moscow air was filled with talk about this endearing initiative, about private enterprise, about a sudden transformation of opera, about new epochs and eras and so on and so forth. The heated talk was followed by heated and excruciating rehearsals, at which Mr. Mamontov, making himself out to be a musical man, became irritated with the reedy voices of his prima donnas and

indignant at the inability of the primary characters to raise their arms at the right time. The rehearsals were followed by performances, and now Moscow has a bad Mamontov Opera in addition to an unsatisfactory Imperial Opera. Everyone is struck by the new opera, but nothing is more striking than the amount of money squandered on it. The décor is magnificent. The scenery, painted by Vasnetsov, Yanov, and Levitan, is splendid; the costumes are of the kind only dreamed of on the Imperial stage; the orchestra is made up of capable musicians very capably conducted, but the male and female singers—heaven help us! The following situation happens in life: you want to smoke; you have matches; you have cigarette paper; you have a cigarette holder; but you don't have what's most important—tobacco! That's how it is with the new opera: you have everything but singers. There isn't a single genuine singer; the main roles, without hesitation or embarrassment, are taken by amateurs and dilettantes who received their musical education at domestic performances, eating-houses, tobacco factories, and so forth. Their singing gets on your nerves and prevents you from hearing the orchestra; their performance makes you depressed.[12]

Mamontov's subsequent productions in 1885—Gounod's *Faust*, Verdi's *Aida*, Glinka's *A Life for the Tsar* (designed by Levitan and Simov), and Rimsky-Korsakov's *The Snow Maiden*—did nothing to change Chekhov's mind. His subsequent reviews repeated his two major themes: Russians make poor opera singers ("They're waiting for the Italians"), and Mamontov was an obscenely rich dilettante who had no business making art. Chekhov scorned the profligacy of it all:

Gold prospectors like those found in Fenimore Cooper or Mayne Reid should head for Savva Mamontov's railroad-opera theater. And don't think that by gold I mean the voice of Miss Liubatovich, the compositions of Mr. Krotkov, or the direction of Mr. Mamontov. By gold I literally mean the gold that pours out of Mr. Mamontov's pockets in a broad stream. When this stream will dry up no one knows. There is a rumor, by the way, that this Maecenas sacrificed around three million on this undertaking. If this is true, then this diligent and boundless stuffing of pockets, on which Mr. Mamontov's singers, comrades-in-arms, and parasites practice, will last at least another year. Those who stuff their pockets around Mamontov are anyone who has the least direct or indirect connection with his opera.[13]

The opportunity to work collaboratively had much to do with Levitan's willingness to do scene painting. He also knew that his livelihood as a painter depended on finding benefactors like Mamontov. But Levitan told Korovin that painting "these enormous canvases made his head hurt and gave him nightmares."[14] Nikolai Kasatkin, another classmate, recalled that painting on such a large scale caused Levitan a great deal of agony because of his love of detail. While Korovin and Nesterov had long associations with Mamontov, Levitan stopped painting for the impresario by March 1886, after the premiere of Krotkov's *The Scarlet Rose*, and he had no further interest in working in the theater. Nevertheless, Levitan's brief stint in theatrical work made his own painting more expansive and bold, evident in the scale of *High Waters* (1885).[15] The painting was over five feet wide, by far his largest work to date.

Levitan arrived at Abramtsevo in early June 1885 to work on *A Life for the Tsar*, which premiered on August 8. He may also have painted a palace scene for *The Snow Maiden*, since Mamontov wrote to Vasnetsov (the opera's designer) on September 10 that it was almost done "but Levitan left and no one is touching it until he returns." Sometime after June 17 Levitan became seriously ill at Abramtsevo and left for Moscow to recover. On June 23 he wrote to Chekhov, "Moscow is hell and the people in it are devils! I've been lying in bed for five days. I have a catarrhal fever according to Dr. Korolevich." Based on the sequence and timing of his symptoms, the hints of promiscuous behavior at Babkino, and the medical condition later developed by Levitan, he may have been suffering from what was known at the time as catarrhal primary syphilis.[16] He complained that his illness would keep him in bed for several more weeks and prevent him from returning to Babkino. He sent a heartfelt bow to everyone: "Tell them that I cannot wait for the minute that I once again see poetic Babkino; this is all I dream of."

Feeling better by early July, Levitan wrote a letter directed individually to each of the three Chekhov brothers: Nikolai, Mikhail, and Anton, who all were now at Babkino. He was overjoyed to learn that Nikolai had gone to a place where he would be able to work more diligently and recover from his "neuralgia," a euphemism for his chronic alcoholism. Nikolai had previously asked Levitan to hire him to help with scene painting work. Levitan told him that given what he had been paid for expenses on set decorations as the head designer for *A Life for the Tsar*, he had too little left after paying his existing assistants and studio workers to add Nikolai to the payroll. He promised to ask Mamontov to give Nikolai his own work, which would be a great deal more profitable. Levitan's note to young Mikhail was brief: he wanted Mikhail to make sure that Pelegea did not overfeed his hunting dog Vesta or else she would not be any good for retrieving.

Levitan told Anton that while he was getting used to being stuck in Moscow, the city still struck him as repulsive. He found it impossible to work on his landscapes. He was desperate to return to the countryside, hopefully within the next two weeks, and to again "see the dear inhabitants of Babkino and also, by the way, your vile physiognomy." But in his note, Levitan also took offense at things, presumably of a sexual nature, that he heard were being said about him in his absence. The huntsman Ivan Gavrilov had been telling lies: "The crocodiles are spreading something over Babkino. [...] I'm not a scoundrel, not a swine and so forth, but a philanthropist, if you will. But all the same, I won't be going to the country. And I'm not living in a bordello."[17]

By mid-July Levitan returned to Babkino. The weather had turned hot, the air smoky from a distant peat fire. Chekhov continued to be amazed by Levitan's skill as a hunter: the household devoured sixteen ducks and a grouse, all shot by Levitan. The artist continued to sketch and paint the River Istra and the Babkino estate; at least half a dozen of these works have survived. He started working on a painting titled *The Birch Grove*, an early foray into impressionism that he reworked and eventually completed four years later.

Chekhov and Levitan had gradually grown closer to each other over the preceding five years, but their summer together at Babkino cemented their relationship. Admittedly Chekhov, in his concern for Levitan's health, was still being the good doctor. And they still addressed each other formally in their correspondence. Levitan's effusive reaction to Babkino had as much to do with the people there as the beauty of the landscape. There was the allure of intelligent young ladies, especially Maria Kiselyova and Maria Chekhova, made more attractive by their devotion to the arts. The infectious, sometimes bawdy, humor of the Chekhov brothers appealed to Levitan in his manic state.

At Babkino, Chekhov came to understand more deeply what Levitan already knew—we perceive nature subjectively, ascribing to it qualities that reflect our state of mind. Chekhov responded to his surroundings that summer enthusiastically, without a trace of irony. Soon after arriving in May, he wrote to Leikin that he felt as if his head were in the clouds. He urged his publisher to visit: "I promise you something that you've never ever seen. The splendor of nature! How I should like to grab and swallow it." Sitting at his desk in front of the window, Chekhov wrote to his brother Mikhail: "Before my eyes unfolds an unusually warm, caressing landscape: a river, the forest in the distance, the village Safontievo, a part of the Kiselyov house . . ." Already aware of the effect that merely looking at the countryside had on him, Chekhov could not help but be struck that Levitan had the ability to use colors, composition, light, and shadow to turn that emotional response into art.

In several stories written that summer, Chekhov started using more subtle metaphorical language to establish a mood through his descriptions of nature. He had anthropomorphized nature in his earlier stories. In *The Shooting Party* (1884), the narrator, a provincial magistrate, borrows trite tropes taken from popular literature, for example the "sleeping lake" or "angry storm." The anthropomorphism at the beginning of "The Huntsman," written at Babkino and likely inspired by the personality of Ivan Gavrilov, came from a much more nuanced voice: "A sultry, stifling midday. Not a cloud in the sky . . . The sunbaked grass had a disconsolate, hopeless look: even if there were rain, it could never be green again . . . The forest stood silent, motionless, as though it were looking at something with its tree-tops or expecting something." By animating nature in a way that created a psychological landscape, Chekhov used words to produce the same effect already recognized in Levitan's work— his paintings were not so much literal representations of nature as reflections of human feelings. In *High Waters*, a cluster of peasant huts lies partially submerged under menacing skies. The feeling is one of abandonment— homes drowned by the overwhelming force of nature. In Chekhov's story the description of the sad, expectant stillness of a hot day sets the emotional stage for a meeting between the huntsman Yegor and the peasant woman Pelegea that is muted but made tense by what is left unsaid—that these two mismatched people are joined together in a hopelessly unresolved relationship. The following year, in a letter to Alexander, Chekhov explicitly outlined his approach to descriptions of nature: they should be brief, very specific so as to create an immediate image in the reader's mind, and anthropomorphic: "Nature becomes animated when you're not squeamish about comparing its phenomena with human actions."[18]

Superficially "The Huntsman" is reminiscent of the vignettes of peasant life in Turgenev's *Notes of a Hunter*. However, while Turgenev's sketches are told by an omniscient narrator-observer, Chekhov disappears into the dialogue between Yegor and Pelegea, a disconnected conversation in which their separate subjective understandings of their relationship form the objective reality of the story: Yegor dismisses the possibility of continuing their relationship given his perceived social superiority; Pelegea feels they are still tied together by the unbreakable bonds of marriage.[19]

Even the rather typical humorous sketch "The Burbot," based on an event that happened while workers were building the bathing hut at Babkino that summer, contains several striking similes. The story begins with a description of a hot, sultry morning. Two workmen are trying to extricate a fish hiding in the submerged roots of a willow. "Feathery clouds stand motionless in the sky looking like snow scattered about." The men become increasingly frustrated as the day progresses: "The sun is baking hot. The shadows begin to grow shorter and draw in on themselves like the horns of a snail." The story "A Dead Body," also written that summer, begins with a description of a still August night. Two peasants are watching over a corpse: "A mist is rising slowly from the fields and casting an opaque veil over everything in sight. Lighted up by the moon, the mist gives the impression at one moment of a calm, boundless sea, at the next of an immense white wall." In these descriptions we see Chekhov maturing as a writer, letting the way nature strikes the eye speak for the author, not unlike the way Chekhov's characters' conversations speak for the author without resorting to an omniscient voice.

At Babkino in 1885 both Chekhov and Levitan were still young artists who had not yet achieved the recognition that instills self-confidence and leads to financial security. Levitan was more committed to his singular path, although he had yet to receive his humiliating second-class diploma from the School of Painting (it would be sent to him in April 1886). Maria Chekhova recalled that he was often frustrated by how his work was received:

> Levitan knew he was traveling the true path, he believed in his path, believed that he could see new beauties in Russian nature, but at the same time it always seemed to him that he was not transmitting part of everything he had found, of everything that lived in his soul. Because of this he sometimes had a tormenting dissatisfaction with himself, but at the same time he had a deep indignation toward his artistic colleagues and the public because they did not understand and did not see anything in what seemed to him to be most true and dear.[20]

As a practicing physician, Chekhov often saw sick peasants from the area surrounding Babkino, but for this he received virtually no payment. He had previously assisted Dr. Rozanov at the Voskresensk hospital, sometimes conducting autopsies. Nevertheless, writing had already become his primary source of income. Chekhov's livelihood depended on the existence of a competitive popular press, rather than the generosity of rich patrons. Paid by the word, he published thirty-three stories between June and October 1885 in the *Petersburg Gazette*, the *Alarm Clock*, and *Fragments*. By his own admission he did not feel he had a talent worthy of respect. He confessed to the writer Dmitri Grigorovich:

> People close to me have always disparaged my writing and have never ceased to give me well-meaning advice not to abandon a proper profession for scribbling. I have hundreds of acquaintances in Moscow, including a few dozen writers, but I cannot remember any of them reading my work or thinking of me as an artist.

When Levitan arrived at Babkino the following summer to stay once again with Chekhov, much had changed over the year for both the writer and the painter.

3

1886

SECOND BABKINO SUMMER

AT THE END OF 1885, LEVITAN moved into a furnished room in the low-rent "England" apartments on Tverskaya Street, where he continued to live over the next four years. His room was well lit, with three windows looking out on the street. He slept in a corner behind a partition. That winter Chekhov was a regular visitor to the apartments, dropping in on Levitan and Alexei Stepanov, a shy, taciturn painter who saw himself as Levitan's disciple and became his constant companion on sketching trips into the countryside. Chekhov joked that he was taking on the role of their biographer and that in the future people would talk about their "English" period.[1] Levitan's initial "English" period verged on Dickensian poverty. He wrote to his sister apologizing for being unable to repay her loan, saying that he had eaten nothing for the past three days. He regularly attended the Saturday soirees of the Moscow Society of Art Lovers and took to selling his sketches at their auctions for a paltry ten or fifteen rubles apiece.[2] He even stooped to going to a drawing instructor on the Arbat who would assign him a subject to sketch, take the drawing, put his own name on it, and sell it for a profit.

The ethnographer-journalist Alexander Prugavin, who lived across the hall, was impressed by Levitan's work habits: "At that time he lived a very isolated existence, spending both his days and nights at home. I admit that I was always surprised and envious of Levitan's unusual devotion to his work. I had the opportunity to observe over a long period of time how he worked from early morning to dusk day after day without putting down his brush."[3] Prugavin was an acquaintance of Lev Tolstoy, who was interested in the ethnographer's study of schismatics and sectarians and occasionally dropped by to see him.[4] Knowing this, Levitan asked Prugavin whether he could come over to meet Tolstoy, by now Russia's most famous public intellectual. Levitan was eager to find out what the great oracle thought of landscape painting. Prugavin encouraged Levitan to visit, saying that Tolstoy always enjoyed meeting new people.

Sometime later, the opportunity arose. Prugavin introduced Levitan to Tolstoy, who looked intently at the young artist's face as they shook hands, then resumed the conversation he was having with Prugavin. Soon afterward Tolstoy said, "Well, I have to go. They're waiting for me." As he showed Tolstoy to the door, Prugavin noticed that Levitan looked unusually embarrassed and agitated. After Tolstoy left, Levitan said, "I'm guilty. I scared off Tolstoy. If I hadn't come, he wouldn't have left here so quickly." Prugavin reassured him that Tolstoy had only dropped by on his way somewhere else. Levitan told Prugavin that he was still curious to know what Tolstoy thought of landscape painting and asked him to bring the question up when the opportunity arose.

Prugavin did ask Tolstoy. "A landscape?" Tolstoy answered with a question. Shrugging his shoulders, he pronounced: "In my opinion, it's just background for a picture." Prugavin was so taken aback by this dismissive response that he decided not to tell Levitan what Tolstoy had said. He knew how sensitive Levitan was about "this form of painting to which he gave his whole being."[5] Tolstoy's attitude toward landscape painting was not markedly different from that of many art critics of the time who felt that a picture must tell a story.

Levitan again became seriously ill. Pereplyotchikov thought that he was suffering from periostitis as a result of working along the Moscow River in freezing weather.[6] Periostitis, an inflammation of the joints, is a symptom of secondary syphilis, and the timing of Levitan's illness was consistent with the disease's progression six months after a possible initial infection the previous summer. Nesterov remembered a late winter night when Chekhov came to look in on the ailing Levitan, whose friends had been taking turns watching over him: "The lamp glowed dimly, two or three easels with unfinished paintings formed shadows along the wall up to the ceiling . . . Occasionally there was a quiet moan from [Levitan] lying behind the partition."[7] Chekhov had recently given Levitan a photograph with the inscription "To Levitasha from A. Chekhov," using an endearment that indicated their growing friendship. In return, Levitan sketched a portrait of Chekhov.

In December, Chekhov made his first trip to St. Petersburg as the guest of his editor Leikin. He seemed genuinely surprised to discover the extent of his fame in the capital, where he was treated, as he described it to his brother Alexander, "like the Shah of Persia." Chekhov was better known in St. Petersburg than in Moscow because he published most of his work in Leikin's *Fragments* and, since the previous May, in the *Petersburg Gazette*. With some exaggeration, he told Alexander: "Don't forget that the whole of Petersburg is keeping tabs on what the Chekhov brothers are producing. I have never seen anything like the reception I received from the Petersburgers Suvorin, Grigorovich, Burenin ... they all showered me with invitations and sang my praises ... and I began to have a bad conscience that I have been such a careless and slovenly writer." Alexei Suvorin invited Chekhov to publish in his newspaper *New Times*, and on February 15, for the first time a story by Chekhov ("The Requiem") appeared under his own name rather than under the pseudonym "Antosha Chekhonte." Chekhov was buoyed by Suvorin's flattering remarks about his work and by the publisher's willingness to give him the time to work at a more measured pace. He wrote Suvorin: "It is a joyous relief that you are not imposing tight deadlines on my contributions. Deadlines always lead to haste and the feeling of having a millstone around one's neck, and I find both inhibiting. Deadlines are a particular problem for me since I am a doctor and have a medical practice ... I can never guarantee that tomorrow I shall not be called away for a whole day." Suvorin became Chekhov's most devoted publisher, and Chekhov felt a rapport with Suvorin that surpassed all other friendships in constancy and honesty until it finally unraveled twelve years later over the Dreyfus affair and Suvorin's increasingly virulent anti-Semitism.

During his stay in St. Petersburg, Chekhov met Victor Bilibin, who was Leikin's editorial secretary and also a contributor to *Fragments*. Close in age, Chekhov and Bilibin immediately hit it off. Bilibin warned Chekhov that although Leikin was introducing Chekhov to other publishers, he was nevertheless intent on preventing him from writing for anyone else.[8] Soon Chekhov was sharing with Bilibin, who himself was about to be married, the details of a secret engagement to Dunya Efros, a school friend of his sister Maria. The pressure to marry was very much on Chekhov's mind. In January he mentioned to his friend Dr. Rozanov a few days after attending the doctor's wedding that he had three friends soon to be married. He jokingly asked Rozanov's new wife to find him a bride or he would shoot himself. He told Rozanov, "It's time I was ruled with a rod of iron as you now are."

But on February 1 Chekhov wrote to Bilibin that the relationship with Efros had fallen apart, in part because of her unwillingness to convert:

> Please thank your fiancée for thinking about me and tell her that my marriage will likely not happen! The censors won't allow it ... My *one and only* is Jewish ["evreika"]. If a rich Jewgirl ["zhidovochka"] has the bravery to convert to Russian Orthodoxy with all its consequences—that's fine; she doesn't and it doesn't matter ... In any case we have already quarreled ... Tomorrow we'll make up and in a week we'll have another argument ... She is so upset that

religion has gotten in the way that she breaks the pencils and photographs on my desk; this is quite in character . . . She has a dreadful temper . . . There is not the slightest doubt that we shall divorce a year or two after we are married . . . Anyhow *finis.*"

From Chekhov's subsequent letter to Bilibin on February 28 it is clear that it was Efros who had called off the engagement: "I'm still not married. I've broken up with my fiancée *definitively.* That is she broke up with me. But I still haven't bought a revolver and I'm not keeping a diary." Chekhov expressed his anger and pessimism with words that have the weight of a cri de coeur: "Everything in life is false, changeable, approximate, and relative." The rejection put Chekhov in a spiteful mood that periodically darkened his thoughts over much of the year.[9] It galled him that she chose her Judaism over him.

In mid-March 1886, Levitan was paid several hundred rubles by Mamontov for his full-scale scene paintings from Korovin's sketches for *The Scarlet Rose.* Within days Levitan left for the Crimea, arriving in Yalta around March 20. He had discussed his plans for going south with Chekhov and the architect Franz Shekhtel, their mutual friend and Levitan's classmate, who would go on to become Moscow's preeminent master of art nouveau architecture. Shekhtel warned Levitan that by going to the Crimea he had abandoned the North, that his passion for the brightness and brilliant colors of the Crimea would "overwhelm the modest but soulful tones of our North."[10] Levitan may simply have wanted to escape what had been a particularly dismal Moscow winter and looked forward to trying his hand at painting nature with a warmer palette.

Levitan was indeed initially enraptured by what he saw in Yalta, but his joy was tempered by the disparity between what he felt and what he was able to convey in a painting. He wrote to Chekhov via Shekhtel on March 24:

> God, it's wonderful here! Imagine bright greenery and a blue sky and what a sky at that! Yesterday evening I clambered up onto a cliff and from that height looked down on the sea, and you know what? I began to cry. I sobbed. Here was eternal beauty; here was where man feels his complete insignificance! But what can words say? This is something you have to see for yourself to understand! I feel terrific, like I haven't felt in a long time, and the work is going well (I have already painted seven sketches and they're very nice), and if this is the way that the work continues to go, I will bring back an entire exhibition.

At the same time Chekhov himself was experiencing his own sense of euphoria. On March 25 Dmitri Grigorovich, Russia's literary patriarch, sent Chekhov a letter proclaiming the budding author's talent—"a talent that sets you far outside the circle of the new generation of writers." Since coming across "The Huntsman" the previous summer, Grigorovich had started to "read everything signed Chekhonte, although inwardly I was angry that a man should so little value himself that he thinks he has to resort to a pseudonym." Among the attributes that he praised in Chekhov was his "mastery of description," the "feeling of plasticity" in his work, and the ability to "give a full picture in a few lines [such as for example] clouds on a dying sunset . . . 'like ash on dying coals.'" He concluded: "your vocation is, I am certain, to write several excellent truly artistic works." Grigorovich's advice was to "stop doing hack work," hold back, and limit himself to stories that were more polished.[11]

Chekhov's response to Grigorovich started with a burst of emotion worthy of Levitan: "Your letter, my kind, ardently loved bringer of good tidings, struck me like lightning. I almost burst into tears. I was profoundly moved and I now feel that it has left a deep trace in my soul." He confessed to having a frivolous attitude about his craft, blaming it on his general disdain of writing for newspapers and on the fact that he was a doctor "still up to my ears in medicine." He couldn't recall having spent more than twenty-four hours working on any story, and confessed that "The Huntsman" was written in the Babkino bathing hut. Chekhov told Grigorovich that it would take time to free himself of his hack work: "There is no easy way to get out of the rut I have fallen into." While he now had little time for writing, "in the summer, when I have more leisure and fewer expenses, I shall take up serious work."

Grigorovich's acclaim had fundamentally changed the way that Chekhov looked at himself as a writer, and he wrote something to that effect to Levitan in the Crimea. In a tone that was becoming typical of his letters to Chekhov, Levitan jokingly commented on both the praise and the criticism coming from Grigorovich: "Don't forget to write me about the content of Grigorovich's letters; this greatly interests me. In general, you are such a talented crocodile, but you write such trivial stuff, dammit!"

Levitan traveled on from Yalta to nearby Alupka. He had requested and finally received by mail his second-class diploma from the Moscow Art Society. He needed the document to legally establish temporary residency in the Crimea. Inevitably euphoria about his surroundings now gave way to dejection. He wrote Chekhov: "I became extremely fed up with Yalta; there is no society there, that is, friends; and nature here only strikes you initially and then becomes extremely boring and I find myself wanting to go north. I have come to Alupka because I didn't work much in Yalta—and, just the same, a new place means that new impressions will suffice for a while, and from here I will undoubtedly head for Babkino." He also wanted Chekhov to tell Shekhtel not to worry: "I love the North more than ever; I have only now come to understand that."

In their three-way correspondence, the men displayed a great deal of sexual swagger, in Shekhtel's case mixed with a morbid fear of catching syphilis. In the Crimea, Shekhtel imagined, Levitan "is, of course, plowing and sighing for his bare-bottomed beauty, but the poor man is only human. How much is he going to have to waste on quicklime, disinfectant, eau de Cologne and all sorts of other ingredients, and how much trouble will it take for him to lard his amorous slut with them to make her fit to receive his thoroughbred charms? By the way, there is a Japanese proverb that says, not without merit, that preparation is the best part of all pleasures." Shekhtel brought this up because he himself was desperate for Dr. Chekhov's help: "In the name of all my current and future chancres, send me the prescription for pills." He was in a hurry because he had become "enamored with an Italian ballerina, an impetuous brunette—a fire-breathing volcano." Without the prescription from Chekhov, "I can only lick my lips and consider this vineyard still unripe."[12] In another letter that spring, Shekhtel continued to complain to Chekhov about an assortment of worrisome ailments: "The sore on my ass has again opened up and I have again taken to drinking your swill—but don't you think it necessary for me to smear it, the awful thing, with something? If this is necessary, please send me a prescription." He also continued to have a pain in his nose and pleaded to Chekhov to tell him honestly: "Is this pain not the result of my *specialty* [fornication]? Is it dangerous to drink up another three or four bottles of your swill?" He told Chekhov that if he lost his nose, "the best decoration on a man's face," he would put a bullet in his skull.[13]

Levitan himself was very discreet about whatever affairs he might have had while in the Crimea. In response to Chekhov's comments on his womanizing, he wrote back from Alupka on April 29: "Tell me, why did you assume that I'd gone off with a woman? There is screwing here, but it was here before I came here. And afterwards, I wasn't looking for any nice, animal screwing; it just happened to be there (and, alas, has gone)."[14]

Levitan arrived back in Moscow "black as an Arab" in late May. Ivan Chekhov told Anton that the painter returned to the "England" carrying "under his arm a small bundle, glory, and money. In the Crimea he cranked out seventy pieces, more paintings than sketches, and in them you see the sea, towns, cliffs, cypresses, and mountains. I saw them all. Moscow artists are ecstatic, saying that no one could draw these things as truthfully as Levitan had. He should arrive at Babkino in a couple of days."[15]

Chekhov had already settled in Babkino earlier in the month together with his mother, sister Maria, and brothers Nikolai and Mikhail. For months he had been urging Shekhtel to spend the summer there as well:

You should be ashamed to remain in stuffy Moscow when there's the possibility of coming to Babkino . . . Living in the city in the summer is worse than pederasty and more immoral than bestiality. It's wonderful here: the birds are singing, Levitan is dressed up as a Chechen, the grass smells, Nikolai is drinking . . . There is so much air and expression in nature that it's impossible to describe it . . . Every twig shouts out and begs to be drawn by the yid Levitan who's running a loan office in Babkino.

Reflecting the growing ease of their friendship, Chekhov's and Levitan's silly dramatics grew more intense and elaborate. Both Maria and Mikhail vividly remembered the pantomime of "the murder of the Muslim Levitan by the Bedouin Chekhov."[16] Levitan put on Oriental robes. Chekhov covered his face with soot and wore a turban. They both went into the field across the river, Levitan riding on a donkey and Chekhov moving into the bushes carrying a rifle. Dismounting the donkey, Levitan spread out a rug on the grass, kneeled, and started praying to the East, bowing his head to the rug. Suddenly Chekhov emerged from the bushes and fired a blank at the praying Levitan, who fell flat on his back.

Around the same time they organized another entertainment—a fake trial with Levitan as the defendant, Alexei Kiselyov as the judge, and Chekhov as the prosecutor. They dressed up in old gilded uniforms that they found in Kiselyov's and Begichev's closets. On June 8, Chekhov again wrote to Shekhtel:

Quit your architecture! We desperately need you. The fact of the matter is that we (Kiselyov, Begichev, and the rest of us) are preparing to put the merchant Levitan on trial with all the legalities of jurisprudence including prosecutors and defense attorneys. He is charged with a) refusing compulsory military service, b) secretly distilling alcohol (Nikolai is apparently drinking at his place, since he's not allowed to drink anywhere else), c) running a secret loan office, d) immorality and so forth. Prepare your testimony in the capacity of a citizen plaintiff.

Begichev played a member of the courtroom audience, weeping with emotion, while Chekhov's closing arguments made the real audience roar with laughter. In addition, Chekhov tacked up a sign on the door of Levitan's chicken-house studio: "Merchant Levitan's Loan Office." Maria Chekhova said that no one could walk past without smiling. These vaudevilles were portrayed as a way to decompress after a hard day's work, and Levitan himself seemed unperturbed by their anti-Semitic tone.

Chekhov's behavior was more callow than intentionally cruel and fit into the general atmosphere of playful mockery of the outside world that presided over summer life at Babkino. Given to exuberance when in a good mood and unafraid to wear his heart on his sleeve (especially in pursuit of women), Levitan acted as if he didn't mind being the villain and victim in Chekhov's pranks. But it also must be said that Levitan's friends sometimes criticized his tendency to retreat into subservience in the presence of his benefactors. Sergei Goloushev, who knew Levitan well and became his first biographer, accepted that Levitan seemed to take things in stride at Babkino. But Goloushev nevertheless found himself wondering how Levitan's soul reacted to "the constant ridicule directed at him."[17] However assimilationist his inclinations were, Levitan was forced to inhabit the role of the alien Jew, the interloper in Russian society. This, together with his conviction from an early age that the world did not really care about landscape painters, only reinforced the feeling of being an outsider.

Chekhov, however, in looking at the work from the Crimea that filled Levitan's small studio, was one of those who greatly admired his landscapes. From Babkino Chekhov wrote a letter to Lily Markova in July congratulating her on her recent marriage ("Your wedding was the best play you ever had a role in") and mentioning that Levitan was spending the summer with him: "He arrived from the Crimea with a mass of remarkable sketches (in the opinion of those who know)—around fifty pieces. His talent is growing not by the day but by the hour." What caught everyone's eye was how different Levitan's Crimean paintings were from the romanticism of his predecessors; his depiction of nature was more expressive while less idealized. Nesterov felt that before Levitan "no Russian painter had ever felt or assimilated the nature of our South with its sea, pensive cypresses, flowering almond trees, and the whole elegiac feeling of the ancient Taurid region. It was as if Levitan was the first to discover the beauty of the southern shore of the Crimea."[18] When his former teacher Polenov visited Yalta the following year, he told his wife that the more he wandered about, the more he appreciated Levitan's sketches. "No one, not Aivazovsky, nor Lagorio, nor Shishkin, nor Myasoyedov, has provided a truer and more characteristic expression of the Crimea than Levitan." In comparison, he found Aivazovsky's work "sickly sweet."[19] Virtually all of Levitan's extant works from 1886 are of Crimean scenes, except for a few pieces depicting the Istra River and the environs of Babkino.

Chekhov's admiration for Levitan did not prevent him from continuing to mock the sloth, dissipation, and pomposity of other Moscow artists, failings he saw in his own brother Nikolai. One of the stories he wrote at Babkino that summer was "Talent," a satirical piece that he sent off to *Fragments* rather than to the *Petersburg Gazette*, where he was starting to publish his more ambitious stories. In "Talent" Yegor Savvich, a genre painter who shares some of Nikolai's vices, is preparing to leave the dacha of the widow Zhilkina, having spent the summer there without producing any work or paying for his stay. Hungover, he is consumed by a sadness that he blames on the coming of autumn. The widow's daughter Katya has fallen in love with him, a development that he finds tiresome, and he yearns to sell his paintings and go abroad: "All you have to do is paint a picture and sell it to a Tretyakov or Botkin [another art patron]." Savvich starts drinking again; the vodka warms his innards and causes him to indulge in reveries on his impending fame: "He was unable to imagine his future works, but he could clearly see how they would talk about them in the press, how they would sell photos of him in art stores, how his friends would look on him with envy."

Savvich receives a visit from his friend the landscape painter Ukleikin and shows him the painting he has been working on, which depicts Katya sitting by an open window that looks out onto a garden. Ukleikin doesn't like it but feels compelled to lie: "There's a lot of air . . . and it's expressive [. . .]. You can sense the background, but . . . this bush screams . . . It's awful how it screams." (Levitan was known to accuse artists of using colors that "screamed.")[20] Toward evening a third artist joins them, the historical painter Kostylev, who is also staying at the dacha. Chekhov the ironist enjoys mocking the pretentiousness of the biblical scene that Kostylev has come up with: "One wants to depict a certain kind of Nero . . . a Herod, or a Clepentian, or something like that . . . and to put in opposition to him the idea of Christianity. On the one hand Rome and on the other, you understand, Christianity . . . But I'm completely unable to find a guiding principle!"

"Something like Siemiradzki's *Torches*?" one of his colleagues asks, referring to Henryk Siemiradzki's massive painting *Nero's Torches*, which depicted the lighting of torches as Nero prepares to burn a group of early Christians at the stake in the presence of Romans lounging in ornate splendor.

"If you please, but in Siemiradzki everything is focused on the gold, mother-of-pearl, external attributes, so to speak, and I want to capture the spirit! The idea! Siemiradzki is a master of effects!"

Although the story revealed a sophisticated knowledge of Moscow artists and their various factions, Chekhov nevertheless came to feel that its satirical tone was excessive. When he revised it for his collected works (1899–1903), he drastically pruned it, deleting the topical references to actual painters. He cut out a paragraph in which the three painters begin a "vicious critique" of contemporary art:

All three vied with each other to prove to the drunken Zhilkina that Russian painting was climbing a mountain, but its talents had strayed from the true path: Shishkin was a herbalist, Kuindzhi sacrificed truth for effects, one Makovsky had become addicted to caricature, the other Makovsky only knew how to paint his wife, Repin's realism was over-salted, etc. The judges who decided what to accept for the Itinerant exhibitions were biased, and the public wasn't worth a damn for anything. The artists criticized and drank, drank like only shoemakers and artists can drink.[21]

In the end Chekhov repeated the observation he had previously made that many young artists lacked talent and were deluding themselves:

If you listened to them, the future, fame, and the happiness of mankind were in their hands. And not one of them would think that this excitement was nothing but a petty, childish playing at art, that time passes, that life day by day heads toward dusk, that they've eaten up a lot of other people's bread and still have nothing to show for it; that all three of them are victims of the intractable law that says that out of hundreds of beginners with high hopes, only two or three will land on their feet, the rest will fall to the wayside and become cannon fodder.

Unlike the shiftless Savvich, Levitan was very productive while staying at Babkino, producing around twenty sketches and paintings during his two summers there. His romantic ardor was tireless as well. One day he surprised Maria Chekhova as she walked along the road from Babkino toward the forest. They chatted for a bit when he suddenly dropped to his knees and declared his love for her. Embarrassed, Maria could think of nothing to say, covered her face with her hands, turned around, and ran off back to the house. She stayed in her room all day, crying. As usual Levitan came to the house for dinner, but Maria didn't leave her room. Chekhov asked why she wasn't at the table. Mikhail mentioned that he had seen her crying earlier in the day. Chekhov got up from the table and went to her room. Maria told him what had happened and admitted that she didn't know what to say to Levitan. Chekhov responded, "Of course, you can, if you want, marry him, but keep in mind that he needs Balzac-aged women, not those like you." Maria recalled: "I was ashamed to admit to my brother that I didn't know what 'a Balzac-aged woman' was and, in truth, I didn't understand the meaning of Anton Pavlovich's phrase, but felt he was warning me about something. I didn't say anything to Levitan, and he again went about Babkino for a week like a gloomy shadow. And I didn't leave the house to go anywhere."[22] Chekhov was alluding to Balzac's novel *A Woman of Thirty* (*La Femme de trente ans*) and Levitan's taste for older women who were sexually promiscuous if not also adulterous. Maria must have wondered about how seriously to take Levitan's declaration given the fact that he was almost comically prone to repeatedly falling in love. Mikhail noted:

His affairs went on publicly and were always tumultuous and turbulent. They had all the stupid things characteristic of love affairs, even including gunshots. If he found a woman who interested him, he would drop everything to pursue her, sometimes quite literally giving chase, even outside Moscow. He would think nothing of kneeling in front of a woman no matter where he happened to be at the moment, whether in a public park or someone's house. Some women liked that about him, but some were afraid to be compromised and avoided him, even though they were secretly drawn to him.[23]

In the long run Levitan's awkward and impulsive declaration to the naïve Maria failed to derail their friendship. She learned not to take him very seriously. The next time he declared himself to her, she jokingly hit him with her shoe. He covered his face with his arms and started crying, but the next day he acted as of nothing had happened.[24]

While visiting Babkino the following winter, Maria felt inspired to paint the view she saw out the Kiselyov's living room window. When she returned to Moscow, she showed her landscape to Levitan, who told her that she had real talent. He offered to give her lessons and she began to take her painting seriously. In his letters to Chekhov, Levitan frequently asked how his sister's painting was progressing and reminded him to urge her to work harder at it.

Neither Levitan nor Maria ever married, and in her old age she fondly recalled that late in his life when he was already gravely ill Levitan confessed to her (and not for the first time): "If I had ever gotten married, it would have been only to you, Mafa."[25]

Levitan's affairs may have inspired "Unhappiness," another story that Chekhov wrote at Babkino that summer. The lawyer Ilyn, who is pursuing Sophia Petrovna, the beautiful young wife of a notary, behaves very much like Levitan and has the same seductive effect on Sophia Petrovna that Mikhail Chekhov noted about women who were the object of Levitan's affections. As the story begins, Ilyn, who is spending the summer at a neighboring dacha, is walking along a wood path with Sophia Petrovna. She begs him: "If you really love and respect me, please make an end of this pursuit of me! You follow me about like a shadow, you are continually looking at me not in a nice way, declaring your love, writing me strange letters, and . . . and I don't know where it's all going to end." She insists that they should be just friends, but he will have none of it and answers, "I am not in the least tempted by friendship with the woman I love." In fact, she is unable to resist the flattery of being loved in such an ardent manner. "It pleased her to see this huge, strong man, with his manly angry face and his big black beard—clever, cultivated and, people said, talented—sit down beside her and bow his head dejectedly."

Ilyn accuses her of leading him on. She admits to herself that there is some truth in what he is saying, that "what gratified her most was that she, an ordinary woman, was talked to by a talented man on 'intellectual' subjects; it afforded her great pleasure, too, to watch the working of his mobile, young face, which was still pale and angry." Her attempted refusal of him only stokes his passion. He threatens to put a bullet through his brains. He drops to his knees before her. "He was clasping her knees, gazing into her face and speaking passionately, hotly, eloquently. In her terror and confusion she did not hear his words; for some reason now, at this dangerous moment, while her knees were being agreeably squeezed and felt as though they were in a warm bath, she was trying with a sort of angry spite, to interpret her own sensations."

Sophia Petrovna finally breaks away, returning to her husband. But when the latter remains unresponsive to her tenderness, she fantasizes about setting off on a train journey with Ilyn secretly accompanying her: "Ilyn would sit, day and night, never taking his eyes off her, wrathful at his own weakness and pale with spiritual agony. He would call himself an immoral schoolboy, would abuse her, tear his hair, but when darkness came on and the passengers were asleep or got out at a station, he would seize the opportunity to kneel before her and embrace her knees as he had at the seat in the woods."

"Unhappiness" was published in August in Suvorin's *New Times*. It was Chekhov's first psychologically complex depiction of an illicit affair. Such love triangles would become a common motif in his later stories.

We know very little about Chekhov's own romance and apparent disappointment that summer—thanks to Chekhov's reticence on the subject and the reluctance of Maria and Mikhail to say anything about their brother's feelings for Dunya Efros—but Anton and Dunya did continue their relationship after she turned down his marriage proposal. From St. Petersburg on April 25 he sent greetings through Mikhail to "Dunechka" and "all my other purgative weaknesses." He wrote to Maria on May 6, "Although Efros has a long nose, I nevertheless respect her."

Soon after Chekhov's return to Moscow in May, Efros left for the Caucasus to take the waters. From there on June 15 she wrote Chekhov complaining that she had sent three letters to Maria, received no reply, and had no idea why. "Could you please convince her to write me or, possibly, make the effort yourself." Chekhov did write back although the letter is lost. From her response on June 27, it is clear that he had invited her to come to Babkino and that in typical fashion he made some sort of joke about needing to marry a rich woman. She fired back in kind:

Anton Pavlovich, I have been thinking about a rich bride for you even before receiving your letter. There is here a certain Moscow merchant's daughter, not bad looking, a bit stout (your taste) and a bit stupid (also a worthy attribute). She's desperate to break loose from her mother's guardianship. I think you'll like her. She is very rich . . . If I arrive in Moscow at the beginning of August, I'll be at your place around the 15th. Only you will have set yourself as an example in vain if I carry out my promises and I don't see you this year at Babkino.[26]

It is likely that Efros did go to Babkino, and that marriage was again discussed. Bilibin, responding in late August to a lost letter from Chekhov, wrote back: "You ask me for my advice regarding marriage. I reply with the words of Apostle Paul who said, 'He that is married cares for the things of the world, how he may please his wife; he that is unmarried cares for how he may please literature.'"[27] The course of Chekhov's life demonstrates that these are words that he took to heart. In late September, after everyone had left Babkino, Chekhov wrote to Maria Kiselyova, "In answer to the question you asked my sister: Did I get married? The answer is no and I'm proud of it. I am above marriage!"

Chekhov left Babkino in a foul mood. He told Maria Kiselyova that he found life to be nothing but alternating rounds of horror, rubbish, and vulgarity. In late summer he sat down to write the story "Mire," about Susanna Rothstein, a wily, unscrupulous, and sexually predatory Jew who ensnares Russian men unable to resist her charms. Although not a literal portrait of Efros, the characterization of Susanna represents a kind of revenge against her.[28]

Alexander Sokolsky, a young lieutenant, calls on Susanna to collect payment of a debt. He finds her in her bedroom sitting in a chair "in an expensive Chinese dressing gown, with her head wrapped up, leaning back on a pillow. Nothing could be seen behind the woolen shawl in which she was muffled but a pale, long, pointed, somewhat aquiline nose, and one large dark eye." She asks him to wait in the drawing room until she gets dressed: "I'll give you the money, though I know you'll abuse me for it afterward. You'll quarrel with your wife after you are married and say: 'If that mangy Jewess hadn't given me the money, I should perhaps have been as free as a bird today.'"

Susanna returns dressed "in a long black dress so slim and tightly laced that her figure looked as though it had been turned on a lathe." She asks him if he likes her rooms, adding: "The ladies about here declare that my rooms always smell of garlic," a common slur regarding Jewish households.[29] She goes on: "With that culinary jibe their stock of wit is exhausted. I hasten to assure you that I've no garlic even in the cellar." Susanna takes him into her study where, as she makes it known, she keeps her money. In a playful mood, she asks Alexander, "Now, Mr. Creditor, trot out the pledge. What a silly thing money is really! How paltry it is, and yet how women love it! I am a Jewess, you know, to the marrow of my bones. I am passionately fond of Shmuels and Yankels, but how I loathe that passion for gain in our Semitic blood. They hoard and what are they hoarding for? One ought to live and enjoy oneself, but they're afraid of spending an extra kopeck." She coyly asks Sokolsky if her accent, her tendency to pronounce "r" as a guttural sound, gives her away. Then she gaily launches into a discourse on the peculiarities of French, German, English, Italian, and Polish. But then her tone suddenly becomes more serious: "You don't like Jews, of course . . . they've many faults, like all nations. I don't dispute that. But are the Jews to blame for it? No, it's not the Jews who are to blame, but the Jewish women! They are narrow-minded, greedy; there's no sort of poetry about them, they're dull . . . You have never lived with a Jewess, so you don't know how charming it is!" Quite suddenly she grabs the pledge from the table, crumples it up in her fist, and tries to shove it into her dress pocket. He grabs her arm and what follows is a sexually charged physical struggle in which Sokolsky "could not help touching her all over and was forced to hurt her and disregard her modesty." He finally forces open her hand only to discover that it is empty. Now that Sokolsky is at her mercy, he finds himself sexually aroused. He tells her he won't leave until he gets his pledge back. Susanna laughs, "Poor fellow! How many days and nights you will have to spend with me, waiting for those pledges!" He is released the next morning, returning to his cousin's home nearby. Both he and his cousin revile Susanna as a wanton woman, but both are overwhelmed by the urge to visit her again.

What are we to make of this nasty story? At this stage in his life, the twenty-six-year-old Chekhov was still writing most often as a satirist, portraying the delusions, weaknesses, and hypocrisy he saw around him. Even as he matured as an artist, he turned again and again to family, friends, and acquaintances to inspire characterizations that he altered and expanded in his stories and plays. He was dismissive of those who claimed to recognize themselves in these characterizations, pointing out the obvious physical differences. While no one took offense at the caricatured artists in "Talent," the same cannot be said of the withering depiction of Susanna in "Mire." The story was published in *New Times* on October 29. The very same day Dunya Efros came to visit Chekhov. He wrote Maria Kiselyova, "I thoroughly irritated her, saying that Jewish youth were worthless. She got offended and left." The story played into its publisher's anti-Semitic agenda. On the "Jewish question" Suvorin's position was that the assimilation of Jews into Russian society was a grave threat, their influence being all out of proportion to their numbers. The portrait of the assimilated

Susanna (she even goes to church) who freely criticizes Jews but neverthe-less still steals from and seduces Russians is consistent with the archetype of the treacherous Jew. As Helena Tolstoy pointed out: "For the readers of the *New Times* the message was familiar. 'They' are dangerous—precisely because 'they' are livelier, more interesting, more attractive, than 'we.'"[30]

Maria Kiselyova was among those friends of Chekhov who hated the story, but her dislike was ostensibly based on the piece's sordid subject matter, not its anti-Semitism. Chekhov sent her a copy in December, joking that it was "about how famous writers are able to utilize their familiarity with 'garlic.'" He added, "The enclosed feuilleton earned me 115 rubles. After this, how is it not possible to be drawn to the Jewish tribe?" She wrote back that she thoroughly disliked the feuilleton. She was disappointed that Chekhov would show the reader only a "pile of dung." Anyone could write about filth and scoundrels, but a gifted writer would be able to find the pearl in the dung. Kiselyova accused Chekhov's editors of complacently sullying his talent by agreeing to publish the story. In response, Chekhov categorically rejected that the role of literature was to find the pearl in the pile of dung: "Literature is accepted as an art because it depicts life as it actually is. Its aim is the truth, unconditional and honest. Limiting its functions to as narrow a field as extracting 'pearls' would be as deadly for art as requiring Levitan to draw a tree without any dirty bark or yellowed leaves." What Chekhov appreciated about Levitan's paintings was that they had turned away from romanticized notions of nature. Chekhov and Levitan both shared the conviction that art mirrors the imperfections in our character, in our aspirations, in the world around us. Chekhov had an easy time deflecting Kiselyova's critique; she did not question the "truth" of the portrait of Susanna, only that it was an unpleasant truth without any redeeming grace. In the same letter Chekhov admitted that the story had generated controversy. Kiselyova's father had liked the story, "but still others are sending Suvorin vituperative letters, rabidly denouncing both the newspaper and me, etc. Well, who is right? Who is the true judge?"

The culmination of Chekhov's literary reworking of his failed relationship with Dunya Efros came a year later with the premiere of his play *Ivanov*. He gave Dunya, now married, a lithographed copy of the play with the inscription: "To Evdokiya Issakovna Konovitser (Efros): to the lady spectator (who was catcalling), from the author."[31] Perhaps with the sympathetic depiction of Ivanov's martyred Jewish wife, Chekhov wanted to both make amends for his much-criticized portrait of Susanna in "Mire" and make it clear to Dunya that their marriage would have never worked even if, like Ivanov's wife, Anna Petrovna (born Sarra Abramson), she had agreed to convert to Orthodoxy. Chekhov himself never expressed any reservations about "Mire," and it can be argued that the two diametrically different portraits of Jewish women were presented in two different genres with different aims—one a caricature in a satirical story, the other a tragic victim of a dangerously neurotic "superfluous man" in a serious drama. There is a parallel between these contradictory portraits of Jewish women (and his conflicted feelings for Dunya Efros) and the contradiction inherent in Chekhov's relationship with Levitan. In his letters to family and close friends, Chekhov matter-of-factly called his friend Levitan a "yid" ("zhid"). In other contexts—in his stories and his letters to professional acquaintances—he used the neutral word "evrei" when mentioning Jews. On the one hand Chekhov saw Levitan as Russia's greatest landscape painter, but on the other hand he felt free to refer to him as a "yid," usually with a comic intent, with all the stereotypical faults of his Semitic tribe. The emotional detachment in Chekhov's personality and his literary technique allowed him to simultaneously view human nature in general and his closest friends in particular with both sympathy and mockery.

After staying at Babkino for most of June and July, Levitan returned to Moscow in early August. Within a few weeks he left on a sketching trip to Savvin village on the Moscow River. He was accompanied by Stepanov and a new painting student—Sophia Kuvshinnikova, the thirty-nine-year-old wife of a police doctor whose eccentrically furnished apartment had become a salon for Moscow artists, writers, and musicians. The fact that Kuvshinnikova, a married woman, had gone off for several weeks with the notorious flirt Levitan raised eyebrows. Chekhov wrote to Maria Kiselyova on September 21 that Levitan was "swirling in a whirlwind," whether from artistic success or love affairs or both is not clear. No sooner had Chekhov finished writing the letter than the "brilliant Levitan" appeared at his door. Chekhov described him to Kiselyova: "He was wearing a roguish hat, a dandyish suit, and an exhausted appearance . . . He had been to *Aida* twice, once to *Rusalka*, was ordering frames, had sold almost all his sketches . . .   And he said he was sad, sad, sad . . . 'God knows, if I could only stay at Babkino for a couple of days!' he exclaims, apparently forgetting how he moped about his last few days there."

The crowning glory of Levitan's year was the Sixth Periodic Exhibition of the Moscow Society of Art Lovers, which opened on December 26 and was second in popularity only to the Itinerant exhibitions. The show included three landscapes Levitan painted at Babkino and over thirty of his Crimean sketches, most of which were sold within the first few days. The burdens of poverty were slowly beginning to lift.

4

1887–1889

ALONG THE STEPPE,
ON THE VOLGA

ON JANUARY 17, 1887, CHEKHOV celebrated his twenty-seventh birthday with a typically theatrical flair. He told a new friend that he had devised an unusual quadrille for the event in which he would dance with his partners Levitan, Shekhtel, and brother Nikolai. He encouraged Maria Kiselyova to attend: "It will be a magnificent ball with Jewgirls [Dunya Efros], turkeys, and Yashenkas [the Yanova sisters]." Such frivolity only temporarily distracted Chekhov from an oppressive feeling that his creative energy was flagging. Once again making an analogy to the way Levitan painted, he complained to his brother Alexander: "I'm sick. Life is boring, and it's hard to start writing because I'm tired and unlike Levitan I can't turn my pictures upside down to give them a fresh critical eye." He came up with a cure—a journey to southern Russia and Taganrog, which he had not seen in almost six years.

Levitan as well felt the urge to travel farther afield than his usual spring and summer excursions within the Moscow region. He was beginning to organize his life around the annual winter and spring exhibitions that were to become the primary venues for displaying and selling his paintings. Most years, Levitan sketched and painted *en plein air* from May through September. He then worked inside in the fall and winter to finish pieces that he intended to have ready for the Itinerant and other annual exhibitions in St. Petersburg and Moscow, which took place from January to May.

Like Chekhov, who needed an advance from Suvorin to make his trip, Levitan was short of money. His colleague Pereplyotchikov, who bumped into him at Daziaro's art supply store in February, noticed that Levitan was in poor spirits: "He lives off his paintings, but they don't especially sell well."[1] But by

March his finances improved. Tretyakov bought two of Levitan's Crimean studies for 150 rubles. And at the end of the month several landscapes sold for twice the asking price at an auction held by the Moscow Society of Art Lovers. He could now afford to make the trip offered to him by the School of Painting six years ago—a journey south to the Volga River.

Interest in the Volga as a source of inspiration for landscape painters first developed in the late 1830s when Tsar Nicholas I commissioned two brothers, Nikanor and Grigory Chernetsov "to draw from nature in panoramic views the beautiful places on both banks of the Volga."[2] These panoramic drawings were turned into a two-thousand-foot cyclorama displayed in a St. Petersburg room made to look like a ship's cabin. However, the problem for painters who hoped the Volga, like the Rhine or Hudson, would yield sublime romantic vistas was that the landscape along the Volga was often flat and dull. Nevertheless, the Volga region served as a backdrop in the work of Levitan's mentor Savrasov and was made famous in Repin's *The Volga Boatmen*. Levitan had high hopes that the river would inspire him as well. At the end of April he went south to Vasilsursk on the Sura River not far from where it flows into the Volga. But two factors conspired to undermine his expectations and plunge him again into depression: he was traveling alone, and the spring weather was unseasonably damp and miserable, rendering the river vistas even more uninteresting.

Earlier, on April 2, Chekhov had left Moscow by train for Taganrog. He quickly tired of his relatives and the town's provinciality. Two weeks later he journeyed across the steppe, first staying at Ragozin Gully, then traveling on to Novocherkassk for a wedding. From there he headed north to the monastery at Svyatye Gory before turning back south to Taganrog. By May 17 he was back in Moscow. Chekhov's time meandering across the steppe inspired him to write stories that reflected a newfound sensitivity to nature and an awareness of its power, its vulnerability to human depredations, and its indifference to human hopes and desires.

Two of these stories, "Happiness" and "Panpipes," were published in 1887. His masterpiece "The Steppe" was written quickly in January 1888 and published in March in the literary thick journal *The Northern Herald*, a first for the author. "The Steppe" resembles not so much a landscape painting as a landscape film, a long tracking shot of the unfolding expanse of the steppe as seen by the nine-year-old Yegorushka from the back of a slow-moving wagon as he travels from his home in Taganrog to Kiev to start his schooling. The steppe moving before his eyes is rendered in ever-changing colors that create a succession of moods. In the early morning, the far hills are "lilac-hued"; sunlight first appears as bright stripes and then completely drenches the grassland in dew. But by mid-day, he writes, "the air grew still and the disappointed steppe took on its despondent July appearance. The grass drooped, the life went out of everything. The sunburned hills, brown-green and—in the distance—violet-colored, with dark hues of peaceful shade [. . .] now seemed endless and numb with misery." Chekhov repeatedly anthropomorphized the changing moods of nature. Toward the end of the day "submissive nature became stunned into silence." As the sun set, "fed up and losing patience, the hills and the air could no longer stand the oppressiveness and tried to cast off its yoke. Behind the hills, a curly ash-gray cloud unexpectedly appeared. It exchanged glances with the steppe, as if to say 'I'm ready' and frowned." In this most "Levitan-like" story, Chekhov found a way to use his imagination and precise observation to make the natural world reflect human feelings.

As he had done before on first seeing the Crimea, Levitan shared his impressions of the Volga in letters to Chekhov. Once again he wrote about the agonizing gap between his ability to sense the divine in nature and his inability to express it in his art:

> I've never so loved nature, never been so sensitive to her, never have so strongly felt this divine something, suffusing everything but not visible to everyone, that you can't even name because it isn't subject to reason, analysis, and is only comprehensible by love. Without this feeling it's not possible to be a real artist. Many people won't understand; they'll call it, if you will, romantic nonsense— so what! They are being sensible . . . But this insight of mine is for me the source of deep suffering. Can anything be more tragic than to feel the eternal beauty of everything that surrounds you, to comprehend a deep secret, to see God in everything and to be unable, recognizing your powerlessness, to express this deep feeling?[3]

Levitan had talked about romanticism with Pereplyotchikov before leaving Moscow. Although a graduate of the School of Painting, Pereplyotchikov had wide-ranging interests—he wrote books and verse and thought of himself as a cultural critic.[4] Some contemporaries, including Chekhov, found him to be insufferably pompous. In his conversation with Levitan, Pereplyotchikov said, "I'm not sympathetic to romanticism; it seems to me that it is not especially truthful even in the most talented examples." Not that Pereplyotchikov accused Levitan of being a romantic. Indeed, he found his paintings to be technically masterful "but the subjects are somehow boring, cold."[5] Such a reaction would have underscored Levitan's sense of failure in being able to make a simple, truthful landscape provoke powerful emotions. He was struggling to find a way to convey "eternal beauty" without resorting to "romantic nonsense."

In "The Steppe" Chekhov's omniscient narrator, without a hint of the author's usual ironic distancing, expresses a sad ecstasy that comes from realizing that nature's beauty is lost on the world. His moonlit reveries are infused with a sense of the "triumph of beauty" in everything around him:

> In this excess of happiness, you feel tension and regret, as if the steppe knows that she is alone, that her wealth and inspiration are lost to the world—unsung, unneeded, and through the joyous hum you hear her sad, hopeless cry: "A poet! A poet!"

There is a difference in how the two artists express this gap between the existence and the expression of natural beauty. Levitan's response is more neurotic, focusing on his own inadequacy in translating perception into art. Chekhov's response is more outwardly directed; it's not that he feels inadequate; it's that the world cares too little for the beauty he sees around him.

Soon after Levitan arrived at the Volga, his enthusiasm predictably gave way to disappointment. Now it all struck him as sad and lifeless, and he wondered whether he should return home immediately. In part it was loneliness and the rain, gray skies, and strong winds. The isolation both focused his creative thinking and made him impatient with his own fits of depression. His letters to Chekhov at this moment, which have come down to us only in copied fragments, are characteristically frank and reflect an unfolding emotional crisis:

> It's hard. I can't sleep. I feel terribly sad . . . and very much envy the peaceful snoring of my two old hosts behind the walls. My nerves are shot; it's simply deadly! But by the way, the hell with me! When will I stop making such a fuss over myself?

> God, when will I be free of discord? When will I start living in harmony with myself? Apparently this will never happen. That is my curse . . . I won't say there wasn't anything interesting during my trip, but it's all overwhelmed by the sorrow of loneliness of a kind that can only be understood here in the backwoods.

> I didn't write you all this time; I didn't want to once again talk about my endless, fruitless sense of discord, but there wasn't anything pleasant . . . Don't wait

for me—I won't come. I won't come because I'm in a state in which I can't see people. I won't come because I am alone. I don't need anyone or anything. I am glad for this almost unbearable spiritual burden because the worse it is, the better, and the sooner, I'm reduced to a common denominator.[6]

Levitan was intimidated, even frightened, by the wide open spaces before him: "Should I not be working sensibly near Moscow ... rather than feel alone in this enormous watery expanse that stretches as far as the eye can see and that simply can kill you?" Yet here he was on the banks of "Mother Volga," where other painters before him had found inspiration. However much the landscape initially disturbed him, Levitan returned several times over the course of the next three years. The Volga enticed him and challenged him to understand the significance of its scale and incorporate it into the way he painted. What had intimidated him on his first trip in 1887—the elemental power of nature—became the very thing he tried to capture on his second trip in 1888. It was not possible for him to depict nature as an epic force without pulling back to a larger canvas, a more expansive frame of reference.

In "The Steppe" Chekhov too used the enormity of the natural landscape to create a sense of awe. Yegorushka is overwhelmed by the road stretching before him: "Instead of a road, something extraordinarily broad, sweeping, and heroic stretched across the steppe. It was a gray band, well-traveled and covered in dust like all roads, but it was dozens of yards wide. Its expansiveness aroused in Yegorushka a sense of wonder and thoughts of a fairy-tale world. Who traveled along it? Who needed all that space? It was strange and inconceivable." Within this huge frame, humans are very small; we feel our insignificance. This contemplation of vastness inevitably leads to melancholy and thoughts of human frailty and impermanence. Yegorushka lies on his back and looks up at the darkening sky:

> When you stare for a long time at the deep sky, for some reason your thoughts and spirit flow together into a sense of loneliness. You begin to feel hopelessly lonely, and everything you previously thought near and dear becomes infinitely remote and worthless. The stars that have looked down from the heavens for thousands of years, the incomprehensible sky itself, and the darkness—all remain indifferent to man's brief life. When you stand before all this and try to find meaning in it, it crushes your spirit with its silence. It makes you think of the silence that awaits all of us in the grave, and the essence of life becomes a feeling of despair and horror.

Evening on the Volga, Levitan's first significant painting to come out of this period, conveys the same sentiments. The painting was probably inspired by his first trip (including the brooding night sky). But it was started in the winter of 1887 and not finished until after his second trip in 1888. He began to paint on larger canvases, this one almost three feet wide. But the human presence is small. In the darkness we see the outlines of four small boats on the near shore and some distant tiny lights on the far shore. What dominates are the expanse of the river and the dense bluish clouds covering up the setting sun and portending a storm. The painting was included in the Eighth Periodic Exhibition of the Moscow Society of Art Lovers at the end of December 1888 (together with nine other paintings) and purchased by Tretyakov for 200 rubles.

Levitan returned to Moscow from his first trip to the Volga in mid-June 1887 and by July he was once again staying with the Chekhovs at Babkino—for the third and last time. His visit was relatively short, and he soon left to spend some time with Polenov at his dacha in Klyazma. The only account we have of Babkino in 1887 is by Maria Kiselyova's sister, Nadezhda Golubyova. She lived in St. Petersburg and spent only a few days at Babkino; much of what she wrote about the Chekhovs was hearsay gathered from her family. But she provides a vivid description of being the victim of yet another of the elaborate theatrical pranks so typical of summers at Babkino. On her arrival she was sitting in the dining room of the Kiselyov house as it started to get dark:

> They lit the lamps and suddenly you could hear a loud noise, an uproar in the corridor that separated the living room from the dining room, as if a crowd of some sort of Asians burst in. Before I was even able to express my surprise, the masqueraders came into the dining room. A terrifying Turk sat on some sort of box; four black Ethiopians were carrying the box and—oh horrors!—they were coming right for me. The Turk took out a dagger and held it over me. I screamed and like a lunatic jumped on the table, which shook and started to fall over when my father managed to grab me. It was funny, stupid, and awkward. The masqueraders looked just as embarrassed as I did, but the Turk lithely jumped off the box and gallantly introduced himself to me: "The artist Levitan." The Ethiopians, taking off their masks, introduced themselves: "The four brothers Chekhov." Among them was Anton Pavlovich.
>
> The charade which they had prepared to act out was undone thanks to my faint-hearted action. So it remained unclear how it was supposed to end. The governess whom my sisters called "Waffles" sat at the piano and humorously snapped at Anton Pavlovich. Undisturbed and serious, he heckled back at her in a manner that you couldn't stop laughing at. Everyone laughed, but he remained serious.[7]

Golubyova offers vignettes of the summer idyll at Babkino: Levitan sketching under an enormous gray umbrella at the edge of the Istra River; Maria Kiselyova getting up at dawn, deceiving even her husband by placing a dummy in her bed, so that she could secretly go into the woods and gather up all the mushrooms before the Chekhov family could get to them; everyone sitting in a field under some pines as Anton Chekhov "let loose with his eloquence, causing us to laugh until we cried." "I found the jokes aimed at Levitan a bit grating, but he, as they said, paid no heed as if they weren't talking about him. He lay on his stomach gobbling up red, juicy wild strawberries."[8]

Toward the end of summer Levitan, just as he had done the previous year, went on a sketching trip to Savvin village with Stepanov and Kuvshinnikova. Stepanov made two sketches of his companions, now looking very much like a couple. In one, both are at work painting, Levitan sitting on a stool under an umbrella with Kuvshinnikova on the grass next to him. In the other, they are walking down a path. Holding on to his arm, she wears a white dress that shows off her trim waist; he is turned solicitously toward her.

Stepanov and Levitan first met Kuvshinnikova when they started attending the popular salons at her state-owned apartment located beneath a police precinct watchtower near the Khitrovka slums, a warren of flop houses, taverns, and street stalls. Her husband, Dmitri, a long-suffering police doctor, indulged her bohemian tastes and insatiable appetite for socializing while quietly devoting himself to treating Khitrovka's crime victims.

The Kuvshinnikovs' four-room apartment was oddly but comfortably furnished. The dining room had benches instead of chairs, its walls lined with primitive shelves, salt shakers, and embroidered towels in the Russian style. While Dmitri's room was Spartan in its simplicity, Sophia's was divided into two levels—the lower level "was draped in the manner of a Persian tent with some kind of Eastern hides; it was very cozy to sit in the enormous tent and hear the music and singing coming from the living room." To get to the top level "you climbed a small winding staircase like that on a ship" to a bedroom that looked more like a stateroom. As Sophia went from room to room, she was followed by a spoiled domesticated crane "at her heels like a dog, dancing to the music, and pecking at anyone she didn't like."[9]

Mikhail Chekhov was a frequent guest. He liked the evenings of loud conversation, music, and singing. When it became generally known that Kuvshinnikova had started accompanying Levitan on his sketching trips, "people around them started to talk but Sophia Petrovna seemed as tender and sincere to her husband as before."[10] Stepanov, who was close to both Kuvshinnikovs, told Mikhail that once after drinking a lot of wine Dmitri poured his heart out to him: "Apparently, he did suspect what was going on, but preferred to suffer in silence." Some of their friends had already concluded that Dmitri acted more like her guardian than her husband. Anton Chekhov, for the most part, stayed away from this social circle. It was obvious to Mikhail that his brother "was critical of Sophia Petrovna and unable to conceal his feelings."[11]

Chekhov knew Levitan well when he had warned Maria that the painter was drawn to older women: Kuvshinnikova was almost thirteen years older than Levitan. The loss of his mother when he was fifteen and his dependence on a woman's touch to nurse him out of his recurring depressions may have contributed to the attraction. Levitan also took comfort in the fact that she was still outwardly devoted to her husband, which constrained her demands on him. He once admitted that he never married because even the best of the women he knew turned out to be too proprietary: "They wanted all or nothing. I can't be that way. I can only completely belong to my gentle, wandering muse. Everything else is worldly vanity."[12]

Kuvshinnikova shared Levitan's passionate devotion to art. While an accomplished pianist, she loved above all to paint, and the relationship began as one between a teacher and student. No one thought her beautiful, but everyone found her interesting. Tatiana Shchepkina-Kupernik, who arrived in Moscow in the early 1890s when the *ménage à trois* was already long known to all, provided a detailed and vivid portrait of Kuvshinnikova in her memoirs: "She was around forty years old, unattractive, with the dark complexion of a mulatto and curly hair (but very soft, not like that of a Negro), and a magnificent figure. She was very well known in Moscow, in fact was a 'leading personality' as they used to say in those days."[13] Her tastes and behavior were considered audacious, but she also retained the good manners and modesty of speech of an older generation. Shchepkina-Kupernik recalled that she had an amusing way of greeting people: "She firmly shook the person's hand like a man and then would continue to hold his hand in hers while she stepped back and intently gave him a critical look from head to toe, giving her opinion as if an inanimate object were before her: 'Take a look, Levitan, there's something dreamy about him.'"[14] She had a habit of calling everyone by their last names. When she was young she liked to dress like a man and once played Hamlet in an amateur production. While both were staying in the countryside, a woman recalled Kuvshinnikova flying toward her on horseback "in a fluttering coat, her hair flying about, with bare legs, all striving, all impulse, the light coat of an Amazon worn right over a naked body."[15]

During her salons, Kuvshinnikova left an album out on a table with an invocation encouraging guests to bring their "spiritual, mental, and artistic material" to the altar of the muses. Over the years her friends added pressed flowers, poems, caricatures, and sketches. Levitan drew a watercolor of a graveyard with the gloomy inscription: "No longer any need for letters or tears." Curiously the album was originally used as a diary that Kuvshinnikova had kept for twenty days in January 1883, when she was staying at her father's estate in Siberia and recovering from an unspecified illness. She seemed not to care that others (Chekhov among them) could read her intimate thoughts, including her description of a brief infatuation with a married political exile. The diary entries confirm what others had noted—she had the ability to express loyalty toward her husband while simultaneously pursuing other men, though not without pangs of guilt. The news that the political exile's wife would be coming to visit him unleashed a burst of self-recrimination in these pages:

> What a vile person I am! Although not deliberately, just the same, I have spoiled things for myself and for others all my life! I go around intoxicated. I know that I have a month to regain my health, and I will have to return to my corner, where a dear person [Dmitri] waits for me, one way or another, and eleven years [of marriage] have passed better than most, not darkened by anything. There were storm clouds, but they didn't hold out . . . and now? Now, minute by minute it becomes more terrible for me . . . I begin to lose faith in myself. I grasp at straws and admit that he [her lover] is unable to hold on to me![16]

In contrast, Kuvshinnikova's published recollections of her time with Levitan contain not a shred of flamboyance. On the contrary, aware that to many she was chiefly known as Levitan's mistress, she was eager to present her bona fides not just as a worthy student of her master but as a painter to be taken seriously in her own right:

> My first sketching trip along the Volga and the Oka with Levitan and the genial genre painter Stepanov gave me what studying in any school for five or six years couldn't . . . Working daily in nature, trading impressions and advice with these gifted colleagues, I advanced rapidly. By 1888 (my second year studying painting) my sketch *Interior of an Ancient Church at Plyos* was acquired by P. M. Tretyakov's gallery. I was a student of Levitan for eight years. My work was shown every year at the periodic exhibitions of the Moscow Society of Art Lovers. This society selected me as an artist-member by accepting my painting *Monastery Gates*. I participated four times in the Petersburg exhibitions of the Academy of Artists. Eight years devoted to the practical study of nature under the direction of Levitan—that was better than any school.[17]

In the second half of April 1888, Levitan, Kuvshinnikova, and Stepanov once again set off on a painting expedition. By now they had grown tired of the area surrounding Savvin and, according to Kuvshinnikova, "were drawn to new places, to new impressions." So they decided to go along the Volga. With familiar companions, better weather, and the discovery of new landscapes, Levitan's second journey to the Volga had a completely different effect on his mood and his artistic output than the first one. They traveled overland to Ryazan, where they boarded a steamboat and sailed down the Oka. At first they tried to stay in the village of Chulkov but Kuvshinnikova said they couldn't tolerate the place for long: "The inhabitants acted very strangely toward us, having never seen 'gentlemen' in their midst. They would follow us in a crowd and stare at us like we were some sort of Aztecs, pawing at our clothes and things." Seeing the "gentlemen" starting to sketch, some of the villagers became alarmed, concerned that there was some sort of evil in their actions. "All this got on our nerves and we hurriedly left."[18] They went on to Nizhny, transferred to another steamboat, and started to head up the Volga.

Finally they reached Plyos. Kuvshinnikova recalled that they were immediately enchanted by the place and decided to stay:

> What attracted us most of all was the small ancient church that afterwards other artists would come to paint as well, and in general the little town turned out to be an attractive little corner, surprisingly beautiful, poetic, and quiet. We found two rooms not far from the riverbank and with the help of some hay, rugs, two tables, and several benches we set up a bivouac. Of course our reckless bohemian life made a deep impression here. An artist turned out to be a rare bird [. . .]. At the bazaar they shared all the news about us: what we were eating, where we were going, etc. But somehow all this soon quieted down. They quickly got used to us and we got used to them. We wandered for whole days along the banks and environs, and every day here, there, and everywhere we planted our enormous white canvas umbrellas which we ourselves had washed with bluing to reduce the harsh light penetrating the umbrella onto the sketch.[19]

The painters continued to strike the locals as exotic creatures. One day Levitan was sketching in the shade of his umbrella by the side of a road outside of town. A group of women returning from a church service stopped to watch him as he worked. "Then a decrepit, partially blind old woman trudged up to him," Kuvshinnikova recalled. "Squinting in the sun, she watched the artist for a long time, then began to cross herself devoutly, took a kopeck coin out of her bag, carefully placed it in the paint box, and quietly went off. God only knows whom she took Levitan to be and what thoughts arose in her old head, but Levitan held onto his coin for a long time."[20]

Intimately familiar with his mood swings, Kuvshinnikova noticed that Levitan had become less subject to bouts of depression, something that was evident even in his paintings. When Chekhov saw the first paintings from Plyos, he said to Levitan, "You know, even your pictures are starting to smile."[21]

It was in Plyos that Levitan began to regularly incorporate churches into his landscapes, occasionally sketching their interiors as well. The associations inspired by cupolas and bell towers rising into the sky complemented the spirituality otherwise achieved by Levitan's ability in his best paintings to make the natural setting and the very air evoke the ineffable. The old church that had drawn them to stop in Plyos became a resonant motif for Levitan, reflecting both spiritual yearning and the sad truth of mutability and decay. The image would eventually find its way into his most famous painting, *Above Eternal Rest*.

Kuvshinnikova was struck by Levitan's newfound interest in the Orthodox service and his sensitivity to its "mystical wonder." She prevailed upon a priest to conduct a service in the old church: "Levitan was here with us and as soon as the service started, he suddenly in agitation started to ask me to show him how and where to place the candles and indeed started to place them before all the icons. And throughout the whole service he stood next to us with an agitated expression and experienced the anxious feeling that was seizing him."[22] With characteristic overwrought emotions, he deeply felt the spirituality of the liturgical ritual. On another occasion he accompanied Kuvshinnikova to a Trinity Day service. She noticed that when the blessing of the flowers begin, he leaned toward her "touched almost to the point of tears" and said: "Listen, this is amazing. My God how good this is! This isn't an Orthodox prayer or from any other religion. This is a universal prayer."[23] Once as young students Levitan and Korovin were in the countryside admiring the dog roses in bloom, their pink flowers shining brightly in the sun. Korovin said, "Let's bow down to them and pray," and the two boys started to make up prayers. "We got wrapped up in our improvisation," recalled Korovin, "both bowing to the dog roses and looking at each other and laughing."[24] For Levitan this playful recognition of the divine in nature evolved and eventually formed the core of his aesthetic beliefs, which reflected an animistic sensibility rather than devotion to any particular religion.

After a two-month stay along the Volga, Levitan briefly returned to Moscow in late June 1888 to retrieve his beloved hunting dog, Vesta. But he also brought with him several pieces that he had painted. He showed them to Goloushev, who told a friend: "In places nature is captured as I've never seen before in his work. And it's in a less studied Levitan-ish manner."[25] Where his fellow artists previously criticized his paintings for being too restrained, they now recognized an emotional power in his work.

Back in Plyos with Vesta at his side, Levitan went off hunting with Kuvshin-nikova for days at a time. She remembered one day when they sat by the water's edge waiting for a boat to take them across the Volga. Levitan paced distract-edly along the shore and noticed some seagulls circling overhead: "Suddenly Levitan raised his rifle, let out a shot—and a poor white bird somersaulted in the air and fell lifeless with a thud on the sandy shore." This thoughtless cruelty upset Kuvshinnikova and she confronted him. At first he started to argue but then admitted that what he had done was "disgusting and awful." According to Kuvshinnikova, he said, "I throw my base act at your feet and promise you that I will never do anything like this again." The row spoiled the day and they returned home where Levitan buried the seagull in the woods. He foolishly promised to quit hunting, but two days later he took off again with Vesta and his rifle.[26]

Kuvshinnikova recounted this incident because "possibly Levitan told Chekhov about it and Anton Pavlovich recalled it when he wrote his *Seagull*." But this is unlikely, especially since a similar incident took place again several years later during the period when Chekhov was writing the play. This gesture of throwing a dead bird at someone's feet appealed to Levitan's flair for the dramatic.

Levitan stayed in Plyos through the early fall and returned to Moscow by the beginning of October. Around this time it was announced that Chekhov had won the Russian Academy's 1888 literature prize (500 rubles) for "The Steppe." In what was becoming a year's end ritual, Levitan too was a prize recipient. While no one received the first prize in the 1888 competition by the Moscow Society of Art Lovers, Levitan was the second prize recipient (200 rubles) for the landscape *Evening Falls*. He showed ten paintings at the society's exhibition; Tretyakov bought two of them for 200 rubles each, as well as a sketch. Kuvshinnikova had two paintings in the exhibition; Tretyakov purchased her *Inside the Peter and Paul Church in Plyos*.

Kuvshinnikova sent Chekhov a note inviting him to her salon on December 24. She mentioned that she hadn't seen him for a long time, probably since early October: "It is thus understandable that I am longing to see you, not as a celebrity, but as a person dear to me."[27] She was aware that Chekhov saw her as "a lover of men of talent," as he had described her to Suvorin. She mentioned that "there will be some nice people such as the Lenskys, Levitan, and other fellow artists." Chekhov did not attend the soiree and wrote back on December 25 apologizing for his absence: "I was sick and nasty like an unclean spirit." But, referring to Tretyakov's purchase of her painting, he did courteously congratulate her "on entering the ranks of the immortals." And then in typical fashion, mixing sincerity and irony, he went on: "It doesn't matter that your painting was small. Kopecks are also small, but when you have a lot of them they make a ruble. Every picture acquired by a gallery and every decent book finding itself in a library, no matter how small they are, serve a great cause— the accumulation of the nation's wealth. See what a patriot I've become!"

In trying to become a friend to Chekhov—something that was impossible given his distaste for her unfaithfulness to her physician husband—Kuvshinnikova presented herself as a devoted admirer of his writing. In February 1889, having just seen *Ivanov* at the Alexandrinsky Theater in St. Petersburg, she wrote Chekhov a letter effusively praising the play. She admitted that she might come across as someone in "a comic, childish state of exaltation," but for her *Ivanov* "made you think; spirits were revived; everyone looked deep inside themselves—recently in the theater most productions offered neither mental nor spiritual enjoyment . . . You have given us all of it." Her only disappointment was that when the audience clamored for the author after the end of the third act, some old man came out on stage and announced that the author wasn't in the theater. Kuvshinnikova also mentioned that before attending the performance she had gone to meet Levitan's train arriving from Moscow: "He was unable to get seats for *Ivanov* and was very disappointed."[28]

Kuvshinnikova's fawning irritated Chekhov. He did not like being treated as a celebrity. He liked his friends not to take him or themselves too seriously. He may have signed his letter to her "with heartfelt devotion," but that is a sentiment he warily held at arm's length.

After a successful winter and spring selling his paintings and having three of his works included in the annual Itinerant exhibition, Levitan left for the third time in the summer of 1889 for the Volga with Kuvshinnikova and Stepanov, staying again primarily in Plyos. Several other fellow-graduates of the School of Painting were also working in the same area. Vasily Baksheev recalled that when he arrived in Plyos, he immediately became discouraged because everything that attracted his artistic eye had already been painted by Levitan and could not be improved upon. It took him a long time to find "non-Levitan motifs" that he could take on as his own. Having known Levitan since their school days, Baksheev was struck in Plyos by Levitan's true qualities as a painter—"an unusually strong love of nature, incredibly demanding on himself, and an unusually powerful visual memory." This did not stop Levitan from once complaining to Baksheev, as he did to everyone, that he was "getting nowhere" because he could not get that which he "saw, felt, and passionately experienced" into a sketch he was making.[29]

In her memoirs Kuvshinnikova provided a revealing example of how Levitan used his dissatisfaction (and his visual memory) as the irritant that eventually produces a pearl. In 1887, while they were staying near Savvin, Levitan fell into one of his depressive states prompted by the "impossibility of expressing on canvas all that vaguely stirred in his soul." He stopped working, said that everything for him was finished, and that he didn't want to go on living:

> I finally convinced Levitan to get out of the house, and we set off along the edge of a pond along the monastery hill. It was getting dark. The sun was close to setting and poured over the monastery the bright light of its last rays, but this beautiful picture aroused nothing in Levitan's soul.
>
> But then the sun began to disappear entirely. Shadows ran along the slope of the hill and covered the monastery wall, and the bell tower glowed in the colors of the sunset with such beauty that a spontaneous joy seized Levitan. Mesmerized, he stood and watched as the tops of the monastery churches more and more strongly glowed red from these rays, and with joy I noticed the familiar fire of passion in Levitan's eyes. Soon the bright colors faded on the white bell towers, and lit by the sunset they reddened slightly in the darkening sky, but the crosses burned with a fiery glow above them. The picture was already different but something even more fascinating . . .
>
> Unwittingly, Levitan started to talk about this beauty, about how you could pray to it like God and ask inspiration of it; belief in yourself and this theme excited us for a long time. It was as if Levitan underwent some kind of transformation, and when we returned home, he was already a different person. He turned once again toward the monastery now pale in the twilight, and he said pensively, "Yes, I believe that some day this will give me a major painting."[30]

The experience did not inspire Levitan to start sketching, and Kuvshin-nikova and Stepanov hesitated to bring the topic up, fearing that it might yet again plunge him into gloom. But two years later, Levitan headed out of Plyos in the direction of nearby Yurevets looking for new subjects to paint. He stumbled across "a small monastery huddled in the woods. It wasn't very pretty and its colors weren't pleasing, but it was the same kind of evening like the one we had in Savvin: the frail bridge stretching across the little river joined the quiet abode to the stormy sea of life, and suddenly in Levitan's head was created one of his best paintings in which his Savvin experiences and what he had just seen and hundreds of other recollections were combined."[31] The resulting painting, *Quiet Abode*, was not finished until the following year.

As he had the previous year, Chekhov spent the summer of 1889 at Luka, the Litvarionov estate near Sumy in the Ukraine. He had heard about the availability of cottages on the estate through Ukrainian musician friends of

Nikolai. On April 24 Chekhov made the train trip to Suma with Nikolai, who was by then terminally ill with tuberculosis. Nikolai's death at age thirty-one at Luka devastated Chekhov—the inescapable toll of the disease on family and friends aroused feelings of dread and doom; he became restless. Grigorovich and Suvorin tried to convince him to join them abroad in Vienna. Chekhov headed to Odessa at the invitation of Alexander Lensky, the actor and theater manager who was there on tour with the Moscow Maly Theater. Initially intending to travel on from there to Vienna, he changed his mind, went to Yalta instead, and from there returned to Luka. By September he was back in Moscow.

In Odessa Chekhov began a friendship with Cleopatra Karatygina, a forty-one-year-old actress with the Maly Theater. Back in Moscow she visited him several times at his house on Sadovaya Street. She remembered that he would lead her into his study and "always take me up to a painting by Levitan. He would roll his hands up into a megaphone while admiring the painting, 'Look! Look! What beauty!'"[32] The painting was *The Oak and the Birch*, which Levitan had given to Chekhov early in their friendship.

By mid-October Levitan was back in Moscow, bringing with him a new set of Volga sketches. He settled into a studio offered to him by the industrialist and amateur painter Sergei Morozov, whom he had met through Polenov. While visiting the Crimea in September 1887, Morozov had taken a few lessons from Polenov. The latter told his own wife that Morozov lacked any real talent for painting: "He over thinks everything and only too well knows the reasons for things, and as a result has very little spontaneity."[33] The Morozovs, like the Mamontovs and Tretyakovs, were a wealthy Old Believer merchant family drawn to supporting the arts. Sergei's more famous and flamboyant brother Savva became a major donor to the Moscow Art Theater. The more taciturn Sergei was eventually drawn to collecting Russian handicrafts. By 1889, Morozov had decided to give up painting and turned over his elegant studio to Levitan. It was an enviably comfortable space on the second story of a wing of the Morozov family's grand mansion located in a secluded part of the city very close to Kuvshinnikova's apartment. The studio had a high ceiling, and indirect light streamed in through its large, north-facing windows.

Levitan had been planning to go abroad, but he suddenly came down with typhus, which seriously undermined his strength. Always concerned when it came to his friend's health, Chekhov wrote a note to Lensky in November saying that it would make him very happy if they went together to visit Levitan in his new studio. Around the same time Polenov's wife dropped in on Levitan as well. She wrote her husband that he had a "charming studio and

Levitan himself has made giant steps since last summer. He is working terribly hard and it's interesting. He himself is sick, although who isn't these days. No household has been left untouched by the flu."[34] Once again a group of Levitan landscapes (seven this time) were displayed at the year-end exhibition of the Moscow Society of Art Lovers, and this time, unlike the previous year, the society decided to award a first prize—to Levitan for his painting *Evening on the Volga*.

5

1890–1891

JEALOUSY

BY THE END OF THE 1880S Levitan and Chekhov had taken to addressing each other using the intimate "you," which up until then Chekhov had reserved for his siblings. As was the case with his brothers, Chekhov mixed concern for Levitan's well-being with a measure of disapproval, particularly when Levitan gave in to his manic-depression and hypersexual behavior.

Levitan's excitability at times left him deaf to social cues and unwittingly exposed him to ridicule. One winter night in 1890 at a gathering of friends at his home, Chekhov spontaneously asked Lensky to do a reading of Chekhov's new one-act farce "The Marriage Proposal." Unprepared for an impromptu reading, Lensky stumbled and lost his place several times. Nevertheless the audience applauded when Lensky finished and called for Chekhov to take a bow. Impulsively Levitan, who had applauded the loudest of all, stood up and announced that he too proposed to do a reading—a recitation of Lermontov's 1,139-line poem "The Demon." Dumbfounded, Chekhov asked apprehensively, "You're thinking of declaiming all of 'The Demon'?" Levitan sputtered that he was and launched into his reading. When, during the course of this lengthy recitation, Levitan choked at one point and had to pause, Chekhov seized the moment and started to applaud. Levitan protested that he had not finished, but Chekhov cut him off and announced to the group: "After the wonderful readings of my comedy and Lermontov's poem, ladies and gentlemen, let's listen to some interesting music. Esteemed performers, if you will . . ." And out came Alexander Ivanenko on the flute and Marian Semashko on the cello to provide a musical conclusion to the evening.[1] Levitan came off as a buffoon in a farce, this time of his own making, with Chekhov as the master of ceremonies.

Winter in Moscow was high season for the city's cultural soirees. In addition to being a regular guest at Chekhov's and Kuvshinnikova's gatherings, Levitan was closely associated with the activities of the Society of Art Lovers, best known for organizing the popular Periodic Exhibitions at which his works were often displayed. The Society's soirees went through an evolution from initial "Fridays" (soon deemed to be too exclusive and therefore boring) to "Saturdays" (hosted by the amateur poet and actor Konstantin Shilovsky, whose generosity in supplying all the food and drink made the attendees feel like moochers), and finally to the "Wednesdays" at the home of the art collector Vladimir Shmarovin.[2]

Shmarovin was an early patron of Levitan going back to the painter's student days. Levitan had brought his early sketches and small paintings to the collector to keep or sell to his friends. One of the earliest works that Shmarovin had bought was the sketch from which Levitan painted *Autumn Day. Sokolniki.* When Tretyakov purchased the painting, Levitan went to Shmarovin and begged him to return the sketch, offering him whatever he wanted in exchange. Shmarovin later regretted selling or thoughtlessly giving away so many pieces, claiming that he otherwise would have amassed the largest collection of Levitan's work.[3]

Shmarovin's "Wednesdays" created an atmosphere where artists felt at home. They paid for their own food and drink through an ingenious lottery sale of pastels that they drew as part of the evening's activities. When the pastels were completed, they were priced from one to five rubles, and tickets were sold for ten kopecks each. Some bought only one ticket, more wealthy attendees bought dozens. Anything remaining was put up for sale at Daziaro's art store on Kuznetsky Bridge.

With the coming of spring, Kuvshinnikova convinced Levitan that they should go to Venice—his first trip to western Europe. When they reached Berlin, they heard that it was unseasonably cold in Italy and decided to head first for Paris, where they arrived on March 7. Levitan was overwhelmed by the city to the point of exhaustion. He wrote Chekhov that he found much of what was popular in Parisian art not to his taste: "Lots of the art here is wonderful, but lots of it is extremely psychopathological," possibly referring to the impressionists, whom most Russian critics dismissed as frivolous exhibitionists. Repin had flirted with impressionism in the 1870s, but he was so thoroughly castigated for it when he returned to Russia that his friends sent him to the countryside to be reeducated as a realist.[4] By the 1890s Repin was characterizing impressionists as nothing but pseudo-artistic dilettantes: "The freshness of direct impressions has gone on to the point of eccentricity, clamorous effects, contrived spotting of iridescent color."[5] Levitan, on the other hand, maintained an ongoing dialogue with impressionism. His landscapes were not steadily evolving from a narrative lyricism toward an impressionist spontaneity. Instead, he was swinging dialectically back and forth between the two. The only "ism" that Levitan consistently adhered to was "plein-air-ism."[6]

In Paris, Levitan complained that the French were so overly self-satisfied that they were "enraptured by what to a healthy person with a healthy head and clear thoughts appears insane," for example Pierre Puvis de Chavannes "before whom they bow and idealize, but you can't even imagine what crap it is." Puvis was immensely popular and held sway over contemporary French art as the head of the Société Nationale des Beaux-Arts. When Nesterov had visited Paris the year before, he was totally enraptured by Puvis, especially his allegorical murals in the Parthenon and the Sorbonne. But understandably Levitan was not drawn to the symbolism, visual flatness, and decorative quality of Puvis's paintings. He much preferred spending his time taking in the old masters, telling Chekhov, "[they were] so touching that they brought tears to your eyes. Here there is greatness of spirit!" Beyond looking at the old masters, he, like Nesterov, influenced by what their teachers Savrasov and Polenov had told them, paid the most attention to the Barbizon School painters.

Levitan could not resist commenting on French women as well, saying that he found them perplexing: "They're either unfinished or completely tarted up by centuries of screwing."[7] Chekhov passed on this tidbit in a deadpan comment to Lensky: "I received Levitan's letter from Paris. He writes mostly about the women. He doesn't like them."

After leaving Paris and before going on to Florence and Venice, Levitan and Kuvshinnikova stayed in Bordighera, the resort town bordering the Côte d'Azur where Claude Monet had lived and painted in 1884. Levitan started sketching but found it difficult to immerse himself in the Mediterranean landscape. Pressing concerns back in Moscow plagued him. And once he surrendered to his bouts of depression, he knew that travel and new impressions could do nothing to change things. He wrote to Polenov that "the source of my sufferings is inside me and a trip to wherever is just a way to run away from myself! A terrifying confession!"

He sent Polenov instructions on how best to hang his paintings included in the Itinerant exhibition that was moving from St. Petersburg to a showing at the Moscow School of Painting. His concern was that since these works (*After a Rain. Plyos* and *Evening. Golden Plyos*, which Tretyakov had already purchased for 2,000 rubles) were not painted in strong light, he did not want them displayed near a window. Levitan asked that his paintings be placed in the figures classroom to the left of the entrance. He worried that if the paintings were not properly displayed, "their absolute failure in Moscow would prove to me the erroneousness of the theory under which they were created." Nesterov later maintained that Levitan's first trip abroad made him more self-assured as an artist because he realized that even if he lived in the West "where art was truly free," he would have painted no differently.[8] But in fact, Levitan was still extremely sensitive to how his work was received and not necessarily confident that the public understood his style and approach. In typical neurotic fashion, after making this very explicit request to Polenov, he concluded that perhaps all that he was asking for was pure nonsense, not necessary, and he would understand if Polenov chose to ignore him.

Levitan also complained to Polenov about malicious rumors circulating in Moscow that he had run away to the West in fear because of an incident that took place at one of Shmarovin's "Wednesdays." Levitan and Goloushev had gotten into an argument at one of the soirees, although what prompted the falling out is unknown. Whatever the cause, Levitan was highly offended that Goloushev had being going around telling people that the incident had caused Levitan to flee Moscow: "The scoundrel. But this careerist-doctor won't get away with it; I demand that this phrase-monger give me an explanation. I will rip the mask of nobility from this fellow!" In the end it was another fit of pique of the type that his friends were used to and often chose to ignore. Goloushev remained a devoted supporter of Levitan and his art.

Levitan returned to Moscow in April bringing with him a series of pastel and watercolor sketches. He made a few paintings from these sketches, but soon he was back to working on Russian motifs. Although he gave several of his studies to friends and showed *Spring in Italy* at the Periodic Exhibition at the end of the year, it was obvious that Italian light and Italian colors were not very compelling as a subject.[9] When Chekhov was in Rome a year later, he found it strange that Levitan did not take to Italy: "If I were a solitary painter and had the money, I would live here in the winter. Not even considering its nature and its warmth, Italy is a unique country where you are convinced that art indeed is the king of everything and this conviction gives you courage." But for Levitan inspiration did not come from the Tuscan hills or the Ligurian Sea but the landscape of northern Russia. As soon as Levitan was back in Moscow, Chekhov tried to entice him to join him on his long-planned journey overland across Siberia to Sakhalin Island on the Pacific, an offer Chekhov would not have made lightly given the length of the trip and his prickliness regarding traveling companions. But Levitan declined for reasons that we can only speculate about and made plans to return to the Volga region with Kuvshinnikova.[10]

Chekhov's reasons for surveying the population of the Sakhalin penal colony and documenting its conditions were multiple and cumulative: Nikolai's death had been a shock, prompting him to change how and where he was living; the poor reception of the play *The Wood Demon* renewed his nagging sense that literary art seemed trivial in comparison to the practical worth of science; he had always admired explorers like Nikolai Przhevalsky, whose obituary he had just written; and not least of all, travel provided an escape from unresolved romantic entanglements.[11]

In the spring of 1889, Lidia ("Lika") Mizinova entered the lives of the Chekhovs. She had just started teaching at the same gymnasium as Maria and the two had become friends. Lika's first visit to the Chekhov house caused a stir among the brothers. While she waited shyly in the entry way for Maria to come down, Anton and Mikhail kept walking up and down the staircase to get a better look at her. Lika later told Maria that her first impression was that there were an awful lot of men in her family. Lika was beautiful, a genuine "Swan Princess" according to the bi-sexual Shchepkina-Kupernik, who was attracted by her "softness and elusive charm."[12] Levitan met Lika at the Chekhovs in the fall of 1889 after returning from Plyos. He immediately became infatuated with her and, as was his habit, declared his love—to no avail.[13]

For her part, Lika was very happy to be accepted into this lively, intelligent family. Chekhov put her to work together with Maria and Olga Kundasova, an eccentric family friend who had once been Chekhov's lover, gathering research for his journey. In the month prior to his departure, Chekhov and Lika spent a great deal of time together, often staying out into the early morning hours. On the day of his departure on April 21, he came by to see Lika at one in the afternoon. After a half-hour spent exchanging pleasantries with her great aunt, the two young people went off together. The aunt was sure that they were romantically involved.

A large crowd gathered that bright evening at the Yaroslavl station to see Chekhov off. On the platform were his mother, his sister, his brothers Ivan and Mikhail, Lika, Levitan, and Kuvshinnikova. Dmitri Kuvshinnikov arrived late, bringing with him a flask of expensive cognac. He hung it around Chekhov's shoulder with orders that he should only drink the cognac once he reached the shores of the Pacific Ocean. The parting was painful for Chekhov's family, who depended so much on his presence as the head of their household. They stood, shifting from one foot to another, feeling that something remained to be said but unable to find the words. Maria and her mother started to cry. It had initially been proposed that the family would accompany him as far as the first stop at Sergeev-Posad, about forty miles away, but they decided that they should stay to avoid the pain of another tearful parting. Instead Chekhov would be accompanied by his brother Ivan, Levitan, the Kuvshinnikovs, and Kundasova. Chekhov gave Lika a photograph inscribed: "To the most kindly creature from whom I am running away to Sakhalin and who scratched my nose. I ask suitors and admirers to wear a thimble on their nose. P. S. This inscription, like an exchange of cards, commits me to nothing." The bell sounded; there were hurried final farewells, and Chekhov and his small entourage climbed into the car. The train blew its whistle and at 8:15 p.m. it pulled away from the station. Maria and her mother hugged each other. Mikhail felt so sad that he decided to leave his family at the station and set off for home alone on foot.

At Yaroslavl Chekhov transferred to the steamboat *Alexander Nevsky* and sailed down the Volga, his first impressions spoiled by the rain. When he woke up the next morning, the sun had come out. He saw flooded fields, monasteries bathed in the light, white churches, "surprising expanses; no matter where you looked, it appeared to be a good place to sit and start fishing." The boat stopped at Plyos "where the languid Levitan lived," he wrote his family. Looking at the dark waters of the river and the overcast sky, Chekhov the doctor told his family that he thought it was unhealthy for Levitan to stay on the Volga: "It makes the soul gloomy. Although it wouldn't be all that bad to have an estate on its shores." But the stop at Plyos also prompted Chekhov to write a note to Kuvshinnikova describing the setting in a way that reflected an understanding of how the landscape inspired the painter: the weather was cold; there were clumps of snow on the shore; he heard the sound of a melancholy accordion; he recognized the church and the house with the red roof above the river from Levitan's *Evening. Golden Plyos*. He thanked Kuvshinnikova for the splendid caviar she gave him, which for lack of company he was eating without an accompanying shot of vodka. He promised to open the cognac on the shores of the Pacific.

Alone among the entourage, Kundasova accompanied him on the Volga. He could not fathom why. When asked, she responded vaguely, with a snort of laughter and a tapping of her feet, about some sort of assignation with someone in a ravine near Kinyoshma. He noticed the strange way she ate—mechanically, as if chomping on oats.

As Chekhov made his way across Siberia, his family and friends left Moscow to spend the summer in the country. In early May, several days after seeing Maria off at the Kursk station for the Lintvaryov estate in the Ukraine, Levitan and Kuvshinnikova left for the Volga to spend their fourth summer together, staying in Plyos, Kinyoshma, and Yurevtsev, where he came across the humble monastery that inspired him to rework the motifs first sketched in Savvin and paint *Quiet Abode*. For his part, Chekhov found little in the Russian landscape to delight him until he reached Lake Baikal and the Yenisei River. He wrote home: "The mountains and the Yenisei have rewarded me with sensations that have paid me back a hundred-fold for all the summersaults I've endured and made me curse Levitan as a fool for the stupidity of not coming with me." Chekhov was seeing the beauty of Siberia through Levitan's eyes, and he felt frustrated that his friend was not there to share it with him as he walked along the "picturesque shore" of Lake Baikal: "Levitan is an idiot for not coming with me. The road was wooded, to the right a forest climbing up into the mountains, to the left a forest descending towards Lake Baikal. What ravines! What cliffs! The hue of Lake Baikal is warm and tender."

After an eighty-one-day journey, Chekhov arrived on Sakhalin Island on July 11 with the goal of visiting every settlement in the penal colony. He filled in thousands of note cards in the course of three months and recorded hundreds of conversations. On October 19 he sailed from Vladivostok on the steamer *Petersburg*, which reached Odessa on December 2. He had with him a pet mongoose that he purchased in Ceylon.

It took Chekhov several years to prepare his notes and impressions for publication—individual chapters began to appear in issues of the journal *Russian Thought* in late 1893 into 1894. He then published the book in its entirety in 1895; it was by far the longest work he was ever to write. *Sakhalin Island* is an exhaustive work of investigative reporting that exposes the corruption of a system established to exploit prisoners as colonizers of inhospitable lands and as a valuable source of free labor. Chekhov mixed statistical information with portraits of prisoners, guards, and settlers. He also included vivid descriptions of the landscape—the unmistakable stamp of an accomplished writer. The land was bleak, damp, and depressing, although he also pointed out that if a landscape painter came to Sakhalin, he would recommend that he visit the Arkovo Valley in the summer with its rich hues and tints, the burdocks, rye, oats, potatoes, sunflowers, and poppies creating a kaleidoscope of colors.[14] The book is also a reflection of the altruism and social activism that were a fundamental part of Chekhov's personality throughout his life, whether as a doctor providing free care, a fund-raiser for the construction of village schools, or as a local organizer during Russia's first national census in 1896. Once back home he immediately enlisted Levitan to ask his patrons to pledge donations to a fund set up to benefit Sakhalin schools.

Excited at Chekhov's impending return to Moscow, Levitan proposed during tea at the Chekhov home that friends and family should host a celebratory banquet for him at a local restaurant. He enthusiastically suggested: "We'll pool the money . . . the cost doesn't matter. It's the feeling! Shall we do it, gentlemen?" At this point Chekhov's father, an inveterate crank, stared at Levitan: "Why have a dinner there? Please don't take Anton away from his family." He then decisively announced: "He will have dinner at home without you!" The group lowered their heads. Levitan turned red and looked to the group for support. But none was forthcoming, and the idea of a banquet was dropped.[15]

Chekhov spent barely a month at home before he went off to St. Petersburg on January 7, 1891, for three weeks of frenetic socializing, briefly taking up with the actress Darya Musina-Pushkina, another of Maria's friends. Two days after his departure, Lika sent Chekhov a letter in which she attempted to move beyond the customary ironic repartee to talk about her true feelings: "I wrote you a long letter today while at the Council, but it's a good thing I wasn't able to send it. I just now reread it and became horrified—nothing but weeping." She imagined (correctly) that he was having a grand time being wined and dined while she was feeling jealous and ill: "When you get back to Moscow, don't forget to drop by the Vaganovo Cemetery and visit my remains."[16] In response, Chekhov gave her nothing but caustic wit, inventing ridiculous names for her presumed suitors: "If you die, Trophim [Levitan] will shoot himself, and Pryshchikov ["Pimply"—the medical student Evgeny Ballas] will suffer from childbirth spasms. Only I will be glad of your death." He hoped that if Trophim did marry her, he would come down with "jaundice, nonstop hiccups, and spasms in his right cheek." He closed the letter: "Farewell, villain of my heart."

Lika countered with a tactic she was starting to employ frequently—parading Levitan as a potential rival: "I just returned from your house. Levitan accompanied me home! [. . .] Don't pay attention to my handwriting. I am writing in the dark and in addition after Levitan has brought me home! And who is accompanying you?" At the same time she still let Chekhov know that she was missing him: "Your letter made me terribly happy today. And I didn't expect such happiness. If you want to make me even happier, then write me again [. . .]. When are you finally returning? Like Pokhlebina [a piano teacher known to be infatuated with Chekhov], I too have been suffering for almost a week." Chekhov knew Levitan well enough not to trust him alone with Lika, yet he sensed from her tone of voice that she was not seriously attracted to the artist.

Lately, Chekhov had been mocking Levitan's increasing coziness with his wealthy supporters. Having worked for almost two years in the nicely appointed studio offered to him by Sergei Morozov, Levitan was invited in 1891 to move into the apartment below the studio. After years of living in one set of furnished rooms after another, he finally had comfortable and convenient living quarters where he could remain for the rest of his life. He enjoyed the patronage of Sophia Golitsyna, whose husband, Prince Vladimir, was appointed deputy mayor of Moscow in 1883. Levitan and other painters often gathered at Vvedenskoe, the manor purchased by the arts patron Count Sergei Sheremetev.[17] In his letters to Lika from St. Petersburg, Chekhov started a running joke that they (and the stationery they were using) did not meet the standards of high society. In his first letter to Maria from the capital, Chekhov sent greetings to his family, friends, Lika, and "the dark-haired Yid from high society." A few days later he told Maria to pass on to the ailing Lika that she should "not eat flour and avoid Levitan. Neither at the Council nor in high society will she find a better admirer of her than I." Lika told Chekhov that during a visit from Maria, both Kuvshinnikova and Levitan dropped by: "What audacity to come to my place together! You would not have done that, of that I am sure." She also joked that she was preparing for her wedding shower "because I have decided to get married *par dépit* [out of pique] (only not to Trophim)." She urged him to get all the partying out of his system: "I want you to have twenty-eight more dinners so that you will be full for the whole year. And you know, if Levitan looked the least bit like you, I would invite him to dinner!!" Chekhov's reply kept up the bantering tone and the allusions to Levitan. He bought the stationery that she had requested: "I think this paper completely satisfies the requirements of high society to which Levitan, Fedotov [her drama teacher], and a horse-drawn tram conductor belong [. . .]. Forgive me that this letter is so sloppily written. I'm agitated, shaking and fearful, that high society will find out about our correspondence. Please do not show my letter to anyone!"

On March 6 Levitan went from being an exhibitor to an elected member of the Association of Itinerant Art Exhibitions. A few days earlier the general committee selected three of Levitan's paintings (*Quiet Abode, Dilapidated Courtyard*, and *Borghetto*) for the Nineteenth Itinerant Exhibition that opened in St. Petersburg on March 9. Chekhov was again in St. Petersburg in mid-March, this time preparing for his first trip to western Europe. A few days before his departure for Vienna, he went to see the Itinerant exhibition. He excitedly reported to his brother Mikhail that "Levitan is celebrating the birthday of his magnificent muse. His picture [*Quiet Abode*] is causing a furor. Grigorovich took me through the exhibition pontificating like Cicero, explaining the virtues and the inadequacies of every painting. He is in raptures over Levitan's landscape. Polonsky finds the bridge to be too long; Pleshcheev sees a discord between the name of the painting and its contents: 'Excuse me, but it's called a quiet abode, but here everything is so filled with the joy of life,' etc. In any case, Levitan's success is out of the ordinary." The press and the critics who had ignored Levitan's paintings in the previous exhibition were now heaping praise on *Quiet Abode*.[18] As usual, the exhibition traveled on to Moscow, and again the critics singled out Levitan's painting for praise.

This was a significant breakthrough for Levitan—the Russian art world had finally come to see him as a fully formed and gifted painter with a rare mastery over the moods and emotions elicited by his works, a quality that Chekhov had long recognized. He re-created the experience of seeing *Quiet Abode* several years later when he wrote "Three Years" (1895). In the story an unhappily married couple take their family to an Itinerant exhibition at the School of Painting. At first the wife, Yulia Sergeevna, imitates her husband's habit of looking at the paintings through his fists, which has the effect of making the subjects look more life-like. She is a lazy observer; many of the paintings look the same to her. Her husband, Alyosha Laptev, fancies himself a critic who notices things, albeit superficially: "'This forest is by Shishkin,' her husband explained to her. 'He always paints one and the same thing . . . But take a look here: you never see violet snow like this . . . And this boy's left arm is shorter than his right.'" She stops in front of a small landscape and gazes at it indifferently:

> In the foreground a small river, a bridge made of logs across it, a path on the other side disappearing into the dark grass, a field, then to the right a piece of forest, a bonfire nearby: it must have been a night watch. And in the distance, the last glow of the sunset.

The scene described is reminiscent of *Quiet Abode* in parts (the small river, the wood bridge across it, the last glow of sunset), but also different. Chekhov may have conflated it with Levitan's *Evening Shadows* (1893), which depicted an open field near dusk with a bit of woods on the right, and added his own element—the watchmen's bonfire. But the impact that the painting has on Yulia Sergeevna precisely describes the way that a Levitan painting affects the viewer:

> Yulia Sergeevna imagined herself walking across the little bridge, then down the path further and further, and it is quiet all around, drowsy landrails cry, the fire flickers far ahead. And for some reason, it suddenly seemed to her that she had seen those same clouds that stretched across the red part of the sky, and the forest, and the fields long ago and many times; she felt lonely, and she wanted to walk, walk, walk down the path; and where the sunset's glow was, there rested the reflection of something unearthly, eternal.

The painting arouses in Yulia Sergeevna a spontaneous emotional response. The landscape evokes in her a mood that is pensive, profoundly moved, and connected to things beyond expression. There is no better description of the impact of a Levitan painting. The art historian Pavel Muratov alluded to a feeling similar to Yulia Sergeevna's sense of melancholic déjà vu when he commented in 1910 that Levitan's landscapes expressed "paeans of the familiar." Levitan's paintings, he wrote, "bring to our minds thousands of remembrances about places, people, events in our lives. Amidst these fields, forests, rivers, summer sunsets, the life history of each of us was played out."[19] In the story Yulia Sergeevna can barely contain her rapture as she looks at the landscape:

> "How well it's painted!" she said, surprised that she had suddenly understood the painting. "Look Alyosha! Do you see how quiet it is here?"
>
> She tried to explain why she liked this landscape so much, but neither her husband nor Kostya [a family friend] understood her. She kept looking at the landscape with a sad smile, and the fact that the others found nothing special in it troubled her; then she began walking around the rooms again and looking at the pictures, she wanted to fully understand them, and it no longer seemed to her that many of the pictures in the exhibition were alike.

This painting has caused her to look at art in a completely new way, as if she could now understand a language that previously sounded to her like noise. She returns home and begins to look with revulsion at the mediocre painting her husband has hung over the grand piano in the drawing room: "Who would want to have such pictures!"

On March 17 Chekhov boarded the express train leaving St. Petersburg for Vienna. In virtually every letter to his family he sent greetings to "the handsome Levitan, golden-haired Lika," and the Kuvshinnikovs. He had broken his pince-nez back home in Moscow and left them with Mikhail to have them repaired. From Paris on April 21 he wrote his brother: "I am simply suffering without my glasses." He visited the annual Salon being held in the Palace of Industry, where the main attractions were the works of Academy painters such as Jean Paul Laurens and Jules Lefebvre. "I didn't see half of what's there thanks to my near-sightedness," he wrote. "By the way, Russian artists are much more serious than French artists. In comparison with the local landscape painters I saw yesterday, Levitan is king."

In May Levitan sold *Quiet Abode* for 600 rubles through the Itinerant Association to a Mr. Alferov. He did not even know Alferov's first name and patronymic and instructed his colleague Yegor Khruslov at the Association to send the painting to the address he had without indicating a name. Responding to Khruslov's mentioning that Nesterov hugely admired the painting, Levitan told him: "Don't believe Nesterov's raptures. He gets carried away like no one I know." Despite having taken very different artistic paths, Levitan and Nesterov remained close and effusively praised each other's work. In *Quiet Abode*, Nesterov undoubtedly saw symbolism and religious feeling in the monastery towers and cupolas simultaneously reflected in the still water and rising up into the early evening sky.

The day after returning to Russia on May 2, Chekhov left with his family for a dacha that Mikhail had found at the last minute near Aleksin on the Oka River in Kaluga province south of Moscow. Anton did not like the place—the house was bleak and small, without latrines, and located not far from a noisy train trestle. For the first few days after their arrival, a strong wind kept them from venturing outside. The family immediately decided to invite "beautiful Lika" to come for a visit. She arrived by boat through Serpukhov with Levitan in tow, presumably hoping to get a rise out of Chekhov. Despite the cramped quarters, Mikhail recalled that the guests filled the house with laughter: "In general it suddenly became a lot more cheerful at our place on the banks of the Oka."[20] Anton had an audience for his inexhaustible and merciless displays of wit; Levitan paraded in front of the ladies with lovesick sighs; the mongoose amused everyone with his antics.

On board the river boat, Lika and Levitan had struck up a conversation with a young local landowner, Evgeny Bylim-Kolosovsky, and mentioned to him that they were on their way to see the writer Chekhov. Two days later two carriages arrived at the dacha to bring the Chekhov entourage on a visit to the young landowner's estate about ten miles away at Bogimovo. Anton fell in love with the place, entranced by the image during their visit of Lika waiting under an awning in front of the house during a brief downpour. Mikhail found it to be a "magnificent, but somewhat rundown estate that boasted a huge stone manor, linden-lined alleys, a charming river, several ponds, and a watermill." He continued, "The rooms inside the house were so spacious that our voices echoed. The living room had columns and the reception hall had a gallery for musicians. Anton was so enchanted with Bogimovo that he decided we should move there."[21] The estate already had summer residents, and Bylim-Kolosovsky offered the Chekhovs the second story of the house.

Lika and Levitan soon left. Prior to their departure, Chekhov and Lika had some sort of a *tête-à-tête*, an emotional one, at least on her part. Chekhov in his first letter to her that summer jokingly referred to the encounter: "Oh, wonderful Lika! When you dampened my right shoulder with a tearful sob (I removed the stain with benzene), and when you ate slice after slice of our bread and meat, we hungrily devoured your face and the back of your neck with our eyes. Oh, Lika, Lika, you devilish beauty." He invited "golden, mother-of-pearl and lisle-threaded Lika" to visit him when he moved into the house of Bylim-Kolosovsky: "The very one who filled you with milk and at the same time forgot to offer you berries [. . .]. Come smell the flowers, fish, stroll, and sob." He mentioned that the mongoose had run away and feared that he was dead. Chekhov finished his letter with a literal jab at his rival, the "Moor" Levitan: "When you are with Trophim at the Alhambra, I hope you accidentally stab him in the eyes with a fork."

Back in Moscow, either by her own design or by mutual agreement, Lika decided to spend most of the summer in the company of Levitan and Kuvshinnikova. Lika had an aunt who lived on an old estate, Pokrovskoe, in Tver province northwest of Moscow. The three of them went there to look for a place where Levitan and Kuvshinnikova could stay for the summer. Levitan found a dacha he liked very much in nearby Zatishie and decided to move in. Lika returned to Moscow for a while before coming back to Pokrovskoe. Since she would have been warmly welcomed by the entire Chekhov family had she accepted Anton's invitation to come to Bogimovo, it is telling that she decided against it. She was frustrated by Chekhov's refusal to commit himself emotionally beyond admiring her at arm's length with a never-ending stream of witticisms and playful endearments. In comparison, while it served her purpose to use Levitan to arouse Chekhov's jealousy, she harbored no deep feelings for him. Kuvshinnikova understood this, and the two women were becoming genuinely fond of each other.

It also served Levitan's purpose—a rival's desire (if only in jest) to be the victorious lover—to goad Chekhov into jealousy. On May 29 Levitan sent a letter to Chekhov from Zatishie: "I am writing to you from that charming corner of the earth where everything, from the air to, God forgive me, the very last small insect on earth is suffused with her, with her, blessed Lika! She is not here yet, but she will be, since she does not love you, you tow-head, but me, dark-haired and volcanic, and she will come only here where I am. It's painful for you to read this, but out of my love for the truth I cannot hide this from you."

Typically for Levitan, his initial enthusiasm for the location as a source of motifs for his painting had given way to a feeling of disappointment: "I walk around and am amazed how I could have liked everything here. I'm a complete psychopath!" Nevertheless he remained in a playful mood in writing to his friend. He wondered whether he made a mistake in not getting a dacha at Bogimovo and begged Chekhov to come visit him, offering to pay for half the costs: "It would be entertaining—the fishing is wonderful and the company would be quite charming, consisting of Sophia Petrovna, me, the Friend [Dmitri Kuvshinnikov], and the Vestal Virgin [Lika]." The letter trailed off with a series of daffy salutations: "Be well and remember that there is a

Levitan who loves you all very much, you scoundrels! [. . .] I kiss you on the tip of your nose and can smell the wildfowl."

Kuvshinnikova made her own separate invitation to Chekhov to visit them, chiding Levitan for failing to pass on her greetings. She asked Chekhov to tell Maria that she wished her a successful summer of painting, noting that her own paintings "for some reason aren't making any progress this year." A bit later she sent another note to Chekhov asking him to send her some quinine powder, and some medicinal drops to treat nerve pain in her teeth.[22]

In early June, Chekhov wrote back to Levitan that Maria had become ill. The news, and the off-hand way Chekhov mentioned it, upset Levitan: "I told Lika about Maria Pavlovna's illness, and she also became very concerned, although she says that if Maria Pavlovna's illness was something serious, you wouldn't have written about it in such a playful tone. She says that if it were something dangerous, you would have telegraphed her. For God's sake, let me know; it's making me very upset." Chekhov also told Levitan, as he had Lika, that the mongoose had run off. This seemed to upset Levitan almost as much as Maria's illness: "How did you let the mongoose get away? That's the damnedest thing! It's simply obscene to bring an animal from Ceylon only to lose it in Kaluga province!!!" Above all, it was Chekhov's unemotional tone, something that frustrated Lika as well, that most exasperated Levitan: "You're a total phlegmatic to write about Maria Pavlovna's illness and about losing the mongoose in such a cold-blooded manner as if that's the normal way to do it!" Given his disapproval of Kuvshinnikova, Chekhov would not have appreciated the fact that she chose to append her own carping to Levitan's letter: "I am adding my anxiousness and disappointment—the first regarding Maria Pavlovna's illness, the second regarding the poor mongoose! I don't understand how it's possible to abandon this tiny foreigner to fate. I simply begin to think that you, Chekhov, were extremely jealous of his success and for that reason consciously didn't protect your rival!" Chekhov must have reacted to this as just so much hyperbole from an eccentric, high-strung couple—Maria soon recovered and left to visit a friend; and the mongoose was found hiding in a quarry on the other side of the Oka River and returned to Bogimovo.

The weather at Zatishie began to improve in June, and Levitan was starting to find some motifs to paint. He made sketches for the painting *Deep Waters* at a mill on the estate of Baroness Woolf in Bernov, where he and Kuvshinnikova would go for picnics. The baroness told them that the mill pond had also inspired Pushkin to write "Rusalka" based on a tragic event that took place there. Her great-grandfather had a young stable hand who fell in love with the daughter of the mill owner. She became pregnant, and when the baron found out about it, he had the young man sent off into the army. The young woman drowned herself in the pond. Pushkin had heard the story while a guest at a neighboring estate. Levitan started with a small sketch but then decided to draw a large study at the site. Kuvshinnikova recalled that "for an entire week every morning we got into a cart—Levitan in the coach box and I in the back seat—and took the study to the mill and back as if it were an icon."[23] Increasingly occupied with his painting, Levitan found it harder to make plans to visit Chekhov as promised. Levitan told him: "I'm thinking of spending time there towards the fall. But more about this later."

In the meantime Levitan continued to sincerely praise and devilishly taunt Chekhov. He told Chekhov that during one stretch of poor weather he stayed inside and "thoughtfully reread" his first two published collections: *Motley Stories* (1886) and *In the Twilight* (1887): "You really struck me as a landscapist. I'm not talking about the mass of very interesting thoughts, but about the landscape paintings in them—they are beyond perfection; for example the pictures of the steppe, the mounds, the sheep in the story 'Happiness' are striking." What drew Levitan to this story was the way that Chekhov used descriptions of the natural setting to create a pensive, languorous mood that echoes the shared realization by an old shepherd and a local overseer, as they converse in the predawn gloom, that life is ultimately disappointing. The sheep "stood with drooping heads, thinking. Their thoughts, lingering and lazy." The broad steppe, the sky, the procession of days and nights crush them into apathy. The two men trade stories of hidden treasures protected by magic spells buried beneath the steppe. The overseer understands that these treasures are the happiness denied in this life. The old shepherd admits that he wouldn't know what to do with a treasure if he actually found one. Their conversation is interrupted by a loud sound resounding across the steppe, "a threatening bang crashing against a rock." The young shepherd accompanying the old man says it is a bucket broken away at the mine pits, an off-stage discordant note that Chekhov used again to similar effect in *The Cherry Orchard*. Silence returns to the steppe as dawn approaches, and the coming of the light, as in "The Steppe," reveals the outlines of a mercilessly uncaring natural world:

> The watch-mounds and burial mounds, which rose here and there above the horizon, and the boundless steppe, had a severe, death-like look; there was a feeling of endless time and utter indifference to man in their immobility and silence; another thousand years would pass, millions of people would die, while they would continue to stand as they have stood, with absolutely no pity for the dead and no interest in the living, and not one soul would ever know why they stood there, and what secret of the steppes was hidden beneath them.

The overseer smiles and says: "What an expanse. Lord have mercy on us! You would have quite a search to find happiness in it!" Here again we see the common aesthetic impulse shared by Chekhov and Levitan—that a landscape precisely observed and contemplated, filtered through words and images, can generate a work of art inseparably containing both beauty and sadness.

Levitan was so taken by "Happiness" that he read it out loud to Kuvshinnikova and Lika. "They were enraptured," he wrote to Chekhov, using the opportunity to stoke their rivalry. "Do you notice what a generous soul I am. I read your stories to Lika and I go into raptures! This is what genuine magnanimity is!"

Almost a month had passed when Lika wrote back to Chekhov on June 10 from Pokrovskoe. Echoing his comic salutations, she started the letter: "Surprising, inimitable Anton Pavlovich." She offered a bow to the mongoose and hoped he would run away again. Lika brought up Kuvshinnikova and Levitan several times, passing on greetings from her and "Trophim." She complained that she only knew how Chekhov and his sister were doing through what Levitan had told her. "Sophia Petrovna is being very nice to me, always inviting me over, but Levitan is gloomy and morose, and I often recall that you would call him the Moor." She closed the letter indicating that her address was the same as Levitan's "only write 'Pokrovskoe village.'" Lika told Chekhov that she terribly wanted to visit him, but her health was preventing it: "I'm getting along pretty badly since I'm almost completely unable to take advantage of summer and my favorite evenings because I can't go out after the sun goes down. I'm not allowed to go swimming and am suffering as a result. I can't even talk loudly or at length thanks to some sort of moist wheezing that I developed before leaving" Moscow. She hoped that she could visit him in the near future and once again "burst out sobbing." In the meantime, Lika tried again unsuccessfully to get Chekhov to change the tone of his letters to her: "Anton Pavlovich, your letters are disgraceful. You write an entire page but in it you say a couple of words, and even they are absolutely idiotic. I would gladly give you a smack on the back of the head for such letters."

Chekhov was in the middle of writing again to Lika when he received her letter. He came close to at least vaguely expressing some sincere feelings for her. His entreaty to have her visit him was cloaked in mock effrontery, but there was also an undertone of frustration in his plea. He found Levitan's proximity to her irritating. At the bottom of the letter he drew a heart with an arrow through it, saying "This is my signature." His desire to see her was deflected onto others:

While amusing yourself with the Circassian Levitan, you have completely forgotten that you promised my brother Ivan to come visit us by July 1, and you have totally failed to reply to my sister's letters. I also wrote to you in Moscow inviting you, but my letter has remained a voice crying in the wilderness. Although you are accepted in the highest circles [. . .] you've just the same been poorly raised, and I don't regret that I once whipped you. You need to understand that waiting for your arrival every day not only wears on us but also costs us money: usually for dinner we only eat yesterday's soup, but when expecting guests, we in addition prepare boiled beef that we buy from the neighboring cooks.

Chekhov went on to describe the beauties of the Bogimovo estate, saying that they often go on walks "during which I usually close my eyes and bend my right arm imagining that you are walking along with me." He sent his greetings to Levitan, but this time without a trace of humor. He was concerned that there might in fact be something going on between them: "Tell him not to write about you in every letter. Firstly, this isn't magnanimous on his part, and secondly, I don't really care how happy he is."

Chekhov appended the letter with reactions to what Lika had just written back to him. With much exaggeration he took her to task for the tone of her letter: "It's absolutely filled with such nice expressions as 'the devil crush you,' 'the devil take it,' 'anathema,' 'smack on the back of the head,' 'scum,' 'scarf up' and so forth. What can I say? Cart drivers like Trophim have had a wonderful influence on you." He also responded with medical advice on how best to recover her health: "You can swim and take evening walks. All this is nonsense. My entire insides are filled with dry and wet wheezing, but I swim and stroll and am still alive. You do need to drink the waters. This I approve of."

Lika replied almost immediately, chastising Chekhov for his bad advice, rudeness, and false suspicions: "As a doctor you don't understand anything. I only have to breathe in a little dampness in order to have a totally sleepless night from coughing, and in the morning I'm completely unable to talk; and as far as swimming is concerned, there is nothing to say since I haven't tried it at all." She then proceeded to set him straight on his attitude toward Kuvshinnikova and Levitan, telling him that Kuvshinnikova now had a grudge against him: "You seemingly ignore her in your letters to Levitan in spite of the fact that she invited you and Masha to visit her; you haven't replied or written to her about this." Where Lika previously sought to play up Levitan as a romantic rival, she now told Chekhov that he had nothing to fear from Levitan "whom I can only lick my lips at, since he doesn't dare come near me, and we're never left alone.

Sophia Petrovna is very nice; she is now very kind and utterly sincere with me. Clearly, she is now quite sure that I cannot be a danger to her." As a result, Lika told Chekhov that "you have no right to write to me about Levitan in that way. You really are anathema. You always spoil everything for me, because I received your letter in Zatishie and had in the presence of Sophia Petrovna to read the phrase 'Amusing yourself with the Circassian Levitan' and so forth." Lika insisted that "absolutely nothing is happening with me or with Levitan when we meet, rest assured!" She maintained: "I desperately want to come soon to Bogimovo, take a stroll, and hang on to your arm while you silently curse me." She added that "when I come, I will be sure to bring a stick with me so that I can teach you some civility."[24]

Somewhat chastened, Chekhov replied to "poor, sick Likisha" that she should delay visiting him for several weeks since Maria was about to leave and would not return before July 3. He continued to give her very specific advice, some serious, some in jest, regarding her health: "Talk less and don't shout when talking to your grandmother and Levitan. In letters to good friends, don't call them idiots." He told her that he had written to Kuvshinnikova and thanked her for her invitation to stay with them, although he gave no indication that he had any plans to leave Bogimovo. Chekhov cryptically told Lika, "I will no longer write to you."

Over the course of the rest of the summer, that statement turned out to be both true and not true. He wrote three short notes to her in June and July, but each time in the guise of another person. In one he took on the persona of an imagined lover Petya, who addressed her in the intimate "you": "Dear Lida! I'm sending you my mugshot." Enclosed was the photograph of an unknown young man with an inscription in Chekhov's hand: "To Lida from Petya." The note continued: "We shall see each other tomorrow. Don't forget your Petka. I kiss you one thousand times!!! I bought Chekhov's stories: how magnificent they are! You should buy them." This was followed by another note, this time in the name of another fictional admirer, Marshal of the Nobility Golovnin-Rtishchev: "Dear Lidia Stakhievna! I love you passionately like a tiger and offer you my hand." Finally at the end July, Chekhov wrote to Lika in the name of his sister Maria, again using the intimate "you" form: "Dear Lika! If you have decided to dissolve your touching triple union for a few days, I will convince my brother to put off his departure. He wanted to go on the fifth of August. Come on the first or second. Oh, if you only knew how much my stomach hurts. Your loving, M. Chekhova." These joking notes underscored Chekhov's growing sense of frustration. Separately Lika and Levitan continued to put off coming to visit him. Their "touching triple union" (with Kuvshinnikova) made him feel excluded.

Yet Chekhov himself seemed disinclined to make the effort to visit Lika and Levitan. Much of his time was taken up with writing—he was both working on the story "The Duel" and organizing his notes from Sakhalin. At Bogimovo he lived in a huge, columned room with a couch that he slept on. In the mornings he worked at the windowsill overlooking the estate grounds usually until about eleven o'clock. After taking a break to go fishing or mushroom hunting, he would have lunch, then return to work around three o'clock and continue until the evening. In mid-July he wrote Levitan asking about the Pushkin poem "Remembrance," which they must have talked about earlier. Levitan, with his much admired knowledge of Russian verse, wrote Chekhov back quoting the poem in its entirety. Chekhov included an excerpt in chapter 17 of "The Duel," in which the poem's meditation on the oppressive weight of remorse is associated with Laevsky and his thoughts on the evening before the duel takes place. In the same letter, Levitan once again said that he very much wanted to visit Chekhov but was currently occupied with a crowd of guests, including Kuvshinnikova's husband and her father.

Levitan and Kuvshinnikova frequently spent their evenings in Pokrovskoe at the Panafidin estate. She often played their piano while Levitan sat outside on the terrace and listened. For her, some of these evenings "were suffused with a special sort of mystical tone." She recalled one night in particular when a guest, a young woman named Natasha, after listening to Kuvshinnikova play, let down her blonde hair, went out onto the terrace, and started screeching like an owl. She "did this with such perfection that after a few minutes real owls would respond, take off toward the house and settling in the trees by the terrace repeated the music with their own cries, and Natasha, like a leader, would support their efforts with their own cries. It resulted in something quite unexpected, and Levitan was in ecstasy, the more so since he was somewhat attracted to Natasha."[25]

Toward the end of summer, Kuvshinnikova abruptly returned to Moscow, possibly after a jealous quarrel with her lover. Levitan was invited to move into the Panafidin house, where Lika was still staying. The large hall was turned into a studio for him. The entire household arranged their day around Levitan's work schedule. They entertained him in the evenings, and when not working he was happy to join them on excursions in the surrounding countryside or on mushroom hunts. Among the work completed at the Pokrovskoe "studio" was a sketch *Autumn*, which he eventually gave to Lika in return for a photograph from her, and an unusual full-length portrait of Nikolai Panafidin, which according to Kuvshinnikova, Levitan always intended to exhibit but never did. He had misgivings about his talents as a portrait painter.

Levitan wrote one more letter to Chekhov that summer, neither one realizing that this would be their last correspondence for over three years. Levitan apologized that a spurt of painting activity was keeping him from going anywhere: "I really awfully want to see you, but I don't know when I can tear myself away—I've undertaken some nice work." Instead, he again invited Chekhov to come visit him: "It would be an extreme joy to see your crocodile physiognomy here in Zatishie. The fishing is terrific here: perch, pike, all kinds of water creatures!" With mock pomposity he signed the letter as the dwarf king "Levitan the VII of the Nibelungs."

On August 18, Chekhov sent off his long story "The Duel" to Suvorin. He had had a productive summer as a writer, but a bitterly disappointing one personally. Since 1885, with the exception of the time on Sakhalin, Chekhov had devoted his summers to dacha life, orchestrating an intensely convivial atmosphere so familiar to us from his plays—a house full of family and guests, many of them men and women in their twenties and thirties bursting with wit and merriment. Inevitably added to the mix was the piquancy of flirtations amid mock rivalries and real jealousies, with Chekhov very much at the center. Not this summer. Despite a string of promises, Levitan and Lika never returned to Bogimovo. To make matters worse, it was evident they were enjoying the lively atmosphere at Zatishie and Pokrovskoe, where at one point there were twenty-three guests staying at the estate. Left alone, Chekhov had plenty of time to stew over his sense of being abandoned by two of his closest friends, and to resent Kuvshinnikova's role in keeping them away. The time spent thinking about this "touching triple union" enjoying themselves without him led to the writing of a story that he started working on as soon as he finished "The Duel." Published in early 1892, "The Grasshopper" severed his relationships with Levitan and the Kuvshinnikovs. The story made it evident that when it came to his writing, as Lika astutely told Chekhov, "you really don't care how people will take what you do."

6

1892

"THE GRASSHOPPER"

THE SAME DAY THAT CHEKHOV sent "The Duel" off to Suvorin, he wrote to the St. Petersburg lawyer Fyodor Chervinsky, asking him to find out how much *The Field* would pay for an "appropriate story" he had in mind. Chervinsky mentioned to Vladimir Tikhonov, who had just become the editor of *The North*, that Chekhov had a story and was looking for a publisher. Tikhonov leaped at the prospect of having Chekhov appear in his publication and wrote to him in September 1891 asking, if he hadn't yet finished the story, could he at least provide a title so that he could boost subscriptions by promoting it as scheduled for his first issue in January. However, Chekhov had not gotten very far in writing the story. He replied to Tikhonov: "I can't tell you what it's going to be called. It's just as hard to name it now as it is to determine the color of a chicken that will be hatched from an egg that hasn't yet been laid." Tikhonov persisted, but Chekhov continued to put him off: "Just call it 'Story' or 'Inhabitants.' Both titles will work." He told Tikhonov "I'm up to my neck right now" and protested that he would not be able to get the story to him until the end of November. He was finishing up "The Wife," which had been promised to the more prestigious *Northern Herald*. Ten days after sending off "The Wife," he mailed a story called "The Great Man" to Tikhonov, explaining with tongue in cheek, "I am sending you a small, tender romance for family reading." Around December 11, Chekhov made some final corrections to the galleys, including changing the title to "The Grasshopper."[1] The story appeared in the January 5 and January 12 issues of *The North*. The critical reviews were few but favorable. Perhaps because it was published in St. Petersburg, there was no immediate reaction among Chekhov's Moscow friends.

Around the same time he was making final changes to "The Grasshopper," Chekhov did something (it is not known what) to offend Kuvshinnikova. He admitted as much in giving her a copy of the new book version of "The Duel" on December 18 with the inscription: "To Sophia Petrovna from the disgraced but unwaveringly devoted author."[2] Levitan and Chekhov were still very much on good terms. While visiting the Chekhov household in December, Levitan drew two pastels that he gave to the family. Both men became involved in raising funds for famine relief following the failure of the harvest in twenty provinces of central Russia that fall. The famine had exposed the cruelty of the state's financial policies toward the peasantry, demanding their surpluses to drive up exports while taxing them heavily at the same time. The peasants had neither financial nor agricultural reserves to fall back on, and the state on its own could not provide adequate relief. It grudgingly allowed private fund-raising. The public felt a sense of shame that Russia, in spite of its rapid industrialization, could so easily become impoverished.[3]

Chekhov approached fellow doctors and writers for donations and even managed to get the conservative Suvorin involved. In "The Wife," a story of marital love-hatred, the couple's competing efforts to organize famine relief become the focus of their enmity. For his part, Levitan donated three landscapes that were sold at a benefit auction organized by the Moscow Society of Art Lovers. One of them, *Winter in the Woods* (1885), was an atypical snowy scene, and even more unusual, the wolf in it had been painted by Stepanov.

At the end of 1891 Polenov painted his magnificent portrait of his former student. Wearing a dress coat, white collar, and cravat, Levitan sits with his arms folded, intently gazing to the side with heavily lidded eyes. His demeanor is introspective and confident. The only sketches that Polenov worked from in preparing his portrait were the studies he had previously done using Levitan as the model for Jesus in his painting *Christ and the Sinner*.[4]

Once again Levitan had a busy winter season of exhibitions that inevitably led to sales of his work. Five of his paintings were included in the Eleventh Periodic Exhibition of the Moscow Society of Art Lovers, including *The Birch Grove*, which he had started working on at Babkino in 1885. After the exhibition closed in February 1892, the painting was purchased by Alexei Langovoi, a medical school classmate of Chekhov's and an art collector, who had just bought his first Levitan piece, *Winter in the Woods*, at the November charity auction. Langovoi was particularly attracted to the way that Levitan created the dappled light in *The Birch Grove*. He boasted that it took four summers of reworking the painting before Levitan felt he had achieved the effect he was striving for, whereas his rival collector Tretyakov had once bought a Volga landscape (*After a Rain*) that Levitan had finished off in a mere five hours. It was common for Levitan to spend months, sometimes years, revising a motif in the studio, making sketch after sketch, before he felt he had a painting that was ready for exhibition. But at that point, he worked quickly, imbuing the final work on canvas with the same spontaneity achieved in his sketches.

Langovoi met Levitan in January when he visited the painter's studio. He recalled the door being opened by a tall, thin man with sad eyes and "an intelligent and extraordinarily expressive face. His voice was pleasant, but with a unique muffled timbre." Levitan took Langovoi up the winding staircase to his studio and started to show him his paintings. Langovoi's eye was caught by a seascape on a rainy, foggy day, painted in Bordighera, Italy. Levitan explained that for him the seas never appeared as depicted, for example by the landscapist Rufin Sudkovsky, with transparent water through which you could see every pebble. "What I saw was a dirty, oily mass," Levitan told Langovoi, who bought the painting on the spot. Langovoi soon became the artist's friend and doctor.[5]

Later that month, Levitan dropped by Nesterov's apartment very early one morning to take a look at his new painting, *The Vision of the Adolescent Bartholomew*. Nesterov wrote his relatives that Levitan was endless in his praise of the highly symbolic painting: "He deeply loved the thing to the extent that he started to speak nonsense and concluded that the picture shouldn't be exhibited here, but sent directly to the Salon" in Paris. Levitan encouraged Tretyakov to take a look at the painting and tried to get him to say what he thought of it after he saw it. Tretyakov initially remained "stubbornly quiet" about whether he was interested in acquiring the work.[6]

In February, Levitan traveled to St. Petersburg to take part in the general meeting of the Itinerant Association. He supported a proposal by Polenov that gave the more talented members of the Association the right to have two paintings accepted without jury approval in the annual exhibitions. In the Twentieth Itinerant Exhibition, which opened in St. Petersburg on February 23, Levitan displayed four paintings, including *Deep Waters*, which he began in Zatishie the previous summer. Tretyakov bought the painting for the astounding sum of 3,000 rubles. By comparison, Langovoi bought *The Birch Grove* for 125 rubles.

Chekhov too now had a sufficient income to act on his desire to buy a country estate. In February, on Anton's behalf, his brother Mikhail bought Melikhovo—nearly six hundred acres of birch woods and pasture with a small wooden house, located forty-five miles south of Moscow. Getting there required taking a train as far as the station at Lopasnya, then traveling six miles by horse or carriage along a very rough country road. Chekhov moved there on March 4. On March 18 Lika wrote to him at Melikhovo, mainly complaining about her poor health, the bad weather, and how miserable she was in Moscow: "I have not been seeing any Moscow people. Levitan came by while I was out, and Sappho hasn't been here at all." Chekhov had decided to start calling Kuvshinnikova "Sappho" after seeing Franz Grillparzer's tragedy of the same name staged at the Maly Theater on February 5. In the play the poet Sappho throws herself into the sea when she discovers that the young Phaon loves not her but the maid Melitta. So Chekhov took to calling Levitan "Phaon," Lika "Melitta," and Kuvshinnikova "Sappho."

Maria Chekhova had invited Lika to Melikhovo for Easter, but Lika told Chekhov that she wasn't coming and asked him for now not to say anything to Maria about it. In turn Chekhov had asked Lika to consider spending the summer at a dacha near Melikhovo: "So, what have you decided regarding the dacha? You're a liar, and I don't believe you: you absolutely don't want to live near us. Your dacha is in the Myasnitska section of town under the fire tower [referring to the Kuvshinnikov apartment]—you are there heart and soul. We are nothing to you. We are last year's starlings whose song has long been forgotten." Chekhov still felt the sting of being left outside the "touching triple union." In his next letter to Lika he addressed her as "sweet Melitta," sending greetings through her to Levitan, and asking her to act as if she were planning to visit Melikhovo: "Don't consign us to oblivion as you did before. At least pretend that you still remember us. Deceive us, Lika. Deception is better than indifference." But Chekhov also continued to treat their relationship as no more than a comic performance: "When will spring come? When, Lika, will spring come? Understand the last question as literal. Don't look for hidden meaning in it. Alas, I am already an old young man. My love is not the sun; it does not make the spring, neither for me nor for the bird I love." Chekhov ended his letter by quoting from a Lermontov poem: "Lika, it is not you I ardently love! I love in you my past sufferings and my lost youth."

In the end Lika did come to Melikhovo for Easter in early April, with Levitan arriving around the same time. On Easter Sunday some of the assembled family and guests took a walk through the melting snow in the garden. Chekhov turned to his friend Gilyarovsky and said to him, "Gilyai, I'm tired. Carry me in the wheelbarrow."[7] Over the past few days Chekhov had become impressed by Gilyarovsky's brawn and unflagging energy: "He wore out all my horses, climbed trees, scared the dogs, and, showing off his strength, chopped wood." Chekhov got in the wheelbarrow and his brother Mikhail joined him, sitting in front. When Gilyarovsky pushed the wheelbarrow up to the front of the house, they asked Levitan to take a picture. Levitan snapped a photo of Anton and Mikhail in the wheelbarrow with Gilyarovsky behind holding them up.

Despite all the effort he expended to get her to Melikhovo, Chekhov didn't pay particular attention to Lika once she was there, spending most of his days off bird-hunting with Levitan. One evening Levitan wounded a woodcock in the wing. It fell into a puddle. Chekhov lifted it up and noticed its "long nose, large black eyes, and beautiful attire. It looked at us with a surprised expression." Levitan frowned, closed his eyes, and asked Chekhov with a quivering voice, "My friend, smash its head with your rifle stock." Chekhov told him he couldn't. Levitan continued to nervously shrug his shoulders, shake his head, and plead for Chekhov to do it. "In the end," Chekhov wrote Suvorin, "I had to do what Levitan asked and I killed it. There was one less beautiful, beloved creature, and the two idiots returned home and sat down for dinner." This incident, and a similar later one, stayed in Chekhov's mind and inspired what he would develop into the central image of *The Seagull.*

In mid-April back in Moscow a scandal erupted regarding "The Grasshopper." Maria blamed Tatiana Shchepkina-Kupernik for provoking the falling out. Shchepkina-Kupernik, who was just eighteen and had not even met Chekhov yet, attended Kuvshinnikova's weekly salon and "sat on the floor at the feet of the mistress of the house, took out her comb, let down her hair, and said loudly, 'I don't understand how Chekhov . . . It's all very strange . . . He's been at your house, enjoyed your hospitality, was considered a friend, and suddenly publishes this disgusting story . . . How is this possible? It's totally incomprehensible.'"[8] When Levitan ran into Chekhov at Korsh's theater, he demanded an explanation. Chekhov sharply replied that he did not owe him any sort of explanation.[9]

What was it about, "this disgusting story" that prompted such outrage? As the story begins, Olga Ivanovna, a flaxen-haired woman of twenty-two, has just married Osip Dymov, a hard-working, thirty-one-year-old doctor, "a simple, very ordinary, and utterly undistinguished man." On the other hand, "[Olga Ivanovna] and her friends and good acquaintances were not completely ordinary people." She had created an "artistic, free-wheeling, and pampered" circle around her that included a gifted actor, a jolly fat opera singer, and several painters, "headed by the genre painter, animal painter, and landscape painter Ryabovsky, a very handsome fair-haired young man of twenty five who had exhibited successfully and had just sold his last painting for 500 rubles." Ryabovsky touched up Olga Ivanovna's paintings and thought she showed promise. She also sang, played the piano, worked with clay, and took part in amateur theatricals. But her greatest talent was "her ability to quickly become acquainted with and form close friendships with famous people." None of the differences in age or external appearance fooled Chekhov's friends— these were thinly disguised portraits of the Kuvshinnikovs and Levitan. The corrections Chekhov made to the galleys confirmed that he felt the need to make the similarities less obvious: he twice appended the description "flaxen haired" to Olga Ivanovna; he added "genre painter" and "animal painter" to his description of Ryabovsky the landscape painter. Some of Kuvshinnikova's other well-known mannerisms were incorporated unchanged: her insincere flattery of her "undistinguished" husband (Olga Ivanovna says to her friends of Dymov, "Just look at him, there's something about him isn't there?"); her habit of addressing people by their last names ("Olga Ivanovna always called her husband by his last name, as she did all the other men she knew"); and her habit of talking to people with a kind of vulgar forthrightness. The description of the way that Olga Ivanovna furnished her apartment closely matched Kuvshinnikova's as described by Shchepkina-Kupernik and Mikhail Chekhov:

> Olga Ivanovna covered all the walls of her drawing room with framed and unframed sketches drawn by herself and others, and created an attractive coziness around her piano and furniture using Chinese parasols, easels, multicolored bits of cloth, daggers, busts, and photographs . . . In the dining room she plastered the walls with cheap prints, hung bast sandals and sickles, placed a scythe and rake in the corner, and achieved a dining room *à la russe*. To make the bedroom look like a cave, she draped the ceiling and walls with a dark cloth, hung a Venetian lantern above the beds, and placed a figure with a halberd by the door.

In his galley corrections of the description of the dining room, Chekhov deleted the mention of "simple clay dishes on the shelves," sensing that he was being too literally accurate. Several years earlier, in the fall of 1888 (around the time Chekhov first visited the Kuvshinnikovs), he mockingly described to Suvorin those who decorated their apartments as she did: "They placed a Japanese figure in the entryway, stuck a Chinese umbrella in the corner, hung a rug on the staircase banister, and consider this to be artistic [. . .]. If an artist in decorating his apartment doesn't go beyond a museum figure with a halberd, shield, and fans on the wall, if all this isn't accidental but thought out and emphasized, then he's not an artist, but a pompous monkey."

Olga Ivanovna's "Wednesdays" sounded very familiar to those who attended Kuvshinnikova's soirees:

> On these evenings the hostess and guests did not play cards or dance, but amused themselves with various artistic activities. The actor from the dramatic theater recited, the singer sang, the artists made sketches in the many albums that Olga Ivanovna had, the cellist played, and the hostess herself drew, modeled clay,

sang, and accompanied musicians. In the intermissions between a recital, the playing of music or singing, everyone talked or argued about literature, theater, and painting. [. . .] Not one evening passed without the hostess getting agitated at every ringing of the doorbell and with a triumphant expression on her face saying, "It's him!," with the understanding that "he" was some newly invited famous person.

In the summer Olga Ivanovna prepared to go on a painting outing on the Volga. Ryabovsky came almost daily to check on how her work was progressing. Chekhov mocks the way the landscape painter critiques her sketch:

> He thrust his hands deep into pockets, firmly pursed his lips, exhaled through his nose and said:
>
> "So . . . your cloud is screaming: it's not lit as if it were evening. The foreground is somehow chewed up, and something, you know, is a bit off . . . And your cottage has choked on something and is mournfully whining . . . and you need to make the corner a bit darker. But in general, it's not bad [. . .]. Nice work.
>
> And the more incomprehensibly he spoke, the easier it was for Olga Ivanovna to understand him.

Soon, the characterization of Ryabovsky as a parody of Levitan comes into focus. On a July night Olga Ivanovna stands on the deck of a Volga steamer with Ryabovsky at her side:

> And he said to her that the black shadows on the water were not shadows, but a dream, that because of this enchanted water with its eerie glitter, because of the endless sky and the sad, brooding shores that spoke of the vanity of our lives and the existence of something higher, more eternal, blessed, it would be good to forget oneself, to die, to become a memory. The past was vulgar and uninteresting, the future insignificant, and this superb night, unique in our lives, would soon end, melt into eternity—so why live?

Ryabovsky displays the exalted highs and the dark lows of a manic depressive. Olga Ivanovna displays the same comically inflated sense of self-importance that Chekhov lampooned earlier in the painter Yegor in the story "Talent":

> She thought she was immortal and would never die. The turquoise color of the water, which she had never seen before, the sky, the shore, the black shadows, and the inexplicable joy that filled her soul—they all said to her that she would

become a great artist and that somewhere out there, beyond the moonlit night, in the endless vastness, success, glory, and the love of the people awaited her ... When she looked for a long time without blinking into the distance, she imagined crowds of people, lights, solemn music, ecstatic shouts, and she herself in a white dress and flowers strewn about her on all sides. She also thought that next to her, his elbows on the railing, stood a genuinely great man, a genius, one of God's chosen.

In the description of Ryabovsky's talent, Chekhov may well have expressed his own sincere thoughts about Levitan's talent:

> Everything he had created up to now was remarkable, new, and unusual, and that which he would create in time, when maturity would strengthen his rare talent, would be striking, immeasurably great, and this was evident in his face, in how he expressed himself, and in his relationship to nature. He spoke so uniquely in his own special language about the shadows, the evening tints, the glint of the moon that you irresistibly felt the spell of his power over nature. He himself was very handsome, original, and his life was independent, free, beyond all that was mundane, not unlike the life of a bird.

In a manner reminiscent of Levitan's impulsive proposals, Ryabovsky whispers to Olga Ivanovna, "I love you madly [...]. Say the word and I'll end my life, quit painting [...]. Love me, love me." It brings to mind Mikhail Chekhov's characterization of Levitan as a man who had a high opinion of his appearance and irresistibility and was given to hanging around women and darkly, coquettishly repeating, "I'm tired [...]. I'm tired."

Summer gives way to autumn, and Ryabovsky's depression deepens. He tells Olga Ivanovna "[that] painting is the most ungrateful and most boring of the arts, that he was not an artist, that only idiots thought he had talent, and suddenly for no reason at all, he grabbed a knife and scratched up his best sketch." As he looks out the window at the Volga, in language reminiscent of what Levitan said to Chekhov on first seeing the river in 1887, the landscape reflects Ryabovsky's sullen mood back to him: "The Volga no longer glittered; it looked dim, dull, and cold. Everything, everything reminded him of the approach of the melancholy, gloomy autumn." It seems to him that the crows flying above the river are taunting him: "Ryabovsky listened to their crowing and felt that he had already dried up and lost his talent, that everything in this world was conditional, relative, and stupid, and that it did not make any sense to have become involved with this woman." Ryabovsky's thoughts repeat almost verbatim how Chekhov expressed his gloom to Bilibin in

February 1886 when Dunya Efros called off their engagement: "I haven't yet bought a revolver and I'm not keeping a diary. Everything in the world is false, changeable, approximate, and relative." Ryabovsky is not just a variation on Levitan; there is bit of Chekhov in him as well. Both artists had read Schopenhauer and absorbed to varying degrees his modernist pessimism— the realization that the human Will eternally strives for the unattainable. In addition, this belief that everything in life is conditional and relative is the quality that ties Chekhov's art to the sensibility of impressionist painting. The act of perception is central to impressionism; *what* is perceived is determined by *how* it is perceived. Chekhov uses a literary device in his late stories to create a similar sense of impressionistic subjectivity. In "The Grasshopper," for example, everything unfolds through the eyes of the protagonists, even when told in the third person. This is achieved through the frequent use of variations of the phrase: "it seemed to him that . . ."[10]

Olga Ivanovna tries to cheer up Ryabovsky by encouraging him to finish a sketch of some woods with cows and geese (Chekhov added the animals in his galley corrections to distance the motif from anything Levitan would likely paint). But nothing dispels Ryabovsky's foul mood, which leads to a fierce argument with Olga Ivanovna, who accuses him of having grown tired of her. Furious, he threatens to throw himself into the Volga, but instead, much like Levitan, he grabs his rifle and goes off hunting alone. Eventually, they leave separately, returning to Moscow. By mid-winter Dymov begins to suspect what everyone already knows—that his wife is having an affair, one that is growing both more contentious and more indiscreet.

Back in his studio, Ryabovsky shifts into a manic phase. Olga Ivanovna's friends talk about how he "was preparing something extraordinary for exhibition, a mixture of landscape with a genre painting in the style of Polenov that was causing everyone who visited his studio to go into ecstasy." Chekhov added the description of the painting as a mixture of landscape and genre when he corrected the galleys, again presumably to make it less resemble Levitan's work. The story then depicts Olga Ivanovna's visit to Ryabovsky's studio: "She found him happy and delighted with his painting, which indeed was magnificent; he skipped about, acted like a fool, and responded to serious questions with joking answers."

Olga Ivanovna continues to ignore Dymov and his accomplishments as a doctor. Ryabovsky starts to have other affairs; Olga Ivanovna makes an unannounced visit to his studio only to find another woman hiding behind one of his paintings. That evening she goes home planning to write a letter that will break off her relationship with Ryabovsky. At home Dymov tells her not to come into his room—he fears that he has caught diphtheria at the hospital—and to summon his doctor friend Korostelyov. Dymov had infected himself by sucking in through a tube some membrane from the throat of a boy he was treating. Olga Ivanovna is overcome by guilt and remorse. She senses that Korostelyov, who knows about her affair, blames her and not the diphtheria for putting Dymov on his deathbed. Korostelyov tells her that Dymov has sacrificed his life for science, that he was a real scientist, a great man. Olga Ivanovna recalls their life together "and she suddenly saw that he really had been an outstanding, rare person: a great man compared with everyone else she had known." In the end, we cannot be certain whether Olga Ivanovna has truly undergone a fundamental transformation or is just temporarily under the spell of the grim celebrity status achieved by her husband's martyrdom.

It would be a mistake to think of "The Grasshopper" as a *roman à clef*. We need know nothing about the prototypes for each character to appreciate the deftness with which Chekhov creates the subjective world as "it seemed" to each of them. Dymov, childish and passive in his personal life, buries himself in his medical research and his devotion to patients to the point of self-oblivion, perhaps even suicide. Ryabovsky, an artist with genuine talent, displays an emotional volatility that gives him permission to be amoral and self-indulgent. Olga Ivanovna, lacking an internal compass, is forever looking and waiting for the "great man" (the original title of the story) to knock at her door, to enter her life and give it meaning.

But thinking about "The Grasshopper" in the context of Chekhov's judgments on art and medicine, on painters and their paintings, and on Lika, Levitan, and the Kuvshinnikovs adds a deeper resonance to the story. "The Grasshopper" is yet another work by Chekhov in which the world of artists is seen as suspect in comparison to the values and virtues of science. Chekhov complained to Suvorin that "science and technology are now living through a tremendous time, while for our brothers [fellow artists] the times are flabby, sour, and boring." It was this conviction that compelled Chekhov to go to Sakhalin and then spend years (including the months in which he wrote this story) laboriously documenting what he saw and learned there. The irony is that fiction is the means by which he makes this contrast between art and science. As we have seen, painters are often the artists most harshly judged, primarily because Chekhov saw painting as a refuge for the delusional and the talentless. Ryabovsky does not fall into that category, but his obliviousness to the effect that his affair has on the good doctor Dymov must have struck Chekhov's friends as the story's most damning criticism of Levitan and his role in the Kuvshinnikov *ménage à trois*. Olga Ivanovna is unmistakably a caricature of Kuvshinnikova, who was in truth a painter of genuine (if modest) talent and who, although given to exaggerated enthusiasms, was nowhere as nearly intellectually lightweight as her literary counterpart. In age and appearance, Olga Ivanovna more closely resembles Lika Mizinova than Kuvshinnikova. The basic dynamic of the story—a flighty young woman dividing her affections between her lover, the painter, and her husband, the doctor—is a reworking of the romantic duel of the previous summer, when Lika at times presented Levitan as a rival for her affections in order to get Chekhov to make some sort of sincere declaration of his feelings for her. As Lika herself commented (and it is a commonplace among writers), the people in Chekhov's life served as raw material to be refashioned to suit the internal logic, structure, and emotional truth of a story. But inescapably, the spark that gave birth to "The Grasshopper" is to be found in Chekhov's annoyance, even jealousy, at the way Lika, Levitan, and Kuvshinnikova carried on and ultimately ignored him as he sat alone at Bogimovo in the summer of 1891.

The flare-up between Levitan and Chekhov came to a head during the last week of April. At some point Chekhov wrote Levitan a letter of explanation, which the latter found unsatisfactory. Levitan personally confronted Chekhov in Moscow some time before April 28, when Chekhov was back in Melikhovo. Maria and Mikhail Chekhov claimed that Levitan was ready to challenge Chekhov to a duel, although Lika made it sound like Levitan was less offended than everyone thought he should be. On April 28, Chekhov wrote a note to Lika about an argument they must have had earlier in the day in Moscow: "You, my dear, got angry at me, but I assure you that it didn't even enter my mind to say something rude or offensive. I was sad that you left. Likusya, let's live peacefully. Write me a couple of lines." Acting nonchalant about the cause of the argument, Chekhov the next day wrote to the children's author Lidia Avilova: "Yesterday, I was in Moscow and almost dropped dead from boredom and all sorts of attacks. Can you imagine, one of my acquaintances, a forty-two-year-old lady, recognized herself in the twenty-year-old heroine of my story "The Grasshopper" [. . .] and all Moscow is accusing me of slander. The main piece of evidence—an external resemblance: the woman paints, her husband is a doctor, and she lives with an artist." Chekhov was loath to admit that exercising his talent demanded a ruthless appropriation of his friends' lives. Lika understood this. Also on April 29, she wrote back to Chekhov responding to his apology for getting into an argument with her about the story:

> You are a strange man, Anton Pavlovich. I don't know what I possibly could have taken offense at from you. I was not offended and in general never get offended. If I allowed myself to say something from which you could conclude that I was angry, then I'm sorry. I know very well that if you either say or do

something offensive, it's not at all out of a desire to do this on purpose, but only because it's absolutely all the same to you how others take what you do. We will live peacefully, and most importantly, we don't imagine what doesn't exist, such as an offense, etc. [. . .] Levitan was here yesterday and again talked about the story. He himself admits that it has all turned out very foolishly. And it's very important to write him another letter. And you cannot consider that writing a letter now doesn't make sense because it would be the same as having written to Kuvshinnikova.

Levitan showed the letter that Chekhov had written him to Lensky, who had already decided (with little justification) to consider himself deeply offended by what he felt was a caricature of him in "The Grasshopper." Among Olga Ivanovna's circle was "a well-known, gifted actor, an elegant, intelligent, modest man who could recite brilliantly and taught Olga Ivanovna elocution." Later, when Dymov visits the cottage along the Volga where Olga Ivanovna is staying, in one of the rooms he finds three men "who were apparently strangers to him." One of the men is described as an actor, "clean-shaven and fat." Possibly Dymov does not recognize the man from his wife's salon, and he is the same actor as previously described, or it is equally likely that it is a different person. In any case, it was hardly an act of calumny that deserved such a strong reaction—Lensky refused to speak to Chekhov for eight years. More likely, Lensky's reaction was the result of his increasingly strained relations with Chekhov. When Chekhov had sent *The Wood Demon* to the Maly Theater in 1889 in the hopes that it would be produced there, Lensky rejected it and told Chekhov to stick to writing short stories.[11] Chekhov took the rejection in stride, thanking Lensky for reading his "vile little play," which he put back in his drawer (the play would later be reshaped into *Uncle Vanya*). As recently as the previous November, they had had some sort of argument. Chekhov wrote Lensky that "[people are saying that] you are angry at me for something," but he assured Lensky that he was drawn to him with all his soul and wanted very much to see him. Lensky replied that people were wrong: he was not offended or indignant at Chekhov but merely "chagrined in proposing a change" that Chekhov declined to make.

Lensky told Levitan that it took him a while to gather his thoughts about Chekhov's letter, but he instinctively sensed that Chekhov's explanations were "false and strained": "I can now tell you what I think and why for me this letter strains credulity from its first word to its last. He calls himself a 'small' or 'petty writer,' I don't remember his exact expression, but we'll keep it in mind; he says that he loves you, and this entirely believable thing we'll also take into account."[12] Chekhov compared what he had done in "The Grasshopper" with Griboyedov's satirical play *Woe from Wit*, whose characters were drawn from 1820s Russian society (most notably the protagonist Chatsky, who was based on the writer and philosopher Pyotr Chaadaev). But Lensky thought that this was mere sophistry. He considered Griboyedov's play to be an honest cry of indignation against society, "a real cry of unbearable pain!" He continued, "And what reasons motivated Anton Pavlovich to write this thing 'The Grasshopper?' . . . They asked him to write 'something' for the first issue of a journal—and only that! And for the sake of this he had no pity on his acquaintances, among whom he was accepted gladly, with love, and he had no pity on the person he 'loved,' making him out to be a vulgar Lovelace! I just don't understand."

Chekhov's defense against those who attacked him was to claim that the story was a trifle, nothing he or anyone else should take very seriously. It was a response entirely consistent with Chekhov's character. As Lika herself knew all too well, make too much of a claim on Chekhov's feelings and he responds by treating the relationship as nothing more than a light-hearted amusement. Lensky used Chekhov's false modesty that he was a "small writer" who produced nothing more than talented 'little nothings" against him, denigrating him in comparison with Griboyedov and Tolstoy, who were "giants who created great works." He brought up *Anna Karenina*, in which Tolstoy "also used real people, but he so skillfully drew portraits of them that you don't hear accusations of slander against Lev Tolstoy." Finally, Lensky mentions that Chekhov also offered the defense that a "painting begins as a portrait and ends as a portrait," which in fact for Chekhov was a fundamental aesthetic stance—a work of art ultimately stands on its own, separate from its references, creating its own reality, internal logic, and truth. "That's true," said Lensky, "but here, as in much else, there is a mass of details and it's all 'relative.'" Lensky did not dispute Chekhov's premise, but he found it impossible to overlook what he saw as the personal harm done by the caricatures in Chekhov's story.

Stepanov, too, was offended by what Chekhov had done, both for Levitan's sake and for his own. He was deeply hurt to discover that his friends recognized his distinctive mannerisms incorporated into Chekhov's characterization of Doctor Korostelyov: "a small man with close-cropped hair and a crumpled face, who, when he spoke with Olga Ivanovna, would, out of embarrassment, button and unbutton his jacket and then start twisting his left moustache with his right hand." It didn't matter that Korostelyov was portrayed sympathetically in the story; Stepanov felt ridiculed and cut off all contact with Chekhov.[13]

No duel was fought between Levitan and Chekhov; no further explanations ensued. Instead, what followed were two and a half years of silence between two men who previously without hesitation told others that they loved each other. The impetuous, meddlesome Shchepkina-Kupernik thought it was a "sad story" in which both men "suffered deeply in their souls," but that seems unlikely in Chekhov's case. He continued to chastise Lika for maintaining her friendship with Levitan and Kuvshinnikova.

On May 12, only two weeks after the scandal over "The Grasshopper" peaked, Levitan left with Kuvshinnikova to spend the summer painting in the vicinity of the village of Gorodok on the Peshka River near Boldino. His first priority was to make some sketches as a guide to retouching *Deep Waters*. Back in February, Repin had told Tretyakov, who had already purchased the painting, that he did not like the piece: "For its scale, it's not completely finished. In general, it's just OK." Having paid a princely sum for it, Tretyakov demanded that Levitan make some changes. The day after he arrived in Gorodok, Levitan wrote Tretyakov: "Don't think that I have forgotten your request and my own acknowledgment to fix the water in my *Deep Waters*. I decided not to retouch it until I was able to validate this motif in nature. I'm drawing several sketches of water, and at the end of May, I'll come to Moscow and begin to rework the painting. If the painting hasn't yet been varnished, please don't do it before I make the corrections."

As usual, Levitan roamed the countryside looking for motifs that caught his eye. One day as he and Kuvshinnikova were returning to Gorodok from hunting, they came out on the old Vladimirsky Road. She recalled that at first they responded to the charm of the scene: "A long stretch of road like a whitish strip ran through a stand of trees into the bluish distance. And in the distance on the road you could see the figures of two pilgrims, and an old rickety icon on a post worn by rains that spoke of long forgotten ancient times. Everything looked so tender and cosy."[14] But then Levitan remembered the grim historical significance of this road: before the coming of the railroad "this [was] the very Vladimirka along which once upon a time so many unfortunate people in shackles headed to Siberia." The quiet poetry of the scene gave way to a deep sadness. They sat by the pedestal of the icon post and started talking "about what painful pictures unfolded on this road, how many sorrowful thoughts were pondered here."

Vladimirka is an unusual painting for Levitan because it is the only one that can be considered to have a hint of social commentary. And even at that, the "commentary" is provided by choosing to connect the historic significance of the road with the mood of the landscape itself: the unsettled and overwhelming gray sky; the endless road rolling over the slightly undulating land as it recedes toward the far horizon; the lonely pilgrim (a rare figure in a Levitan painting, here more implied than defined) turned toward the icon post; the distant white walls of a church almost lost in the expanse of sky and earth.

Levitan gave one of his sketches for *Vladimirka* to Mikhail Chekhov, who was offended by its inscription, "to the future prosecutor." At the time Mikhail was in law school, and he felt the dedication implied with misguided humor that he would become the kind of jurist who would send people in chains down this road toward Siberia; he gave the sketch away.[15] Levitan tried to give the painting itself to Gilyarovsky, who had written a poem inspired by the work. But Gilyarovsky would not take it, even after Levitan told him that he could get five hundred rubles for it. A comic exchange ensued—Levitan went to the trouble of bringing it to Gilyarovsky's apartment and leaving it there while he was out, only to discover that it was sitting again back in his studio by the time he returned home. Tretyakov refused to buy *Vladimirka*, and two years later Levitan decided to donate it to his Gallery, where today it is displayed in the hall devoted to Levitan.[16]

During the summer of 1892, Lika, having assured Chekhov that she had not been offended by "The Grasshopper," chose the moment to pursue him more insistently. She stayed in Melikhovo for a week in early June and then went on to Rzhev to spend the rest of the summer at the estate of Nikolai Basov, a distant relative. Something happened between Lika and Chekhov during the last night of her stay at Melikhovo, most likely a sign of affection from Chekhov, meant in jest, which so upset her that she wrote him about it as soon as she arrived in Rzhev: "Throwing all false pride aside, I will say that I'm very unhappy and I very much want to see you. I'm unhappy, Anton Pavlovich, because you apparently were very surprised and did not like my behavior the evening before my departure. I admit that I behaved too much like a little girl and this bothers me a great deal." She felt embarrassed that she so "forgot herself that she didn't get the joke and took it seriously." Mixed together with this was a conversation they had about possibly going to the Caucasus together. Lika leaped at this proposal, admitting that she was incapable of doing anything halfway. "There will be tickets to the Caucasus, that is, separate ones for you and me, only don't think that after what we talked about, you absolutely have to come with me! I'm going in any case—alone or not—but I'm going." She told him the tickets would be ready on the first of August and begged him to tell no one about them or her invitation.

Chekhov responded as usual, refusing to take anything she wrote seriously and initially acting as if they were not in any way tied together emotionally. In his eyes her letters "did not have the significance of documents, but rather only of sweet-smelling flowers." He asked her to tell those she was staying with to be reassured that he was not their rival: "We Chekhovs [. . .] don't interfere in the lives of young ladies. It's a principle for us. So, you are free." This was not the reassurance she was looking for. On top of this, he told her they should call off the trip to the Caucasus because of the threat of cholera in the region.

But in the very same letter, Chekhov upbraided Lika for continuing her friendship with Levitan and Kuvshinnikova, which he playfully claimed aroused his jealousy: "Are you dreaming of Levitan with his dark eyes full of African passion? Are you still getting letters from your seventy-year-old rival [Kuvshinnikova] and hypocritically answering them? Lika, there is an enormous crocodile sitting inside you, and truly it's a good thing that I listen to my common sense and not my heart, which you have stung." Lika snapped back: "Why do you so urgently want to remind me of Levitan and about my 'dreams.' I'm not thinking *about anyone*. I don't want or need anyone."[17]

Lika and Chekhov continued to write to each other with a convoluted mix of sincerity and jest, creating an emotional muddle that exploded into anger and frustration on her part and spiteful humor on his part. He continued to needle her with allusions to Sappho and her Jewish lover:

> Lika, you're always finding fault. In every word of my letters you see irony or spite. What can I say, you have a wonderful nature. In vain do you think that you will become an old maid. I bet that in time you will turn into a nasty, shrill old lady, who can loan money with interest and box the ears of neighboring children. The unlucky titular councilor in a red dressing gown, who will have the honor of calling you his spouse, will nevertheless steal your liqueur and drown with it the bitterness of family life. I often imagine, like two worthy personages, you and Sappho are sitting at a table drinking up the liqueur, recalling the past, while in the next room your titular councilor sits by the fire with a meek and guilty appearance, and plays checkers with a bald little Jew whose name I would rather not recall.

He urged Lika to come and stay at Melikhovo for the winter: "I will take charge of your upbringing and beat your bad habits out of you. And most importantly, I will shield you from Sappho." For the moment, Lika grew tired of Chekhov's teasing, threatening to stop writing him entirely. She stayed away from him for the rest of the summer. But Chekhov persisted in his mock jealousy of Levitan, sending Lika a fake note intended for the painter signed by "Lika's lover."

> Trophim! If you, you son of a bitch, don't stop courting Lika, I'll shove a corkscrew up that spot that rhymes with Europe, you scumbag [in Russian *zhopa*—"ass"—rhymes with *Evropa*]. Oh, you're such an obscenity! Don't you know that Lika belongs to me and that we already have two children, you pig snout!

Levitan returned with Kuvshinnikova to Moscow in late summer, but he was not to stay there for long. The Bolshoi Opera tenor Lavrenty Donskoy recalled dropping in on the Kuvshinnikovs at that time to find everyone in the apartment upset and agitated; a few people were even crying. Levitan himself arrived in a gloomy mood. "What's the matter? What's going on?" Donskoy asked. Someone replied, "Don't you know? Levitan has been forbidden entry into Moscow. He's being expelled."[18] For the second time, Levitan was caught up in a general expulsion of Jews from Moscow. His friends feared it would be permanent and were prepared to close down his studio, pack up his works, and send them off to an as yet unknown destination.[19]

Levitan had been well aware of the increased hostility to Jews in the city, which started when the reactionary Grand Prince Sergei Alexandrovich, brother of Tsar Alexander III, became governor general of Moscow in February 1891. The grand prince promulgated a decree that ordered the expulsion of Jews to take place in phases, starting with artisans, brewers, and distillers. It was initially unclear exactly when this phased expulsion would be implemented. In April 1892 the painter Leonid Pasternak wrote his wife: "A sense of panic reigns among Jews [. . .]. It's horrible, horrible! Yesterday, for example, I bumped into Levitan at the Polenovs, and then we bumbled around the city for nearly half a day, the whole time singing one and the same sad note about the expulsion of Jews."[20]

Levitan might have thought he would escape banishment because of his fame as an artist. But unlike members of wealthy Jewish families, he had never been given permanent legal residency in the city, and the local authorities had started to abuse their prerogatives and expel classes of Jews not named in the decree. Samuel Vermel, a prominent Jewish journalist and acquaintance of Levitan, recalled: "No one was spared. No condition, no reason was taken into consideration. They didn't extend anyone's time frame for an hour. On the designated day, the police inspector showed up in a Jewish apartment and reminded everyone that the designated day had come and they had to leave immediately. Pleas, efforts, attempts to protect someone—nothing worked."[21] Vermel heard a story about a Jew who was doing electrical repairs to the grand prince's house. When the grand prince was looking over the almost completed work and expressing satisfaction, the electrician decided to take advantage of the situation and told his client that he might not be able to finish the work. When the grand prince asked why, he responded: "I'm a Jew and I'm about to have to leave Moscow." The grand prince was at first taken aback, but then said, "Well, then work faster" and quickly left the hall.

About 38,000 Moscow Jews were expelled and only about 7,000 were allowed to remain. Many Jews decided to leave Russia: 42,145 in 1891 and 76,417 in

1892.[22] Levitan decided to go back to Boldino, where he had spent the summer, and waited while his friends pleaded his case to government officials.[23] Prince Vladimir Golitsyn, whose wife was a patron of Levitan, approached the grand prince, saying that "we have only one Levitan in all of Russia."[24] Ironically, but not surprisingly, the magnanimous Kuvshinnikov was credited with finally successfully arranging for Levitan to be temporarily allowed to return to Moscow in early December.

Levitan resumed his usual frenetic pace of winter activities. After serving as a judge in a competition sponsored by the Moscow Society of Art Lovers, he went to St. Petersburg to the Academy of Art to help in the selection of pieces for the Russian section of the Chicago World Exposition, which opened to the public in May 1893 and included his 1892 painting *Evening Bells*. That winter Valentin Serov painted his famous portrait of Levitan in his studio.

Isaac Levitan, standing, and Sergei Korovin. Detail from a group portrait of the participants in the first student exhibition (1878) of the Moscow School of Painting, Sculpture, and Architecture.

Autumn Day. Sokolniki (1879). The first of twenty Levitan paintings purchased by Pavel Tretyakov for his collection.

High Waters (1885)—with its peasant huts submerged under menacing skies—evokes the feeling of abandonment.

Levitan's *Portrait of Anton Chekhov* (1886), a study painted at Babkino.

Evening on the Volga (1887–1888). Painting along the Volga River challenged Levitan to find motifs that captured its vast scale.

Levitan's *Portrait of Sophia Kuvshinnikova* (1888).

The Birch Grove (1889) is an early example of Levitan's use of impressionist techniques.

In Chekhov's "Three Years," the unhappily married Yulia Sergeevna is moved by a painting remarkably similar to Levitan's *Quiet Abode* (1890).

Osip Braz's *Portrait of A. P. Chekhov* (1898). Although Levitan reassured Tretyakov that the painting was a good likeness, Chekhov himself told a friend that the portrait made him look like he had just inhaled a lot of horseradish.

Levitan used a large canvas to lend the landscape in *Deep Waters* (1892) a more forceful symbolism.

Vladimirka (1892) depicts the road along which prisoners had been transported to Siberia.

Chekhov's family and friends in April 1890 before he left for Sakhalin. Middle row: Lika Mizinova (second from left) and Maria Chekhova (third from left). Front row (from left): Mikhail Chekhov and Anton Chekhov.

Portrait of the writer Tatiana Shchepkina-Kupernik (1914) by Ilya Repin.

The actress Lidia Yavorskaya.

Levitan said of *Above Eternal Rest* (1894): "All of me is in it, all of my psyche, all of my substance."

Radiating joy at the coming of spring, *March* (1895) marks a change from the somber motifs of the Volga paintings.

The vibrant *Golden Autumn* (1895) captures a wide tonal range from the bright yellow of turning leaves to the dark water mirroring the sky.

The exuberance of the short, swirling brush strokes in *Stormy Day* (1897) is a dramatic contrast to the more finished, melancholic tone of *Above Eternal Rest*.

The Last Rays of Sun (1899), with its flat planes and monochromatic palette, presages a movement toward greater abstraction.

The Lake (Rus) (1900) remained unfinished, a painting in which Levitan synthesized impressionistic spontaneity with a sense of spiritual peace.

7

1893–1894

TANGLED AFFAIRS

LEVITAN'S STATUS AS A Jew without residency rights continued to plague him. Thanks to Kuvshinnikov's intercession, the police no longer bothered him about living in Moscow. But in the spring of 1893 he started thinking about where to go painting in the summer, and for that he needed a temporary passport to live outside the city. This time Pavel Briullov, a fellow Itinerant, influential academician, and later curator of the Russian Museum, smoothed the way so that Levitan could submit the necessary papers to the office of the police chief. In his letter of thanks to Briullov, Levitan provided a glimpse of the anger and frustration he long felt but rarely expressed openly: "All this red tape, constraints, and efforts drive me crazy. It seems to me that my matter will never end."[1]

After the closing in Moscow on May 9 of the Twenty-First Itinerant Exhibition, which included the painting *Vladimirka* and Serov's portrait, Levitan returned to Tver Province, where he had spent the two previous summers. Initially Levitan and Kuvshinnikova stayed at an estate on the Msta River belonging to Donskoy, but then they moved on to the Ushakov family estate on the shore of Ostrovno Lake. They settled into two rooms with bright white walls on the second floor with a view of the lake. The ancient house was built in the Empire Style with bluish-green glass in the windows and broad stairs descending in several flights from the upstairs balcony down to the garden. The lilacs spreading out over the grounds were almost as old as the house itself, which is depicted in Levitan's *Spring. White Lilacs* (1894).[2] The Ushakovs did everything they could to avoid disturbing Levitan. They moved out of the house into an annex and even locked up the guard dogs in a distant garden pavilion during the day. While he worked, Levitan enjoyed having Kuvshinnikova play the piano, particularly pieces by Beethoven. When

Levitan stopped working, he joined in the activities of the others, going for walks, visiting neighboring estates, fishing, hunting, and gathering mushrooms with his dog, whom he had taught to sniff out and bark at fly agaric, a poisonous Amanita mushroom.[3]

When Levitan looked out his window, he could see between the house and the lake an old wooden church constructed in 1778. He started making sketches for what would become his most famous painting, *Above Eternal Rest*. Although Kuvshinnikova maintained that the motif was "painted from nature during our riding excursions" along Udomlya Lake,[4] which was about four miles east of Ostrovno Lake, the work was inspired by elements from several locations along the two lakes, as well as by sketches made several years earlier of the derelict church he visited so often in Plyos. Levitan's student Wittold Byalynitsky-Birulya recalled that on the shore of Ostrovno Lake there was a raised area with an old wooden church half buried in the ground.[5] Next to it was an overgrown cemetery with bent-over wooden crosses covered in moss. One of the pastels that Levitan drew in Udomlya in 1893, called *The Forgotten* (now lost), depicted a cemetery sitting on high ground with bent crosses. He had long been attracted to drawing this particular motif. For Levitan, an abandoned cemetery had the same significance that the burial mounds on the steppe had for Chekhov—evidence of past lives gradually worn away by the implacable forces of nature.[6]

Levitan started the painting that summer but finished it in Moscow in December or the very beginning of 1894. When Nesterov suggested that he should incorporate the beloved old church he had painted in Plyos into *Above Eternal Rest*, Levitan borrowed a sketch of the church that he had already sold to Tretyakov, who decided to let him keep it.[7] *Above Eternal Rest* was displayed at the Twenty-Second Itinerant Exhibition and then purchased by Tretyakov, which made Levitan "unspeakably happy." While critics were far from unanimous in praising the painting, Levitan told Tretyakov that it "affects me so very strongly because all of me is in it, all of my psyche, all of my substance, and it would be painful to the point of tears if it was not included in your colossal collection."

Painted in a literal style similar to that of his teacher Savrasov, *Above Eternal Rest* is a didactic painting that reflects Levitan's belief in the power of nature to overwhelm all human endeavors. A faint light shines from the small window of a church at the edge of a promontory that resembles the prow of a ship heading off into the unknown. A strong wind bends the trees behind the church. The cemetery is overgrown, some crosses have been knocked over. Both church and cemetery look small and huddled against the vastness of the landscape; they are surrounded by the broad lake, its waters raked by the wind;

they are frail before the looming sky and the massive dark clouds portending an approaching storm. The painting conveys a sense of the insubstantiality of man and his spiritual yearnings. We are reminded of Yegorushka in Chekhov's "The Steppe" lying on his back, looking at the night sky, sensing its indifference to man's brief life and "that solitariness awaiting us all in the grave."

Around the same time that *Above Eternal Rest* was first being exhibited in St. Petersburg and Moscow, Chekhov wrote "The Student," a short story which, like Levitan's painting, is often cited as a work that reveals the essence of his artistic sensibility. Toward evening, Ivan Velikopolsky, a seminary student, is making his way home on Good Friday. A spring-like day has given way to an icy winter night; light has been overcome by darkness; hope has turned to despair. Ivan is overwhelmed by a feeling of pessimism on a vast historical scale:

> And now, shrugging from the cold, the student thought about the fact that this very wind blew in the time of Ryurik, and of Ivan the Terrible, and of Peter the Great, and in their day there was the same ferocious poverty, hunger, the same dilapidated thatched roofs, ignorance, misery, the same empty expanse all around, the same gloom and feeling of oppression—all these horrors had existed, exist now, and will continue to exist, and even when another thousand years pass, life will not become any better. He didn't want to go home.

But then Ivan comes upon a bonfire being tended in a field owned by two widows, a mother and daughter. As he holds his hands toward the flames, he tells the widows that it was on a cold night such as this that the Apostle Peter warmed himself by a fire. He then proceeds to retell with great empathy the Gospel story of Peter's betrayal of Jesus that had been read in church the day before. Much to his surprise the story brings the mother to tears. The daughter, mute from a husband who beat her, stares at Ivan, blushes, and becomes "distressed and tense like someone who is holding back a terrible pain." Ivan is startled that the story he has told about something that happened nineteen centuries ago has had such meaning for these women in their present lives:

> And joy suddenly welled up in his soul, and he even stopped for a minute to catch his breath. The past, he thought, is joined to the present by an unbroken chain of events, one flowing out of the other. And it seemed to him that he had just seen both ends of this chain: When he touched one end, the other end vibrated.

Ivan has realized that his story of compassion for Peter's human weakness has touched on something eternal. Ivan the student is a religiously pure version

of Chekhov the writer, whose stories and plays about the imperfect, the irra-
tional, and even the ridiculous in people arouse in readers and audiences a
shared recognition of, and sympathy for, our flawed lives. In Levitan's art we
see a natural landscape that, at times, is indifferent to human failings; people are noticeably absent from his paintings. Chekhov, on the other hand,
embraced those failings and made them central to his art.

Chekhov spent most of 1893 ensconced in Melikhovo, withdrawn from the
social life of Moscow. He told Suvorin: "This summer I continuously stayed
in one spot; I visited the sick, treated them, expected there to be cholera.
[. . .] I saw a thousand sick people, wasted a lot of time, and the cholera never
came. I didn't write anything but only took walks in my spare time, read, and
whipped my unwieldy *Sakhalin* into shape." He found himself overcome with
the desire to cut loose and socialize. In August the writer Ignaty Potapenko
came to visit him in Melikhovo. The two men had first met in Odessa in the
summer of 1889 when Chekhov was passing through. At the time Chekhov
had found him to be the "God of boredom." Potapenko recalled that he
had felt inadequate in Chekhov's presence; he had "stared into [Chekhov's]
mouth," passively waiting for the famous writer to impart his wisdom. Later
Potapenko understood that this expectation invariably caused Chekhov to
withdraw and say nothing.[8] But Chekhov now realized that his first impression
had been wrong. They found themselves enjoying each other's company, and
Chekhov was particularly impressed by Potapenko's ability to play the violin
and sing romances. To Potapenko it seemed that their relationship developed
slowly; it was not easy to feel certain that you had Chekhov's friendship.
He had the kind of irresistible charm that made people act very openly in
front of him, "but he never revealed his soul to anyone." Potapenko felt that
Chekhov's reticence sprang from his total devotion to his creative work, which
was always "completely hidden from the eyes of others." And since he was
always creating, even when interacting with people, he was always holding
something back, "and that is why even the people closest to him felt a certain
distance between them and him."[9]

By now, Lika had come to the same conclusion. After years of failed
attempts to penetrate Chekhov's inscrutable feelings, she had reached the
point of exasperation. She wrote to him on August 22:

> Your letter was completely saturated with such egotism! You only need people
> so that when the weather gets bad and the evenings get long, and there's noth-
> ing to do, and it's too early to go to bed, then there will be someone around
> to relieve your boredom. But then time passes and you no longer give them a

thought [. . .]. I'm convinced that if in the course of a year for some reason I never visited you, you wouldn't make the slightest effort to see me.

When Lika came to Melikhovo, she turned her attentions toward Potapenko in the same way that she had with Levitan—as way of making Chekhov jealous. But this time, Chekhov refused to take the bait. In December Lika wrote to Chekhov: "I have finally fallen in love . . . with Potapenko! What's to be done, papa? You'll always be able to get rid of me and pounce on someone else!" There was a note of resignation and a sense of abandonment in her voice.

Joining the circle of Chekhov family friends in the fall of 1893 was the nineteen-year-old Shchepkina-Kupernik. Maria Chekhova had met her through Lika and then introduced her to Chekhov. According to Mikhail Chekhov, Anton, at least initially, valued her talents as a versifier and was charmed by her youthful impetuousness, which she quickly used to make her way into Moscow cultural life soon after arriving from Kiev. Already part of Kuvshinnikova's Wednesday soirees, in the summer of 1893 she added a poem "Toward a Portrait of Levitan," written in pencil in proper schoolgirl handwriting, into the hostess's album. In his looks, dress, and demeanor, Levitan struck Shchepkina-Kupernik as the very quintessence of a painter:

He came reluctantly into the everyday world
Like someone from an ancient Van Dyke portrait.
Looking as if he had once worn a black velvet coat,
He seemed as if everything about him
Was from those bygone years:
A pointed beard,
Expressive dark eyes, dissipated and meek,
That look without noticing you,
His stern features
Covered by a bronze tan.
But not for nothing do you see
So much childish goodness in his smile.
A lover of pure art,
Shunning people and the world,
He doesn't conceal other earthly feelings in his soul.
He will not live without freedom
And he's happy in the forest depths.
He's familiar with the language of nature
And knows no other.[10]

That summer Shchepkina-Kupernik's rising celebrity turned notorious as word of her lesbianism spread. Taking advantage of the fame of her actor-grandfather, she had been given minor roles to play in Korsh's theater, where she met another actress, Lidia Yavorskaya, who both in her acting style and personal life modeled herself after Sarah Bernhardt. Shchepkina-Kupernik had known Yavorskaya's parents in Kiev, but by then their daughter (who was three years older than Shchepkina-Kupernik) had already graduated from the gymnasium, married and divorced a teacher, and left for drama school in St. Petersburg. The two women began a very open and tempestuous affair. A swarm of artists gravitated toward their rooms in the adjoining Hotel Madrid and Hotel Louvre, including Lika, Potapenko, Chekhov, and Levitan (but only when Chekhov was absent). Chekhov, in turn, found Levitan's behavior toward his "little girls" (as he called them) off-putting.[11] When Shchepkina-Kupernik returned to Kiev for the Christmas holidays, Yavorskaya wrote to her "petite Sappho" that she profoundly missed her and the charming company of their mutual friends Chekhov and Lika. Although Yavorskaya asked Shchepkina-Kupernik for Levitan's address, she confessed that she didn't much like him "and I think the feeling has been mutual from the first time we met" ("Levitan ne m'a pas plu, ainsi que moi de même je pense les sentiments sont réciproques des premiers coup d'oeil").[12] Lika then discovered that Yavorskaya was also pursuing Chekhov, and this prompted her to seek revenge in Potapenko's arms. By the end of February 1894, Lika was pregnant with Potapenko's child, a troubling development complicated by the fact that he was already married.

Shchepkina-Kupernik maintained that Chekhov and Yavorskaya were enjoying nothing more than a light flirtation. While this initially might have been true, Chekhov succumbed eventually to the actress's charms. The essence of the dynamic among the three of them was captured in a photograph that Chekhov called "The Temptation of St. Anthony." The photograph came about because the editor Fyodor Kumanin liked to include portraits of the authors in a series of small books of poetry and prose he published. Kumanin sent the three of them, Lika, and a mutual friend of theirs (the future opera singer Varvara Eberle) to a studio where they were photographed individually and in groups. The last shot was of Shchepkina-Kupernik, Yavorskaya, and Chekhov together. When the photographer said "Look into the camera," Chekhov turned and made a stone face, which caused the women to lean forward and burst out laughing.[13] In the resulting photograph, Chekhov faces the camera with an inscrutable look while the two women, seemingly infatuated, gaze intently at him.

The irrepressible Shchepkina-Kupernik also asked Chekhov to contribute an inscription for an engraved silver blotting pad to be given to Yavorskaya following a benefit performance at Korsh's theater. Provocatively, she gave as an example Levitan's inscription: "Believe in yourself" (a clearly unnecessary injunction to the diva Yavorskaya). Chekhov refused, saying that to take part would offend other actresses who had appeared in his plays and for whom he had not offered a comparable tribute.[14]

In early January 1894, again through the intercession of Briullov, Levitan, after twenty-three years, finally received formal permission to live outside the Pale of Settlement, which made him a legal permanent resident of Moscow. Levitan thanked Briullov effusively, saying his gratitude was beyond words: "Your assistance has saved me from an enormous amount of unpleasantness." To help his own cause, Levitan made efforts to ensure that his popularity among the ruling elite was known to all. When Grand Prince Sergei, who had been responsible for his banishment, came with his wife to tour Levitan's studio, Levitan wrote Efim Konovitser, Dunya Efros's husband, asking him to mention this in his newspaper *The Courier*.[15] The grand prince purchased *The Forgotten*, Levitan's painting of the overgrown cemetery.

Recognition of the quality of Levitan's work continued to grow, both with the public and among his fellow artists. Pereplyotchikov no longer criticized his paintings as "cold." Pereplyotchikov loved having long conversations with Korovin in his studio, but he felt that Korovin's work, unlike Levitan's, wasn't progressing, even though in the beginning Levitan had borrowed much from Korovin. Pereplyotchikov recalled as prophetic a past incident when the artist Lev Kamenev dropped in on the landlady Gorbacheva's house where at the time "almost all of Moscow's landscape painters lived." Kamenev looked at Levitan's studies and then at Pereplyotchikov's and said: "It's time for all of us together with Savrasov to drop dead."

When Levitan was feeling manic and discussing the work of his peers, his opinions were strong and unequivocal, ecstatic in praising those he admired, dismissive of those he did not. Donskoy described what it was like to see Levitan in this state:

> He would have unusual heightened moods, and this would happen to him when arguing about art [. . .]. I can see him now before me, alive and in the heat of an argument . . . Thin, bony, with restrained gestures full of internal fire and surprisingly glistening eyes. His conversation at such moments was fireworks, and he rained on his opponent an endless flow of glittering ideas . . . Where did this come from?[16]

Pereplyotchikov, too, found Levitan's personality to be mercurial, noting in his diary:

Levitan is a person who has already suffered much in the struggle for existence. He's not stupid, but a skeptical individualist who judges people often when he's not feeling himself: he's a man of the moment, of impressions, nervous, a sensualist. At times the best features of his nature come forward, and then he makes a good impression.[17]

In March everyone abandoned Moscow. Rumors of orgies had compelled the management of the Hotel Louvre and Madrid to ask Shchepkina-Kupernik and Yavorskaya to leave.[18] Shchepkina-Kupernik and Yavorskaya went to the Kursk station with a bouquet of tulips and hyacinths to see Chekhov off for the Crimea. Yavorskaya left for Europe the next day. Feeling abandoned, Shchepkina-Kupernik talked "grandfather" Sablin, the editor of *The Russian Gazette*, into funding her to join Yavorskaya in exchange for writing a series of feuilletons for his newspaper. Lika and Eberle went to Paris to take singing lessons, joining Potapenko, who was already there with his wife. Levitan was set to take his second trip abroad but first had several matters to attend to related to his paintings included in the spring Itinerant exhibition at the School of Painting. He instructed Ostroukhov on how he wanted paintings hung in Moscow. He asked Khruslov to send two paintings from the Itinerant show to the London World Exhibition. And he wrote Tretyakov expressing deep regret that he would not be able to attend the celebration set for April 23, when Tretyakov officially turned over his private gallery to the city of Moscow.

On March 13 Levitan left for Vienna and then went on to Lake Como in Italy. As usual he was more apprehensive than enthusiastic about traveling to the West. In part he was worried about his health. He told Tretyakov before he left, "I feel so terrible, I admit, that if I were to stay here in our climate this spring, I would stay forever. Maybe it's my hypochondria, but that's the way it is." He sought out Langovoi for medical advice. The doctor found Levitan's condition puzzling: "From my first examination, I diagnosed a serious ailment of his aorta that was completely unexpected at his age and with his healthy lifestyle. In addition, I noticed that he had a significant nervous temperament and a tendency for melancholy moods."[19]

Levitan made the trip without Kuvshinnikova, in one of several signs that their relationship was deteriorating. The previous year she had given him a photo with the inscription "in memory of our last happy summer at Gorodka." In writing to Vasnetsov on April 9 from Nice, Levitan continued to express concern about his health. He also admitted, as had happened during his first trip to the West, that traveling through the landscape of southern Europe, rather than inspiring him with new motifs, only served to provoke a deep nostalgia for Russia:

I'm feeling a little better, although still not all that great. I'm not going to Italy, but in a week or two I will be going to Paris to look at some exhibitions, and then off for home.

I'm imagining how glorious it is now in Russia—the rivers are overflowing, everything is coming to life . . . There is no better country than Russia! Only in Russia is it possible to be a genuine landscape painter.

It's also nice here, but they can have it.

A week later Levitan wrote an even more deeply confessional letter to Nikolai Medyntsev from Mont Baron, where the majesty of the French Alps surrounding him only served to remind him how much he missed Russia. Medyntsev was an acquaintance at whose home Levitan and his painter friends often gathered; Stepanov married his daughter. Levitan not only pined for the Russian landscape, he also hungered for the spiritual regeneration associated with Russian Easter. He embraced the potent symbolism of a resurrection linked to the coming of spring:

I am writing to you at the very same time that you undoubtedly, having just returned from abroad, are sitting amidst your family on the eve of the Easter holiday—the harbinger of spring, and I envy you, as awful as that is, and just the same with all my soul I wish you all the best.

Undoubtedly in an hour or so the church bells will ring out. Oh, how I love those minutes, the minutes that speak the truths about life, not speaking about a factual resurrection, but about the triumph of divine truth. However, all this is possibly not the case. Tell me, my dear friend, why am I here? What do I need in a foreign land, when at the very same time I am drawn to Russia and so desperately want to see the melting snow, the birch tree? . . . The devil knows what kind of person I am—I am drawn to everything that is unknown, and having tasted it, an unspoken sadness remains and a desire to return to the past . . . I'll stop, or else all this will descend into a sentimentality that is boring for others to read.

In the same letter Levitan continued to mention his health concerns: "I feel physically stronger although I haven't gained a bit of weight." He had considered going to Rome "but the heat scares me, and the thought of being overwhelmed by the impressions." Levitan asked Medyntsev whether he had seen the Kuvshinnikovs, whom he had yet to hear from.

Potapenko wrote to Maria Chekhova that on May 30 Levitan suddenly appeared in Paris, where he "amazed the boulevardiers with his stylish Moscow attire."[20] Potapenko also reported that Yavorskaya was "enraptured by the arrival of her girlfriend Tania" and had organized a celebratory evening in her honor. Lika, three months pregnant, was there as well, feeling too sick to take her singing lessons, and seeing Potapenko only briefly and in secret when he was able to get away from his wife. Although Levitan mentioned to friends that he hoped to see several exhibitions in Paris, we only know that he attended a salon exhibition of James Jacques Josef Tissot's realistic illustrations for *The Life of Christ*. Levitan told Pereplyotchikov that he was enthralled by these pictures, but that no other paintings made any particular impression on him.

While his friends converged in Paris, Chekhov was back in Melikhovo after a month-long stay in Yalta. But even at a distance, he had not been spared from the turmoil of their tangled affairs. He received a letter from Yavorskaya in Italy pleading for him to use his influence to silence a jilted lover who had written to her father telling him his daughter had gone off to Italy with Shchepkina-Kupernik, and that their lesbian relationship had become a "nasty Moscow fable." Yavorskaya asked Chekhov to write to the customs department in St. Petersburg, where the perpetrator worked, "to stop him from making a nuisance of himself."[21] In mid-June, eager to get away from the demands of his family in Melikhovo, Chekhov went to Moscow to spend three days with Suvorin, whom he had not seen for four months.[22] Always candid in sharing his thoughts with Suvorin, Chekhov regaled him in a letter with a ribald description of the sexual dalliances of his Moscow circle, himself included. He insisted that his friends greatly exaggerated how often they had sex with respectable women: "All this is just words, when in fact they are having sex with cooks or going to one-ruble whore houses. All writers lie. Having sex with a lady in a city isn't as easy as in books." Chekhov proceeded to write in seven sentences an entire short story on the subject:

> Romancing a lady from proper circles is a long procedure. First, it has to be night. Second, you go to the Hermitage Hotel. Third, at the Hermitage they tell you there are no rooms available, and you go searching for another refuge. Fourth, in the hotel room your lady loses courage, starts shaking, and exclaims, "Oh, my God, what am I doing?! No! No!" The right time for undressing and words passes. Fifth, on the way back your lady has an expression on her face as if you had raped her and is constantly mumbling, "No, I will never forgive myself for this!"[23]

Levitan was back in Russia toward the end of June. During the first week of July he and Kuvshinnikova returned to the Ushakov estate on Lake Ostrovno for the summer. Their relationship had not yet totally fallen apart.

Kuvshinnikova invited Shchepkina-Kupernik and her young friend Natasha Blagovolenskaya, "a slender girl with naïve eyes and thick curls" who taught in a theatrical school, to spend the summer with them. Shchepkina-Kupernik said that Kuvshinnikova "loved to surround herself with young faces; she did not envy youth, she was charmed by it." Kuvshinnikova knew that having the young women around would delight Levitan and deflect the growing tension between them. The first part of the summer, as recalled by Shchepkina-Kupernik, was idyllic: "Levitan really loved us, called us 'little girls,' played with us like little kittens, drew us in our Empire outfits." Shchepkina-Kupernik did not much like the result: "Genre painting was not his strength." He would row them out to one of the little islands on the lake and leave them there for the whole day: "We were left alone on this island and lived the lives of wood nymphs: we swam, dried ourselves in the sun, swam again, and picked strawberries which lay scattered right under our noses." Natasha recited monologues and Tatiana wrote verse:

> This feeling of isolation and being at one with nature was intoxicating. When the splash of oars broke the silence of dusk across the lake, we threw on our clothes and ran to the shore where we could already hear Levitan's cheery voice from the lake:
>
> "Girls, it's dinner! We have crawfish and raspberries today . . ."
>
> Sophia Petrovna was affectionate, cheerful, went about in a sort of improbably Greek tunic, the color of which, we laughed, was a mix of tulip, orange, sunset, and criminal passion; or she wore an exaggerated caftan in the style of Vasnetsov, and in the evenings she would play "Moonlight Sonata" or "Apassionata" while Levitan listened, squeezing his eyes shut from pleasure and, as was his custom, sighing deeply.[24]

Shchepkina-Kupernik was struck by Levitan's devotion to his painting. He and Kuvshinnikova would leave early in the morning, "grabbing umbrellas, sketchbooks, and some kind of snack," and be gone the whole day. Once, Kuvshinnikova returned alone around five o'clock, perturbed: "He's completely obsessed! I just couldn't tear him away." When she went back to look for him, she could not find him; he had moved on to another location. "She became agitated, and she had red and white patches on her dark face." They sent one of the house staff with two setters off to search for him. They did not return until sunset with the "guilty" Levitan, who "had a tired but satisfied look on his face. 'I got a lot of work done today. And I'm as hungry as a wolf,' he announced excitedly, putting all his things in the corner of the terrace and going off to wash up."

In early July, Anna Turchaninova, the wife of a prominent St. Petersburg official, arrived at a neighboring estate accompanied by her three daughters. Varvara and Sophia were already young ladies, and little Anna (whom they also called Lyulya) was around fourteen. Knowing that the famous painter Levitan was staying with the Ushakovs, Turchaninova made a visit; possibly she had already met him previously in Petersburg.[25] Shchepkina-Kupernik thought her a preening socialite. She "was around Sophia Petrovna's age, but very *soignée* with painted lips (Sophia Petrovna disliked makeup), with an elegantly correct toilette, and with the reticence and grace of a St. Petersburg coquette (she always struck me as looking like Lavretsky's wife in *A Nest of Gentlefolk*). And so began a battle." Tatiana and Natasha continued to enjoy their half-childish lives, but they could not help but notice the drama that was unfolding in front of their eyes: "Levitan frowned, and more and more often went off 'hunting' with his [dog] Vesta. Sophia Petrovna went about with an inflamed face and sometimes with tears in her eyes . . . We felt sorry for her, but with the thoughtless cruelty of youth we were surprised that people fell in love at this age . . . and joked that when we turned forty, we would either die or go to a monastery!"

A more detailed, fictionalized description of what happened can be gleaned from Shchepkina-Kupernik's short story "The Elders," which she published in 1911.[26] The story's characters closely match their real-life counterparts. Tavochka is a seventeen-year-old girl who, together with her friend, is staying at an estate as a guest of a woman named Irina and her lover, a famous painter, whom the girls call Uncle Leva. The painter is described in a manner similar to Shchepkina-Kupernik's verse portrait of Levitan: "He looked like someone in an old Spanish portrait—with his pointed dark beard with glittering gray streaks, his pale yellow face and dark eyes." Irina agrees: "Oh, he's a real Velasquez!" He asks the young girls what they think of his landscape paintings, and Tavochka answers: "Good . . . only sad!" She goes on to say that "never did a single painting of his arouse in me a smile or happiness. But this sadness was better than any sort of joy." When she asks him why his paintings are always so sad, he replies: "Nature in Russia, no matter how beautiful it is, can arouse only sadness in the soul. The sadness of powers lost in vain and unrealized hopes."

Their newly arrived neighbors come to visit: "It was a mother and two daughters; the father, a well-known St. Petersburg bureaucrat, came rarely, so the women lived alone." The young girls find the mother (Polina) repulsive: "She looked like a gypsy. Her eyelids were dark brown, as if singed, and her lips were bright like a red pepper [. . .]. She always wore white, and she always smelled so sweetly and strongly that even the cups from which she drank smelled of perfume . . . She was always gracious to everyone, [. . .] but she had evil eyes."

One day Polina's two girls appear and invite everyone over to their place since their mother is not feeling well. Irina declines, but Uncle Leva suddenly announces that he thinks the activity would liven him up. He tells the girls he is coming with them, informing Irina that he will probably be back for dinner. But Uncle Leva fails to return. A terrible thunderstorm strikes and everyone goes to bed. Tavochka wakes up in the middle of the night and hears the sound of the piano. From upstairs she sees Irina playing Chopin: "Suddenly she stopped playing and cried out in a strange voice, 'Oh, God' and put her face in her hands and started crying. Then she heard the balcony door slam and Uncle Leva came into the hall. Irina turned around and shook as if in fright, then she threw herself at him, not imperiously as usual but somehow in despair and she shouted out, 'Finally.' And he took her hand and sternly, not the way he normally spoke during the day, said: 'Mad woman!'"

The atmosphere in the house becomes tense. Uncle Leva "went off hunting with his dog. We didn't know what he was shooting because he never brought anything back. Occasionally we would hear gunshots resounding over the lake, and this would make Irina shudder and turn pale."

Soon afterward Polina organizes a dinner celebrating her birthday. Uncle Leva and Irina argue when she appears "in a Greek tunic the color of nasturtium with golden clasps on her shoulders." "Looking sideways at her, Uncle Leva asked, 'Are you going like that?' She blushed, 'You don't like these colors anymore?' He became confused, coughed, and replied, 'No it's very nice, but . . . in company? It's going to be a dinner, a lot of people have been invited.'"

Uncle Leva sets off for the dinner early, leaving everyone else behind. Irina tells the girls to go ahead on their own, that she has decided not to go. At the dinner Uncle Leva, who has just given Polina his latest painting, is the honored guest, sitting next to the mistress. Soon Irina appears, having changed into a white dress like the one being worn by Polina. Irina sits next to Polina's husband, who is there for the occasion, and flirts with him while drinking glass after glass. Afterward there are fireworks on the lake. Standing next to Uncle Leva, Irina "timidly threaded her arm under his elbow, but he moved away and said in a quiet, but nasty voice: 'You were rude.' 'But you are driving me to despair!' 'Stop the comedy.' He walked away. She stood for a moment as if lost and then quickly left."

At home Irina and Uncle Leva avoid each other. Tavochka comes across Irina in the garden. She has been crying again and then begins wailing. Tavochka asks her what is wrong. Irina gathers herself and tells her: "Never fall in love, Tavochka, never!" and quickly walks away.

Shchepkina-Kupernik's story captures both the nature and the events of the breakup between Kuvshinnikova and Levitan, as she openly admitted in her

memoirs.[27] She wrote that the battle "ended with a complete victory for the
St. Petersburg lioness and utter defeat for the poor, sincere Sophia Petrovna."
Kuvshinnikova left Ostrovno, taking the young girls with her. Shchepkina-
Kupernik wrote:

> After the breakup with Levitan, Sophia Petrovna's life seemed to become lack-
> luster [. . .]. As before, friends gathered at her Russian table for modest dinners;
> as before, artists drew sketches in her album; she had love affairs . . . but it just
> wasn't the same. Her memories of Levitan forever remained the most precious
> in her life, and the pages she wrote about him after his death were unusually
> touching and wonderful: she didn't let any personal offense color her memories
> of him.[28]

While the tumult of abandoning Kuvshinnikova for Turchaninova distressed
Levitan, it did not drive him into depression. On July 9 he wrote to the
younger Nikolai Medyntsev that he had "settled in and begun to work" but
asked him to tell his father that "I've become bogged down. He'll understand
what I mean by this," referring to his difficulties with Kuvshinnikova. Still, he
managed to joke with the younger Medyntsev about his amorous adventures:
"I'm thinking, as before, you are flying around various dachas and swallow-
ing up the hearts of credulous dacha ladies? Oh, you ravenous crocodile and
devourer of hearts!" By August, after Kuvshinnikova had moved out, Levitan
moved into Turchaninova's estate, Gorka, where she had set up a studio for
him. He worked hard painting a series of landscapes, still lives, and pastels
despite feeling emotionally unmoored. Toward the end of summer he wrote to
Shchepkina-Kupernik with some exaggeration that "my personal unpleasantness, which I'm going through now, has knocked me off my feet and pushed
everything else aside. At some point we will talk about this in Moscow. I am
living uneasily . . . Everything in the world is coming to an end . . . and for what
reason the devil only knows." At the same time, Levitan was telling Medyntsev
that he was "working a lot and reading even more." At Gorka he had at his disposal Turchaninova's enormous library filled with forbidden books that were
of great interest to him.

Chekhov spent most of July and August with Potapenko, much to the
distress of his sister Maria, who could not forgive Potapenko for seducing
Lika and abandoning her in Europe. The two men traveled down the Volga
together and on to Taganrog. Lika was in Paris, desperately unhappy, stuck
with Potapenko's wife, whom she considered a "bitch."[29] Lika blamed Chekhov
for not stopping her from going to Europe with Potapenko. She was glad that
Chekhov's "girl friends" Shchepkina-Kupernik and Yavorskaya had left: she

had grown tired of their boasting of Chekhov's attentions. In September, Chekhov made his second trip to Europe, accompanied by Suvorin. They left for Vienna from Odessa and went on to Abbazia (a resort on the Adriatic), Venice, Nice, and Paris. Lika, seven months pregnant, was now in Montreux, Switzerland, pleading for Chekhov to come visit her. He wrote that he could not, that he was forced to accompany Suvorin to Paris. Aware of Lika's condition, Chekhov wrote his sister that Potapenko was "a Yid and a swine." By the time she returned to Paris to have her baby, Chekhov had already left for Moscow. Potapenko was present in November when Lika gave birth to a daughter, Christina, but left soon afterward, never to see Lika again.

Short on money and "sitting like a crab stuck at low tide," Levitan ended up staying at Gorka longer than he intended. When he finally returned to Moscow and saw Shchepkina-Kupernik, she was busy with a production of Edmond Rostand's *Les Romanesques*, a play she had translated for Yavorskaya to perform at Korsh's theater. In late November Chekhov invited Shchepkina-Kupernik to come to Melikhovo: "I will be thrilled if you come visit me, but I fear that your tasty cartilage and bones will be knocked out of joint. The road is terrible. The carriage will leap about in tormenting pain and its wheels will drop off at every step. The last time I came from the station, my heart was shaken along the route and ripped away, and as a result I am no longer able to love."

Shchepkina-Kupernik arrived for her first visit to Melikhovo on December 3, accompanied by Maria. Not surprisingly, given her lively nature, she immediately embraced the spirited atmosphere of the Chekhov household. With Chekhov's father away and Anton's encouragement, she took to writing the daily entries in Pavel Egorovich's diary, mischievously imitating his bland, laconic style. After her second visit, Shchepkina-Kupernik was given a list of things to bring from Moscow at New Year's.

Just before Christmas, while visiting Ivan in Moscow, Chekhov sat down in one of the cold classrooms where his brother taught and read a story by Shchepkina-Kupernik that had just been published in *The Weekly*. He had previously congratulated her on the work being accepted by such a "solid, attractive journal" and now wrote her a note praising the story in his typically backhanded fashion: "I read your 'Loneliness' and forgave you for all your sins. The story is quite good and without a doubt you are intelligent and thoroughly sly. I was especially struck by the artistry of the story. By the way, you don't understand anything." In a postscript he added: "You were unable to hold yourself back and on page 180 you describe Sophia Petrovna [Kuvshinnikova]." But in her memoirs she maintained he was wrong in teasing her about this; she had not described Kuvshinnikova in this story but, rather, waited another sixteen years before doing so in "The Elders."

Shchepkina-Kupernik felt emboldened by Chekhov's praise and attention. On January 1, 1895, she and Yavorskaya sent a mock decree to him as the "Literary General and Knight of the Orders of the Sacred Names of Tatiana and Lidia the First, and Private of our Personal Escorts."[30] The next day on her way to her third visit to Melikhovo, Shchepkina-Kupernik decided to drop by Levitan's studio. He had promised to show her the sketches he made at Ostrovno the previous summer. She was loaded down with all sorts of packages for the Chekhov family and in a lively mood:

> When Levitan found out where I was going, he exhaled deeply, as was his habit, and told me how hard this stupid rift was for him and how much he would like to go there.
>
> "Why does it have to be that way?" I said with the energy and impetuousness of youth. "If you want to, then you have to go. Come with me right now!"
>
> "What? Now? Just go?"
>
> "Yes, just go, but first wash your hands!" (He was covered in paint.)
>
> "But what if it's inappropriate? And suddenly he doesn't understand?"
>
> "I'll take the blame if it's inappropriate!" I decided categorically.
>
> Levitan became agitated, fired up . . . then suddenly made up his mind. He threw down his brushes, washed his hands—and in a few hours we arrived along the winter road at the humble house at Melikhovo. Along the entire way Levitan was agitated, breathing heavily, and would ask excitedly:
>
> "Tanichka, what if we're impulsively doing something stupid?" (He had a way of very pleasantly rolling his "r's.")
>
> I calmed him down, but his agitation spontaneously also infected me, and my heart started to pound: what if I'm suddenly leading him toward an unpleasant moment? Although on the other hand, knowing Anton Pavlovich, I was sure nothing of the sort would happen.[31]

Shchepkina-Kupernik, who played a big part in stirring up the animosity between the two men, was now about to bring them together again.

8 | 1895

"I'M SICK OF MYSELF"

IT WAS LATE EVENING BY the time Levitan and Shchepkina-Kupernik approached the house at Melikhovo. Chekhov's parents were already in bed. Shchepkina-Kupernik described the reunion:

> The dogs barked at the sleigh bells . . . Masha ran onto the porch . . . [Chekhov] came out, looking like he had been drinking. He peered into the darkness to see who was with me—there was a brief pause, and suddenly they both flung themselves towards each other, very, very strongly clasped each other's hand—and . . . started talking about the most everyday things: about the road, the weather, Moscow—as if nothing had happened. At dinner, when I saw how Levitan's beautiful eyes were wet and glistening and how Chekhov's normally pensive eyes were radiating happiness, I was terribly pleased with myself.[1]

Knowing that his friend was planning to go to Moscow the next day, Levitan left in the morning before Chekhov got up. He wrote a note on a visiting card: "I'm sorry that I won't see you today. Will you drop in on me? I am unspeakably happy to be here again among the Chekhovs. I have returned again to that which was dear to me and indeed never stopped being dear to me." The family's hired hand took Levitan to the train station. Shchepkina-Kupernik stayed another three days.

On January 4 Chekhov settled into the Great Moscow Hotel just north of Red Square for two weeks. Shchepkina-Kupernik and Yavorskaya lavished their attentions on him. They jointly sent him a love note: "Come immediately, Antosha!" Shchepkina-Kupernik wrote. "We thirst to see and adore you. This is me writing for Yavorskaya, I just love you." Yavorskaya added: "I am awfully sad parting with you, as if the best part of my heart is being torn out [. . .].

Don't forget the woman who loves only you [. . .]. I'm lonely without you . . .
I'm in despair. Come, darling."[2] Her flirtation had turned into a seduction.
From Paris, recalling how the two sirens had talked endlessly during their
time there about their affection for Chekhov, Lika correctly surmised what
was happening now that they were back in Moscow. She wrote Chekhov:
"Well, has Tania settled in Melikhovo and occupied my place on the divan?
Is your wedding to Yavorskaya soon?"[3] Her tone was ironic; she knew from
her own bitter experience that nothing chilled Chekhov's ardor more than
declarations of love. Still angry at him, Lika wrote Maria telling her that she
was her only remaining genuine friend: "I had the idiotic fantasy to also think
of Anton Pavlovich as a friend, but this certainly turned out to be only a silly
fantasy!" However close she felt to Maria, Lika was still unable to confide in her
about the birth of her child. She concealed her misery, joking about a French
admirer who sang gypsy songs to her on a guitar and gossiping about their
mutual friends. She had received a letter in verse from Shchepkina-Kupernik
about her visits to Melikhovo: "Have Tania and Yavorskaya again made up?
And your brother with Levitan? How surprising!" She had been meaning
to write to him and told Maria that if a reconciliation between Levitan and
Kuvshinnikova ever took place, "you would have to throw your hands up in
the air and no longer be surprised by anything in the world!"[4]

Chekhov accepted Levitan's invitation and visited him at his studio, a short
walk from his hotel. The brilliance of Levitan's recent work and the obvious
physical and emotional toll that Levitan's romantic entanglements had taken
made a strong impression on the writer. It was apparent that Levitan's health
had deteriorated over the two years since their falling out. Chekhov told
Suvorin: "He is Russia's finest landscape painter, but, as you can imagine, he
is no longer young. He no longer paints in a youthful way, but with bravura.
I think women have worn him out. These wonderful creations give their
love, and they don't take much from a man—only his youth. It's impossible
to paint a landscape without pathos, without enthusiasm, and enthusiasm is
impossible if a man has stuffed himself full. If I were a landscape painter, I
would lead an almost ascetic life: I would have sex once a year and would eat
only once a day."

At the time, Levitan was preparing paintings and pastels for the Twenty-
Third Itinerant Exhibition in St. Petersburg in February. They included works
from Europe (*Lake Como* and *Corniche. South of France*) and from Udomlya
(*On the Lake*). Levitan must have also told his friend about his difficulties
separating from Kuvshinnikova, who was showering him with reproaches
and demanding that he send back all her letters to him.[5] But Chekhov had
his own reasons for complaining about how women inevitably undermine

an artist's creative energy and focus. During his Moscow stay while he was having an affair with Yavorskaya, Chekhov scolded Shchepkina-Kupernik about her unabashed lesbianism in a way that deeply offended her. On January 20, back in Melikhovo, he tried to make amends, sending her a note: "Don't be angry with me. Come to Melikhovo today or tomorrow. We'll drink to peace—and *basta*. You be a good girl." He signed the note "Resident of 'The Louvre' (No. 54)," referring to the hotel room he used to stay in adjacent to Shchepkina-Kupernik and Yavorskaya. But in truth he was still angry with her. He wrote Suvorin the next day:

> She is a talented little girl, but I doubt that you will find her likeable. I am sorry for her because I am annoyed with myself: three days a week I find her loathsome. She is sly as the devil, but her motives are so petty that it turns out she's not a devil, but a rat. Yavorskaya is quite a different matter. She is a very good woman and an actress who might have amounted to something if she hadn't been spoiled by her training.

In her memoirs, Shchepkina-Kupernik insisted that Yavorskaya was not as easily seduced as most men assumed and mistakenly concluded that when Chekhov realized that his relationship with Yavorskaya "would not go beyond flirting, he seemingly acted offended by this."[6] She saw both Chekhov and Yavorskaya as sexual rivals.

Understandably wary of what Chekhov actually thought of her, Shchepkina-Kupernik replied to Chekhov's invitation: "I am very glad, Anton Pavlovich, that your unusually strange mood has left you." Nevertheless, she was still stunned that he had judged her behavior so priggishly. "This has caused a minor revolution in my entire view of things," she added. Still, she concluded that if his apology was sincere, she would come to Melikhovo as soon as she was able to.[7]

Shchepkina-Kupernik immediately regretted sending the note off. She wrote again to Chekhov to "apologize for the stupid, childish feeling that compelled me to write you such an answer in my last note." But since their relationship had shifted so rapidly from his encouragement of her to his disapproval, she continued to agonize over how this had happened:

> Tell me directly, simply. What alienated you from me? What were you dissatisfied about? What? Do you really think that just *words* alone were all that I said to you in sweet, dear Melikhovo . . . I will always, always do everything to make amends for my poor manners, if that's what they are, and again be in your good favor. Allow me to look right into your good, honest eyes: they cannot lie; they

cannot be mistaken—they will see that I was never against you in either word or thought and I will never be, that I love you, and if I see in you a coldness or enmity—it's very, very hard on me.[8]

But Chekhov did remain cool toward her. Shchepkina-Kupernik next came to Melikhovo over two months later when she accompanied Maria there for Easter.

Levitan arrived in Melikhovo on January 22, still wrapped up in a melancholia so apparent to everyone that when he left four days later, Pavel Egorovich wrote in his diary "the psychiatric patient has left."[9] A few days later Levitan asked his friend and intermediary Nikolai Medyntsev if he had succeeded in returning Kuvshinnikova's letters, and if not, if he would then send them back to him. He twice cancelled plans to go hunting with Langovoi: "Something that I cannot put off has arisen. God only knows, it's as if fate is tormenting me. Sorry."

Levitan's relationship with Shchepkina-Kupernik and Yavorskaya remained light and flirtatious. But he hadn't abandoned his feelings for Maria. The previous October, Maria experienced an unexplained "sad event," as she described it to Shchepkina-Kupernik, which could have been prompted by a visit by Levitan soon after his return from Gorka.[10] In Moscow on January 18, after seeing Levitan, she wrote a note to Shchepkina-Kupernik passing on an invitation from Levitan to visit him the next afternoon. Maria added playfully, "I'm not jealous."[11] Maria and Levitan's ongoing affection for each other was no secret. At the end of January, Lika wrote Maria asking her if she planned to marry Levitan now that Kuvshinnikova had left him.[12] On February 4 Levitan accompanied Maria to a benefit performance in honor of Yavorskaya of *The Battle for Happiness*, a play by Sophia Kovalevskaya and the Swedish writer Anna Leffler. Shchepkina-Kupernik had worked with Yavorskaya to improve the translation. After the performance, Yavorskaya invited Levitan and Maria to her rooms at the Louvre Hotel to revel in its success, although Maria later privately told her brother that the benefit "was something awful."[13] The gathered group, which included the writer Dmitri Mamin-Sibiryak and the newspaper editor Mikhail Sablin, sent a celebratory telegram to Chekhov, who was in St. Petersburg: "The flowers are fragrant here and remind us of you. We love you and all eight of us send you our greetings."[14]

Two days later Maria found herself defending Levitan to a furious Mamin-Sibiryak. She was having dinner with the writer (who was known as a heavy drinker) and Sablin at the Hermitage Restaurant after an impromptu visit to the circus. In the course of their conversation, she mentioned Levitan and praised his talents as a landscape painter. Much to her surprise Mamin-Sibiryak became enraged that she considered him a "Russian" landscape artist. It was not unusual for critics to disparage Levitan as a Jew incapable of being a truly Russian artist. Back in Melikhovo, she wrote to her brother: "When you return, I'll tell you everything. He really gave it to me!"[15]

While Levitan and Maria's relationship became more relaxed now that he and her brother were friends again and socializing, the breakup with Kuvshinnikova was still weighing on him. He told Tretyakov on March 2: "I don't know where I'm going to spend the summer. My nerves are so shot that it's difficult to make plans for the future." He did, however, decide to leave Moscow in mid-March and join Turchaninova at Gorka for several weeks. And the outcome of that visit was one of his masterpieces, the painting *March*. Despite Levitan's bouts of melancholia, the painting radiates simple joy at the coming of spring. The sky is a bright, cloudless blue. The high contrast of sunlight turns the melting snow into various shades of gray with brilliant white highlights. The horse and empty sleigh waiting at the side of the house evoke a feeling of arrival, as does the sharp shadow across the welcoming open door. Much of *March* was painted *en plein air* rather than reworked in his studio, giving it a decidedly impressionistic feel. Lyulya, Turchaninova's youngest daughter, watched Levitan as he worked on *March*. She carried his paint box for him (he was starting to complain about his weak heart) and listened to him while watching in fascination as he prepared the canvas with whitewash and brushed on the colors that turned the sky into a deep, bottomless blue.[16] To make it easier for Levitan to decide to return for the summer, Turchaninova ordered the construction of a separate studio for him on the shore of the lake where he could be alone and have the space to work on large pieces.

Back in Moscow at the end of March, Levitan dropped in on Alexander Sredin, a protégé of Korovin and Serov, to discuss a proposed exhibition being planned separate from the Itinerant Association. Formed as a group that seceded from the St. Petersburg Academy, the Association, now hidebound in its ways, had rejoined the Academy in 1893. A small contingent of the original members took it upon themselves to be the sole judges of whom to admit to the exhibitions, effectively excluding the younger generation of painters. This decision drove Repin to resign from the Association.[17] Nesterov recalled that he, Levitan, and Serov increasingly felt like outcasts. Not finding Sredin at home, Levitan wrote him that he had changed his mind about being able to help organize the exhibition: "I'm telling you truthfully, for me, a sick man physically and morally beaten down, the thought of the work in front of me simply begins to frighten me. Hardly knowing whether I will be able to do something tomorrow, how can I promise to do something several months from now?" Levitan apologized for "refusing to take part in this really necessary matter," but "art is such a voracious hydra and so jealous that it consumes the whole person, leaving him nothing of his physical and moral savings." He left open the possibility of either devoting his energy to planning the exhibition in the fall, or cajoling Ostroukhov, who had by now become a major art collector, to take his place. Ironically, one of the events looming before Levitan was the opening of the latest Itinerant exhibition in Moscow on April 3, and on April 7 he went to St. Petersburg to attend the general meeting of the Itinerant membership.

On April 29 Levitan was again Chekhov's guest at Melikhovo. The birches were beginning to leaf out, and he accompanied Anton and Maria on a long walk in the woods, not returning until late in the evening. Chekhov gave Levitan a copy of *Sakhalin Island*, which had recently been published in book form, and added the inscription: "I give this book to dear Levitasha in the event that he murders someone out of jealousy and ends up on this island."

On their walk Levitan undoubtedly talked to Anton and Maria about his imminent summer plans to go to Gorka to stay with the Turchaninovs and invited them to visit him there at his new studio. Levitan left Melikhovo on May 1 and by May 4 he was at Gorka. From there he immediately wrote to Chekhov, asking him to help Dr. Lev Berchansky, the brother of his sister Tereza's husband, get his plays passed by the censors: "there is nothing that needs to be censored with respect to undermining social or governmental authority (I have read one of his plays), but nevertheless the plays have been banned." When Levitan was still a desperately poor student at the School of Painting, Lev Berchansky had helped him sell some of his paintings, and for that he was eternally grateful. But Levitan did not wait for Chekhov to respond to his letter; two days later he again visited Melikhovo briefly, returning to Gorka the next day.

His restlessness reflected a turmoil in his personal life that was coming to a head: Anna Turchaninova's eighteen-year-old daughter Varya had fallen in love with him. The situation was evident to everyone at Gorka. Mother and daughter were locked in battle. Levitan either did not want to or was not able to discourage this dual affair. One night Varya went to Levitan's studio and said that she was ready to secretly elope with him. He refused and Anna found out about it. Distraught, on June 21 Levitan put a pistol to his head and managed to angle it in such a way that the bullet only grazed his skull. Anna immediately sent her daughter back home to St. Petersburg for a few days.[18]

On June 23, without mentioning the suicide attempt, Levitan wrote to Chekhov:

For god's sake, if at all possible, come visit me, if only for a few days. I'm feeling terrible like never before. I would come myself to you, but I simply don't have the energy. Don't refuse me in this. A large room will be at your disposal in the house where I'm living alone in the woods on the shore of a lake. All the comforts will be at your disposal: wonderful fishing, a boat. If for some reason money is an issue for you now, don't think about it, I can lend it to you [. . .].

Come, my dear one, you will make me very happy, and I think you yourself will enjoy it.

Chekhov ignored Levitan's plea. Long familiar with the cycles of his friend's manic depression, he likely concluded that Levitan's mood would lift in a few days' time without any intervention on his part. On July 1, much to his surprise, Chekhov received a letter from Anna Turchaninova:

I don't know you, most esteemed Anton Vasilievich [*sic*], I am contacting you with a big request on the insistence of the doctor treating Isaac Ilich. Levitan is suffering from the most extreme melancholia, which has led him to the most horrible condition. In a moment of despair he tried to kill himself on June 21st. Fortunately he managed to be saved. The wound is no longer dangerous, but Levitan now requires careful, heart-felt, and tender nursing. Knowing from conversations that you are friendly with and close to Levitan, I decided to write you, asking that you quickly come see the patient. The life of a man depends on your arrival. You, only you, can save him and pull him out of his complete indifference to life and temporarily mad decision to kill himself.

Isaac Ilich wrote to you, but didn't receive an answer.

Please do not tell anyone about what has happened. Take pity on the unhappy man. Be so good as to answer me immediately. I will send horses for you.[19]

News of the suicide attempt and Turchaninova's appeal to him as a doctor made it impossible for Chekhov to ignore the summons. He told Leikin that he was sitting at home tending his roses, organizing the hay cutting, and pondering where he should spend the rest of the summer "when suddenly—bang! I received a telegram, and I woke up on the shores of one of the lakes about forty or fifty miles from the Bologoe station." He arrived at Gorka on July 5 and initially planned to stay for as many as ten days. Chekhov wrote Suvorin on the same day, respecting Turchaninova's request to keep the purpose of his visit confidential: "I've just arrived here and settled into a two-story house, newly chopped from an old forest on the shores of a lake. I've been summoned here to tend to a sick person." He found the place dreary: "Here on the lake the weather is depressing, cloudy. The roads are sour, the hay is mangy, and the children have a sickly look." He told Suvorin: "The place is swampy. It smells of Polovetsians and Pechenegs," evoking the image of wild, nomadic Central Asian marauders.

Chekhov witnessed an atmosphere of hysteria in the Turchaninov household. Levitan was wearing a black bandage, which earlier during an encounter with mother and daughter he had angrily ripped off his head and thrown to the floor. He then stormed out of the house toward the lake with a shotgun in his hand. He returned carrying a dead seagull, "which he had shot for no reason," and threw it at Anna Turchaninova's feet.[20] Chekhov stayed for less than a week, but the lakeside estate and the drama that played out before his eyes made an indelible impression on him. At the time Chekhov was considering writing a play. At Gorka he gave Levitan one by Maeterlinck to read, sharing his own fascination with emerging symbolist drama; Levitan found the work to be "a very interesting thing."

On July 13, Levitan wrote to Langovoi explaining what had happened to him:

> I can tell you, as my doctor and a good friend, the whole truth, knowing that this will go no further. My melancholia has progressed to the point that I shot myself; I remain alive, but for a month already a doctor has been coming to clean the wound and change the bandages. This is what has become of your obedient servant! I go about with a bandaged head, occasionally an awful pain in my head brings me to despair. Just the same, every day I get better. I think I will try to work. I've done almost nothing this summer and apparently won't get anything done. In general, unhappy thoughts fill my head.
>
> I have been taking the medicine you prescribed.

Levitan added a postscript: "I can't think about hunting. For me the sound of a shot is unbearable."

By now many of Chekhov's friends considered Levitan's suicide attempts more melodramatic than life-threatening. According to his brother Mikhail, even after getting the letter from Turchaninova, Chekhov made the trip to Gorka reluctantly, assuming that Levitan had only made it look as if he wanted to kill himself. When Levitan later complained to Maria about the dramatic events at Gorka, she shot back at him that it sounded to her like something he had read in a Guy de Maupassant novel, referring to *Fort comme la mort*, in which a painter falls in love with both a mother and her daughter.[21] Back in 1891 the musician Ivanenko had joked with Chekhov about the kind of sadness one feels when "an earthquake has happened or Levitan has shot himself."[22] Toward the end of the year Ivan Troyanovsky, an art collector and another of Levitan's doctors, wrote a friend that Levitan had told him about the attempted suicide at Gorka, but Troyanovsky could find no signs of a wound and considered the whole affair a "tragicomedy."[23] Several weeks after Chekhov left Gorka, Levitan wrote him that his bouts of overwhelming melancholia had returned:

> Once again I've become depressed and depressed beyond measure and bounds, depressed to the point of stupefaction, of horror. If you only knew how terrible I feel now in my soul. I've been pierced by sadness and despondency. What am I to do? With each day I have less will to fight against my dark mood. I should go somewhere, but I can't because it's impossible for me to make a decision; I vacillate endlessly. I need to be taken somewhere, but who will take this on themselves? Despite my condition, I observe myself constantly, and I can see that I'm finally breaking down. And I'm sick of myself, completely sick!
>
> I don't know why, but those few days that you spent with me were the most peaceful of the entire summer.

The letter was in part a plea for Chekhov to come visit him again: "Here everyone just about fell in love with you and awaits you as promised." Chekhov responded, suggesting that Levitan come to Melikhovo first, and then the two of them would go together to Gorka as long as Chekhov could be back by August 15 for Maria's birthday. But for some reason Chekhov's letter only arrived on August 8, when Levitan felt that it was too late to fit the proposed joint visits into Chekhov's schedule. In addition, much to his own delight, Levitan was starting to paint again and working on a subject that he could let slip if Chekhov visited: "I'm painting flowering lilies that have already faded." In the meantime Chekhov had arranged to visit Tolstoy at Yasnaya Polyana on August 8 and 9.

Levitan urged Chekhov to come see him after August 15: "Not just talking about myself, everyone at Gorka is anxiously awaiting you. You're such a crocodile, managing to charm everyone in just three days. Varya asked me to write that they're all bored without you. I'm damned jealous. Come and stay longer. Bring some work with you."

What Chekhov had been working on was his play. Percolating in his imagination were the personal dramas consuming Potapenko, Mizinova, Yavorskaya, and Levitan. At the end of January, Lika found out that Potapenko had told Maria about their child. On February 3 Lika wrote a shattering, confessional letter to Maria, finally revealing her abject state: "It's been almost a year that I've forgotten what it means to have peace, happiness, and other pleasant things! From almost my first day in Paris there began torment, lies, concealing, etc. Then at the most difficult time for me, it turned out that there was nothing for me to hope for and I was in such a state that, no joking, I thought of ending it all."[24] When Potapenko left after the birth of the child, Lika realized "in my heart I knew that the parting was forever. And that is how I live. Why and what for I don't know." Yet Lika begged Maria not to blame Potapenko for what happened: "Oh, this is all so repulsive and when I tell you everything, you'll be surprised that Ignaty hasn't yet shot himself. I feel so sorry for him and I so painfully love him! Why this happened, I don't know. Apparently because no one has ever loved me as he has, without hesitation, without reason!" In May Lika left her child with a wet nurse in Paris and returned to Russia for a brief visit, seeing Chekhov in Moscow and staying at Melikhovo twice. On May 5 Chekhov wrote Suvorin that the play he was writing was "something strange."

That spring Chekhov was free of Yavorskaya's effusive declarations of love—she was off touring with Korsh's theater. In March, with her characteristic "theatrical egocentrism,"[25] she described to Chekhov her triumphs in Nizhny Novgorod and St. Petersburg. Chekhov encouraged Suvorin to go see her in *Madame Sans-Gène*: "She is intelligent and nicely dressed, occasionally witty [. . .]. If it weren't for her screeching and certain mannerisms (also her affectations), she would be a genuine artist."

Having made a few notes about his new play before summer, Chekhov began working intensively on the piece only after returning to Melikhovo after visiting Levitan. What Chekhov saw at Gorka inspired the theme, structure, and setting for the play. He wrote in his notebook: "She signed her letters The Seagull." And: "An actress, seeing the pond, broke into tears recalling her childhood."[26] Unlike "The Grasshopper," *The Seagull* much more subtly reshaped the attributes, behavior, and actions of his friends (and himself), although not so much so that they would not be able to recognize at least aspects of themselves in the characters on stage. Similarly the "landscape" (Chekhov used this very word) of the play transformed the dreariness he saw at Gorka into what Dr. Dorn calls an "enchanted lake" that casts a spell of nervous romantic longing over those visiting the Sorin estate. Hanging on Chekhov's living room wall at Melikhovo was a sketch given to him by Levitan of *Lake Ostrovno* (1895) with its village and church in the background.[27] Both painter and writer in their own ways bestowed a mood and meaning to the mundane lake setting.

In Act I Nina Zarechnaya tells Treplev: "I am drawn here to this lake like a seagull." Treplev's symbolist play in the style of Maeterlinck invokes the ghosts hovering over the lake to "bring us dreams of things as they will be two hundred thousand years from now" (to which Sorin caustically replies:

"There will be just nothing"). Chekhov conjures the heightened emotional atmosphere that he witnessed at Turchaninova's estate. The sound of singing from across the lake prompts a reverie by Arkadina: "Ten or fifteen years ago you could always hear music and singing on the lake—almost every night. There are six country houses around the lake [as there were around Ostrovno]. I remember such laughter, and noise, and shooting—and love affairs all the time . . . And the *jeune premier* and idol of all those houses was . . . allow me to introduce him," pointing toward Dorn. "He's fascinating still, but in those days he was irresistible."

In creating the literary and romantic antagonists Treplev and Trigorin, Chekhov drew upon the personalities and behavior of Levitan, Potapenko, and himself. He appreciated the layered symbolism of Levitan tossing the dead seagull at Turchaninova's feet. In Act II Treplev puts the dead seagull at Zarechnaya's feet: "Soon I shall kill myself in the same way." When Zarechnaya points out the seagull to Trigorin, it gives the writer an idea that he jots down in his notebook: "A plot for a short story: a young girl like you lives on the shore of a lake since childhood; she loves the lake like a seagull, and she is happy and free like the seagull. But by chance a man appears, sees her, and having nothing better to do, destroys her, just like this seagull."

Act III begins after a failed suicide attempt by Treplev. While his mother Arkadina is changing the bandage wrapped around his head, they get into an argument about Trigorin and start insulting each other ("Decadent!" "Skinflint!" "Beggar!" "Nonentity!"). Treplev rips the bandage off his head just as Levitan had done. At the end of the act Zarechnaya runs off to become an actress and carry on an affair with Trigorin, echoing Varya Turchaninova's invitation to Levitan to elope, but also Lika's decision to go to Paris for voice lessons and to carry on her affair with Potapenko. Like Lika, Zarechnaya has a child, and prophetically, the child dies (Lika's daughter, Christina, died in November 1896, just a month after the play's premiere). After attending the disastrous premiere at the Alexandrinsky Theater in St. Petersburg (the audience for the benefit performance had come expecting a farce), Lika wrote to Chekhov: "Yes, everyone here is saying that *The Seagull* is taken from my life and also that you did a good job on a certain someone,"[28] referring to Trigorin as an unflattering portrait of Potapenko.

Suvorin too recognized Potapenko when he first read the play in December 1895. Chekhov responded, "If indeed it looks like Potapenko is depicted in it, then of course it shouldn't be produced or printed." But no such thing happened. There is no evidence that Potapenko recognized his unhappy affair with Lika in Zarechnaya's love for Trigorin or, if he did, was offended in any way. In fact, Potapenko took the lead in guiding *The Seagull* through its review by the censors, who were bothered by Treplev's indifference to his mother's love affairs and were demanding cuts.[29] Like Trigorin, Potapenko was a popular and prolific writer, but not one motivated to innovate—he had a current wife, a former wife, and two children to support. Trigorin confesses to Zarechnaya: "For some reason, as soon as I've finished one novel, I must start writing another . . . I write in a rush, without stopping, and can't do anything else." He tells her that his readers find his work to be charming, but nothing more: "And when I die, my friends as they pass by my grave, will say: 'Here lies Trigorin. He was a good writer, but not as good as Turgenev.'" He feels incapable of moving beyond the picturesque. Standing on the lake's edge, he says: "I love this water, the trees, the sky; I have a feeling for nature; it arouses a passion in me, an irresistible desire to write. But I'm not just a landscape painter, I'm also a citizen; I love my country, its people; I feel that if I'm a writer, then I must speak about the people, about their sufferings, about their future, and about science, the rights of man, and so on and so forth." But he feels badgered into being a prolific writer rather than a talented one, and this has turned him into the literary equivalent of an inferior version of Levitan: "And in the end I feel that I am only able to paint landscapes, and in everything else, I'm false, false to the very marrow of my bones."

Yet the self-deprecating Chekhov was unafraid to give this writer *manqué* some of his own attributes. On a superficial level there was Trigorin's mania for fishing. On a more significant level, he ascribed to Trigorin his own artistic technique of substituting an effect for its cause. Treplev jealously praises the way in which Trigorin would depict a moonlit scene, using an example that is almost a direct quote from Chekhov's advice in a letter to his brother Alexander in 1886: "Trigorin has worked out his own methods. It comes easily to him . . . He would just mention the neck of a broken bottle glistening on the dam and the black shadow of a mill wheel—and there you'd have a moonlit night."

Having long ago chided Chekhov for his indifference to his friends' feelings when they recognized themselves in his works, Lika was not about to criticize him again for how she was transformed into Zarechnaya. Her letters to him and Maria from Paris and Switzerland after she was abandoned by Potapenko inspired the depiction of Zarechnaya as a tragic victim of Trigorin's eventual indifference. But Chekhov did not hesitate to also portray Zarechnaya as an earnest, but mostly talentless actress—an opinion that Lika knew Chekhov held of her as well. Toward the end of the play, when Zarechnaya returns to the Sorin estate after losing her child, Treplev tells Dorn: "As far as I can tell from what I've heard, Nina's personal life turned out to be a complete failure [. . .]. She started acting in a small theater at some holiday place near Moscow, and then went to the provinces [. . .]. She would always take on big parts, but she acted them crudely, without distinction, with false intonations and violent gestures. There were moments when she showed talent—when she uttered a cry, or died on stage—but they were only moments."

Early in their friendship, Chekhov made it clear to Lika that he saw her artistic talents as limited. He was unsympathetic to what he felt was her unwillingness to work hard. He wrote her on July 27, 1892: "You completely lack the impulse to do proper work. [. . .] That's why you young ladies are only capable of giving insignificant lessons and learning nonsense from Fedotov," a Moscow theater impresario from whom Lika was taking acting classes. Lika gave a heart-felt response, suggesting that in Chekhov's case his work ethic was also the source of his maddening diffidence. She said that he was partially correct: "I'm unable to properly work on several things at the same time. Once I take on one thing—I devote my interest and enthusiasm to it alone, and since I have this one thing, everything else, of course, falls into the background. I'm unable like you to devote myself equally to everything and everyone. This is possibly a major failing, but just the same I prefer to be this way. I at least have one thing that's especially dear to me, but for you nothing is ever dear to you."[30]

If *The Seagull* presents a tableau of insecure artists struggling to find their place in the world, Irina Arkadina is the self-deluding *grande dame* in their midst, an epigone demanding everyone's full confidence in her talents. Her son Treplev says of her: "You mustn't praise anyone but her, you must acclaim her and go into raptures over her wonderful acting in *The Lady with the Camellias*, or the *Fumes of Life*." There is much about her self-intoxication, and her origins in Odessa and Kiev, that recall Yavorskaya. Shchepkina-Kupernik painted an ambivalent portrait of her in her memoirs: "She was a restless female figure with a nervous, sharp, slightly hoarse voice, carrying on intrigues with her snake-like grace and striking in her ability to be a tigress down to her fingertips."[31] She remembered a time when Chekhov came to see Yavorskaya in her hotel room: "She struck the pose of a Hindu heroine, dropped to her knees on the rug, stretching her thin arm out to Chekhov exclaiming: 'The unique . . . the inscrutable . . . the charming . . .'" In *The Seagull* Arkadina kneels before Trigorin, calling him "Wonderful, charming, amazing, unique."

Levitan was unable to entice Chekhov to visit him again at Gorka. And, as was often the case, his depression gave way to a period of intense creativity. At the height of summer's splendor, Levitan devoted himself to several stylistically varied studies of flowers and plants, often using pastels. He sketched roses in a watercolor that he gave to Sophia Turchaninova, the middle daughter. Levitan painted the water lilies he mentioned to Chekhov with the precision of a botanical illustration and using an unusual foreshortened perspective, from above. Because of his weakened heart, he had little Lyulya row him out to the lilies; they anchored the boat with a rock tied to a rope so it wouldn't move while he worked. Lyulya recalled another painting session that summer: "Isaac Ilich thought of painting a picture of *Lilies on a White Night*, and he needed to see them lit up by a white night. I, as always, rowed. Several lilies got tangled in an oar and were lifted up toward him. He grabbed one lily and kissed it. I said to him that the lilies would soon fade and that I would like them as a souvenir in my album." Levitan obligingly sketched some lilies in her album.[32]

As fall approached, Levitan turned his attention to an impressionistic rendering of ferns fading to yellow and brown deep in the forest. Belying all the recent tumult was his second great work from Gorka—the bright and serene *Golden Autumn*, painted with the same vibrant splashes of color seen in *March*. Mood is created through capturing contrasting colors on a sunny early autumn day—the intense yellow of the turning leaves at one end of the spectrum, the dark, opaque water mirroring the reeds and the sky at the other end.

Levitan returned to Moscow from Gorka on October 9 and immediately went to Melikhovo for two days. He had hoped to see Maria there, but she left the day he arrived, perhaps not wanting to endure the rehashing of his romantic entanglement with the Turchaninovs. Chekhov invited him to go badger hunting; they had no success and ended up planting tulip bulbs instead. Knowing Levitan's connections among his wealthy patrons, Chekhov asked him to help find a sponsor to save the journal *Surgical Annals*, which despite increasing subscriptions was losing money. Levitan dropped in on the industrialist and art collector Kozma Soldatenkov, but the latter turned out to be abroad, as was Sergei Morozov, so Levitan told Chekhov, "we will have to wait." Awaiting Levitan in Moscow was an even more pressing request for money from his sister Tereza, who assumed that it would be easy for Levitan to ask the Turchaninovs for a loan. He told her that he was in no position to help out: "My affairs this year are thoroughly awful. I've sold nothing at the exhibition, but I can't change my lifestyle, that is decrease expenses, since the most important thing, Tereza, is my studio, which I simply can't do without [. . .]. I can't get anything from Turchaninov or anyone else. There are things that seem easy to do, but this is only from a distance. If I manage to sell something, I'll send whatever I can. At the present moment I absolutely cannot send anything."

By the end of October Levitan once again descended into depression. Hoping that getting out of Moscow again would lift his spirits, he decided to write to Polenov to see whether he could visit him at his estate, Borok: "I've had such a bout of melancholia, such terrifying despair the likes of which I've never experienced before and which, I suspect, I won't be able to endure if I stay in the city, where I feel myself more alone than in the woods. Fear not, you won't see my sad figure—I'll wander about. I can't work; I can't read; music irritates; people are boring and I don't need them. All that remains is to withdraw from life, but I can't repeat this after my summer attempt, God knows why, and so I don't have the strength to live or die. What to do with myself?!!" Polenov responded sympathetically: "Of course, come visit us and breathe the ozone, which we have lots of from the melting snow. I too am a sick person and suffer from the same ailment that you have, and am treating myself for this awful illness that you call melancholia, but is now called neurasthenia [. . .]. The main medicine is clean air, cold water, a shovel, saw, and axe. And after three months of this mixture you feel almost like a healthy person, and even seemingly forget that there is on earth such a thing as painting; this joy, this poison."[33] But for Levitan putting aside painting could never serve as treatment for his depression. On the contrary, a renewed desire to paint invariably lifted his melancholia. He told Polenov that he had been set to come visit him "when suddenly, and I mean suddenly, I had a strong urge to work. I gave in to it and now it's already been a week that I haven't been able to tear myself away from the canvas." His nerves calmed down "and the world didn't seem so awful." Responding to Polenov's comment that their shared affliction should be called neurasthenia rather than melancholia, Levitan replied, "in the words of Shakespeare's Romeo: 'A rose by any other name would smell just as sweet.'" Levitan also commiserated with Polenov, his former teacher, for the disappointment of not having been chosen as a professor of the "new Academy" (now merged with the Itinerants) when a lesser talent like Alexander Makovsky ("the same Makovsky whom we didn't accept into the auction of the Society of Lovers of Art") had been named "an Academy painter with the right to travel abroad." Levitan considered this "flagrant cynicism," given that other Itinerants such as Repin and Shishkin had been admitted.

Sitting in his studio in the garden at Melikhovo, away from the distractions in the main house, Chekhov finished writing the first version of *The Seagull* in November. He told Suvorin: "I'm writing it not without pleasure, although I'm violating terribly the rules of stagecraft. It's a comedy, three female roles, six male roles, four acts, a landscape (a view out onto a lake); lots of conversation about literature, little action, and five pounds of love." On December 1 he sent the manuscript to Moscow to be typed. A few days later Chekhov himself went to Moscow, where he read the play for the first time to a large group of people in Yavorskaya's blue living room. Shchepkina-Kupernik recalled that Yavorskaya, whose tastes ran to French drama in the style of Dumas, did not like it at all, although she feigned delight. The impresario Korsh said it was bad theater to have a man shoot himself offstage and not even let him give a speech before he died. Shchepkina-Kupernik herself said she was unable to respond to the play objectively because "it seemed to me that its heroine was based on a girl whom I was close to and was also close to Anton Pavlovich, and who at this time had gone through a difficult and sad affair with a writer. And I was most of all bothered by the thought: would her fate turn out to be just as sad as that of the poor Seagull?" Chekhov responded to the noise and arguments following his reading with an expression on his face that was both embarrassed and stern.[34] He told Suvorin that his play had failed without even being performed.

With *The Seagull* completed, Chekhov was still in a frame of mind to write about artists, their sensibilities, and his own ambivalence about their self-absorption in the face of pressing social needs. He started working on "The House with a Mezzanine" (subtitled "An Artist's Story")—a first-person narrative about a landscape painter who one summer meets two sisters living at a neighboring estate. The manor house he is living in has much in common with Bogimovo, where Chekhov stayed in the summer of 1891—the enormous colonnaded ballroom, the long couch he slept on while the young landowner stayed in a cottage in the garden. But then the painter chances upon the much more modest house with a mezzanine, which, like the house in *The Seagull*, recalls the Turchaninov estate, Gorka. Looking at the house for the first time, he finds himself "[catching] the enchanting breath of something dear and familiar as if I had seen this landscape as a child," in a moment that echoes the nostalgic reverie of Nina Zarechnaya. Living at the house is the Volchaninov family—a mother and two daughters, Lida and Zhenya. Like Gorka, the estate has grounds for tennis and croquet, a pharmacy for dispensing medicine to local peasants, and a church with a bell tower, the "cross on it glittering in the setting sun," as in a Levitan painting. When the painter first meets Lida, who has come to his house to collect donations for victims of a fire in the village, she says to him that if he "wants to meet some admirers of his work and cares to look us up, Mother and I will be delighted." During his first visit the mother "hurriedly called to mind two or three of my landscapes she had seen in Moscow exhibitions. Now she wanted to know what I was trying to express in them."

The painter feels drawn to "this small, comfortable house" and the young sisters who "seemed like a breath of fresh air about the place—it was all thoroughly civilized." Like Levitan, the narrator is prone to melancholia. He visits the Volchaninovs often, sitting on the bottom step of the terrace, "depressed, dissatisfied with [himself], and full of regrets about [his] life passing so rapidly and unexcitingly." He muses, "My heart felt heavy within me and I kept thinking how wonderful it would be if I could only rip it out of my breast somehow." He soon realizes that the severe Lida, busy devoting herself to improving the lives of the local peasants, dislikes him "as a landscape painter who did not portray peasant hardship." In return he feels disdain for what he sees as her acts of *noblesse oblige* and criticizes her for playing doctor, dispensing medicines to the peasants: "After all, who couldn't play lady bountiful on five thousand acres of her own land?" Instead, he finds himself attracted to the younger Zhenya, who is carefree and lives a life of idleness. Charmed by Zhenya and her mother eating breakfast on the terrace on Sunday mornings, he remarks, "Everyone is so gay, so delightfully dressed. And you know that all these healthy, well-nourished, good-looking people are going to do nothing all day long. At such times you find yourself wishing that life was always like this. I thought so now as I strolled around the garden, prepared to wander in this way, aimless and unoccupied, all day or all summer."

While there are echoes of Levitan and even of Chekhov himself in the characterization of the painter, his philosophical stance and his indolence represent neither one of them. He has Levitan-like moods: "Since I was quite young, I've been racked with envy, fed up with myself, and disillusioned with my work." Like Chekhov, he has traveled to the shores of Lake Baikal. But the ideological battle between the narrator and the Tolstoyan Lida is another example of Chekhov's ability to stand aside and let his protagonists present themselves on their own terms, as humans with both admirable ideals and flawed justifications of those ideals. The narrator's argument against Lida's good works is that they do nothing to change the root causes of poverty and misery. His solution is a redistribution of labor that would lessen everyone's burden: "And we'd all join in devoting our leisure to science and the arts. We'd unite in a communal quest for truth and the meaning of life." Lida counters that "Those are the sort of charming things people usually say to excuse their own apathy. Rejecting hospitals and schools is easier than healing or teaching." She continues: "Though you've just been sneering so hard at all these libraries and dispensaries, I rate the least perfect of them higher than all the landscapes ever painted."

Stung by Lida's rebuke, the narrator takes solace in his growing love for Zhenya, realizing that it sprang in part from her childlike devotion to him: "Zhenya liked me as an artist. Having won her love by my art, I longed to paint for her alone. I thought of her as my young princess who would reign with me over these trees and field, over this mist and sunset, and over this wondrously enchanting world of nature where I had so far felt utterly lonely and unwanted." As Zhenya waits by the gate to see him off that night, he kisses her and declares his love. In her naïveté, she feels she must tell her mother and Lida at once about the declaration. The next day he calls on the Volchaninovs in the afternoon. He finds only Lida there, and she curtly tells him that her mother and Zhenya have left for Penza province and will go on from there to Europe for the winter.

He never sees the Volchaninovs again. The story ends elegiacally: "at sad, lonely moments, vague memories awake, and gradually I seem to feel that I am remembered and expected—that we shall meet again . . . Zhenya, where are you?"

Lida has prevailed upon her mother to thwart their love. But the narrator has deluded himself into believing that his love was something more than the desire to be worshipped by a passive woman-child after being so summarily dismissed by her more strong-willed and intelligent older sister. The drama of Turchaninov mother and daughter feuding over Levitan at Gorka the previous summer, which ended with Anna Turchaninova sending Varya away after she tried to elope with him, must have been in Chekhov's mind as he wrote the story. Chekhov was convinced that romantic entanglements of the kind that constantly plagued Levitan sap an artist of his creative drive. He told Suvorin: "Women take away your youth, but not in my case. In my life I have been just a sales-clerk, not the boss, and fate has rarely toyed with me. I have had few romances, and I'm no more like Catherine the Great than a walnut is like a battleship."

9

1896

"SUPERB SKETCHES AND A PASSIONATE THIRST FOR LIFE"

DESPITE THEIR RECONCILIATION, the friendship between Chekhov and Levitan was never again to be as close as it had been before Chekhov wrote "The Grasshopper." Stepanov could not forgive Levitan for his rapprochement with the author of that story and stopped seeing his old friend.[1] Chekhov and Levitan never again spent their summers together or seriously considered each other romantic rivals. Both were at the height of their careers, and the demands of their work kept them apart. For Levitan, 1895 had been tumultuous but productive. By virtue of the strong body of work he was now ready to show, 1896 proved to be a year in which his paintings were widely exhibited and sold well.

In February, ten Levitan landscapes were part of the Twenty-Fourth St. Petersburg Itinerant Exhibition, including *March, Golden Autumn*, and *Fresh Wind. Volga*. (The latter was a painting he started in 1891 and reworked for years in his studio until he felt it was finished.) In its exuberance and bright palette, *Fresh Wind. Volga* more closely resembles *March* and *Golden Autumn* than his earlier Volga paintings, with their more muted colors; Goloushev claimed that by the time Levitan settled on the final motif for the painting, it only took him two or three hours to complete the painting.[2] When the exhibition came to Moscow at the end of March, Tretyakov bought *March*, and Mikhail Morozov purchased *Fresh Wind. Volga*. When the exhibition closed, Tretyakov also bought *Golden Autumn*. In April and May, Levitan had his first and only private exhibition during his lifetime, sharing a space in Odessa with the scene-decorator Victor Simov and the Academy painter Alexander Popov.[3]

Around the same time, Levitan received an invitation, thanks to the efforts of Alexandre Benois, to take part in an upcoming Munich Secession exhibition. In response, he sent three pieces—*Thunderstorm, Cloudy Day*, and *Threshing Floor*—and agreed to make the paintings available for sale.[4] This was the first indication that Levitan was beginning to associate himself tentatively with the progressive young critics and painters in St. Petersburg who would go on to form the World of Art movement, spearheaded by Sergei Diaghilev. Benois, a prolific artist and influential critic who came from a well-connected family of architects, first met Diaghilev in 1890, when the latter still considered himself a budding composer. That ambition was crushed in 1894 when Nikolai Rimsky-Korsakov told him to his face that his compositions were "absurd."[5] By the spring of 1895 Diaghilev had found a new passion—collecting and exhibiting art. When Diaghilev went to western Europe on a buying trip, Benois put him in touch with Hans Bartels and Franz von Lenbach, both associated with the Munich Secession, an alternative exhibition society that was formed when eleven artists broke away from the Munich *Genossenschaft* in 1892.[6] Diaghilev's tastes were far from radical: among the paintings he came back with were works by the realist von Lenbach and the ever popular symbolist Puvis de Chavannes.

Together and separately, Benois and Diaghilev, through their writings and exhibitions, began to devote considerable energy to dismissing the Itinerants and their staunchest champion, the critic Vladimir Stasov, as tired proponents of a tendentious realism that was now no longer relevant. Though their critical positions were far from identical, they shared a common conviction that, as Diaghilev put it, a work of art "is useful only to itself," that its inherent beauty transcended ethics, ideology, and even nationality.[7] They came to the defense of the younger painters—notably Serov, Levitan, Nesterov, and Korovin—who had never felt comfortable among the more didactic Itinerants; Stasov in his critical writings had mostly ignored Levitan. Benois and Diaghilev saw an opening to woo these painters away from the Itinerants and into their camp.

Levitan visited Chekhov at Melikhovo only once in 1896, arriving on April 29 together with Maria and with Dunya (Efros) Konovitser, Chekhov's former fiancée. Chekhov remained friends with Dunya even after she married the lawyer Efim Konovitser. The Konovitsers had rented a dacha on the neighboring Vaskino estate and were frequent visitors to Melikhovo. Chekhov had left for Moscow that same day but returned when he found out that Levitan and Dunya had come for a visit. But they did not stay long. The weather was bleak—windy with a cold rain—and the guests left on May 1. Levitan set off for Gorka to paint and to see Turchaninova. He made five sketches of a blooming apple orchard, inscribing one of the sketches to Turchaninova's "sweet child

Anyurka from the old fogey I. Levitan."[8] He also started sketching the spring flooding, which would evolve into the painting *Spring. High Waters*, completed in 1897. Back in Moscow on May 18, Levitan made three paintings of what for him was a highly unusual motif: a nighttime cityscape of the illumination of the Kremlin walls and towers in celebration of the coronation of the new Tsar Nicholas II. The Moscow Electric Light Company had used twelve thousand lamps and eleven projectors to lend a fairytale quality to the heart of the city.[9]

On May 28, the All-Russian Industrial and Art Exhibition opened in Nizhny Novgorod. Levitan initially planned to attend the opening but decided against it, most likely because it would be a distraction from his normal regimen of devoting late spring and summer to finding new locations and new motifs. The exhibition was the largest ever held in prerevolutionary Russia, attracting more than one million visitors before it closed in October. Sponsored by Nicholas II, who visited the site for three days with Tsarina Alexandra, the exhibition, consisting of 70 buildings and 120 pavilions (several designed by Shekhtel), spread out over two hundred acres. The event showcased the newest technological achievements to be found in Russia. On display were the world's first radio receiver and Russia's first automobile. Motion picture films by the Lumière brothers were screened. Visitors rode electric trams and took a funicular from the lower to the upper part of the city.

Alexandre Benois's brother Albert was in charge of the main art pavilion, for which Savva Mamontov commissioned Mikhail Vrubel to produce two murals: *The Princess of the Dream* and *Mikula Selyaninovich*. When the jurists rejected both murals, Mamontov built a separate pavilion to exhibit them. He also hired Korovin to design a separate neo-Russian style Far North pavilion hewn from logs.[10] Mamontov had already formed a grandiose plan to build a rail line that would extend to Arkhangelsk, and he sent Korovin and Serov on painting expeditions along the proposed route. Korovin produced specifically for the pavilion ten panels, some as large as twelve feet, depicting life in the far north. The jurists did select 230 Itinerant paintings and 325 Academy paintings for the main pavilion. Among them were eighteen paintings by Levitan, the most comprehensive exhibition of his work to date, for the first time making it possible for visitors to see the breadth and quality of his work since 1888.

Rather than go to Nizhny, Levitan sought a dramatic change of scenery to take him in a new direction. He made preparations to go to Siberia. After all, Chekhov was adamant that Levitan had been foolish in not accompanying him on his journey to Sakhalin; he was sure that the landscape of Siberia would profoundly excite Levitan. But in the end Levitan decided, possibly out of concern for his health, to make a less arduous journey to Finland instead.

He may have been influenced by seeing the Finnish landscape painters that Diaghilev was championing, and by Korovin's and Serov's recent travels to the far north. Levitan set off in mid-June, expecting to find strong motifs among the cliffs rising from the Gulf of Finland. Although he did run into Pereplyotchikov, he mostly traveled alone. The decision to go by himself did not bode well: Levitan needed the company of others to lift him out of his recurring bouts of depression. On July 3 toward the end of his trip, he wrote Chekhov that he had found nothing "but melancholia cubed. God only knows why this is so—either my artistic receptivity has dried up or nature here is simply mediocre." He concluded it was the latter, which drove him to feelings of impotence and boredom: "Everything is monotonously the same to the point of vileness. If only the trees at least started to grow upside down." He began to feel overwhelmed by a sense of existential dread:

> I wandered for days in the hills. The cliffs were completely smooth without a single angular form. As we know, they were worn smooth during the Ice Age, over many centuries, thousands of years, and inevitably I started to think about this. Centuries. The meaning of this word is simply tragic. Centuries. This is something into which millions of people have sunk, and will still sink into again without end. What horror, what sadness! It's an old thought and an old fear, but it just rattles my skull. The vanity, the insignificance of everything becomes clear!

When nature failed to provide Levitan with artistic inspiration, when he could not feel immersed in nature, what remained was a sense of lonely isolation, a terrifying awareness of the indifference of geological time to the pitifully unimportant life of any individual. Even attempts at playful small talk with Chekhov failed to dispel his gloom:

> How are you? How are you working? Are you running after anyone? Is she interesting? Pfoo, how boring it all is!
> So long, be well and happy if possible—I can't. It's apparent the curse of the Wandering Jew hangs over me, but that is as it should be—I too am a Semite.

Levitan wrote an almost identical letter to a new correspondent, Elena Karzinkina, similarly describing his fear of the "terrifying eternity into which generations have sunk and will continue to sink." Levitan was romantically pursuing Karzinkina, an artist who started studying at the Moscow School of Painting several years after Levitan had left. There is no evidence, however, that she was similarly attracted to him. In his letter to her, Levitan acknowledged the disparity in their personalities. He knew that his ranting about "the tragic meaning of the word 'centuries'" was antithetical to her balanced nature. He envied her ability to drive such thoughts away and retain her happiness.

Karzinkina met Levitan when he started to attend her brother's literary-artistic salon after the two men became acquainted through Troyanovsky. In her memoirs, written in 1940, she maintains a rather demure tone in talking about Levitan: "He very much liked to talk about love in general, but I never talked to him about his personal life. He was very sensitive and, I would say, reticent and was afraid to offend anyone." She allowed that "many considered Levitan handsome. But I will just say that he had remarkable yellowish-chestnut eyes that were unusually expressive." What she recalled was "a man of medium height, nicely proportioned in a well-made dark blue jacket and soft tie. He never wore black and in general didn't like the color black, saying that it gave off unflattering reflections." He was very particular about how his women friends looked. He told Karzinkina what materials to use in sewing a new dress. She noticed that Kuvshinnikova, as we can see in Levitan's portrait of her, "always dressed according to his taste, wore single-colored dresses, never high collars or starched collars, which were accepted in those days, and always a collar trimmed with lace, more or less open."[11]

After leaving Finland and before returning to Moscow, Levitan spent a week in the vicinity of Lake Ladoga just north of St. Petersburg. He wrote Chekhov that he was going to see the monks at Valaam Monastery, located on the largest island on the lake. As it turned out, the journey north had not been as fruitless as he claimed. He returned with a series of sketches of fortresses, cliff-side ruins, the sea, and lakes, some of which he would rework into paintings. Goloushev had high praise for his Finnish landscape *Forest Lake*, with its pines "in the distance, illuminated by the last rays of sunset, so believable, so suffused with poetic atmosphere that it feels like you see nature itself before you."[12] Nevertheless, Levitan told friends that the excursion had been a failure. Back in Moscow he wrote Vasnetsov that he had been right to say that he would not like Finland: "for almost a whole month I loafed around Finland, finally crawled away, drew nothing, and I feel like something you wouldn't even wish on an evil Tatar. But that's an old thing with me! Depression and dejection are my constant companions. I'll now settle in somewhere around Moscow and attempt to work."

Similarly, he wrote to the painter Elizaveta Zvantseva that in Finland he "didn't accomplish anything and felt damned depressed." Levitan told Zvantseva: "Now I'm looking for a dacha, I want to settle in, I'm too tired to take any trips. I still don't know where I'll end up. I would like to visit you, but I don't have the energy for such a big trip." He told her that he was still putting off going to the All-Russian Exhibition, likely until the fall: "My nerves are too shot to view the exhibition, and the heat is now unbearable."[13] Zvantseva was a student of Repin, who had fallen madly in love with her. He painted five portraits of her, only one of which survives. She also had a long acquaintance with Chekhov. When she was on her way to visit him in Yalta in 1903, Olga Knipper told her husband to be nice to Zvantseva when she arrived: "She's delicate and very nice. She's been in love with you for fifteen years. Be attentive. Don't be heartless."[14]

Because it was Levitan's nature to resist complacency and to constantly seek ways to make his art simpler and more expressive, he continued to be curious about those artists and critics who were rebelling against the status quo. He found himself interested in aligning himself with those established Moscow painters, many of whom had flourished under the wing of Savva Mamontov, who were getting to know Diaghilev and starting to talk about the idea of forming a new society of young painters.[15] However, when the conversation turned to plans to organize an exhibition and publish a journal devoted to new art, Levitan together with Nesterov balked; they were not yet prepared to directly confront the Itinerant Association and jeopardize their standing in the organization. Korovin and Serov, on the other hand, had no qualms. Diaghilev continued to champion Levitan as a Russian painter who could hold his own against the best European artists. On August 26, Diaghilev published a review of the Munich Secession exhibition in a St. Petersburg newspaper in which he claimed that the works of the Russian painters took European audiences by surprise: "They expected from them neo-Byzantine 'mystical paintings,' in effect they expected a Byzantine Puvis de Chavannes." They did not expect from Russia "those grayish landscapes that gloomily stared out of the corners." Diaghilev was convinced that anyone looking at Levitan's *Quiet Abode* or *Above Eternal Rest* (both displayed in the 1898 Secession exhibition) would have "to agree that we have our own unique poetry" and, at the same time, that those paintings were significant "participants in the progress of universal art."[16]

Levitan finally attended the All-Russian Exhibition in Nizhny Novgorod in September. After it closed, the painting *Golden Autumn* was shipped to Kharkov for the November Itinerant Exhibition, where it was damaged and sent back to Levitan in Moscow. He wrote Tretyakov that he thought he could fix it: "I don't completely understand how this could have happened. I'll do it in a couple of days and then let you know or bring it to you myself." Sometime during the first week in November, Levitan became seriously ill, collapsing as he made his way up the steps of the Historical Museum to see an exhibition.[17] He was taken home and Morozov called for a doctor. The symptoms of heart disease that Langovoi had diagnosed two years earlier were becoming worse.

Levitan referred to his poor health in a letter to Polenov on November 22, apologizing that he was unable to join in the celebrations taking place in Moscow honoring Polenov's twenty-five years of artistic creativity. Levitan expressed his deep respect for him "as a most talented artist" and added, "my thanks to you as my teacher and as a good, responsive person. I would have gone and personally told you this, but I am ill, seriously ill [. . .]. As soon as I get better, I will without fail go see you so that I can tell you everything that I think in this regard; to write about it is literally hard—I am weak."

For years Levitan's friends had mocked his habit of looking balefully into the eyes of his female admirers and telling them how very tired he was. Chekhov parodied this in "The Grasshopper" when on the deck of the Volga steamer the artist Ryabovsky sits on a bench gazing adoringly at Olga Ivanovna; he closes his eyes, smiles languidly, and says, "I'm tired." But Levitan's exhaustion was no romantic affectation but, rather, a medical condition—the ballooning of his aorta was pulling apart his aortic valve, causing blood to leak back into his heart. On December 18, Chekhov wrote to Shekhtel that "there are rumors that Levitan is seriously ill." The day before, Langovoi had tried to visit Levitan but was told he was too tired to receive him. Nesterov told Albert Benois that Levitan "has suddenly been found to have the most serious heart disease. The doctors don't promise any sort of good outcome. I feel sorry for him. He's a good man and a gifted artist. I personally have a special sympathy for him as a school mate whom I've known since we were seventeen. I know his life and know with what energy and what difficulty he made his way and fought for his place."[18]

Chekhov himself was back home in Melikhovo licking his wounds from the poorly received premiere of *The Seagull* in St. Petersburg on October 17. Lika had been in attendance, sitting in Suvorin's box, and she accompanied Maria back to Melikhovo to make sure Chekhov would do no harm to himself.[19] Once again their correspondence became affectionate, but as always, humor masked their true feelings. On October 25 Lika wrote him: "Every day I mark off my calendar. Only 310 days remain until I attain my bliss." Chekhov replied: "You write that we will attain our bliss in 310 days [. . .]. I'm glad, but could we put off this bliss for another two or three years? It really frightens me!" Lika responded more seriously that Kuvshinnikova had been right when she said that "you hope that I don't have the patience to wait three years for you."[20] Two weeks after she wrote this letter, Lika's daughter, Christina, died.

On December 20 Chekhov went to Moscow to treat Levitan at his home.[21] The two men had not seen each other for eight months. Levitan eagerly showed off his latest work. The next day back in Melikhovo Chekhov wrote in his notebook: "Levitan has a distended aorta. He has mud plasters on his chest. Superb sketches and a passionate thirst for life."[22] He invited Levitan to come spend New Year's with his family at Melikhovo. Levitan replied on December 26 that he was unsure whether he had the stamina to make the trip:

> I feel better, dear Anton Pavlovich, although the thought of traveling by train strikes me as unpleasant, and most importantly, I don't know how Maria Pavlovna's health is and whether I would inhibit things with my visit. Let me know.

Chekhov also invited Lika: "Since you are coming to us to celebrate New Year's, I have a request of you: at Andreev's on Tverskaya, buy a large bottle of red wine, Christy No. 17, and bring it. Only I beg you, don't drink it up on the way. [. . .] Be well, cantaloupe." Levitan did not come. Lika arrived at Melikhovo together with the landscape painter Prokofy Seryogin. The only other non-family member there was Sasha Selivanova, a friend from Taganrog days. At midnight they feasted on pie. In the kitchen the servants told fortunes by divining the shapes created by melting candle wax.[23] What the future held for Chekhov within the next few months was a health crisis nearly as severe as that experienced by Levitan. Over the next few years the two men, already joined together by friendship and an appreciation of each other's art, would also be bound by a shared awareness that both of their lives were about to be cut short.

10 1897
"I LOVE HIM"

LEVITAN BEGAN TO SUFFER from a loss of stamina at the very moment he felt drawn toward the ferment created by Diaghilev's anti-Itinerant writing and exhibitions. On January 4, Levitan wrote Benois that because of his weak heart he would be unable to participate in his St. Petersburg watercolor exhibition.[1] In fact, Benois and Diaghilev were mounting competing shows. Benois's exhibition featured pieces from Princess Maria Tenisheva's collection, which Diaghilev could not resist branding as "deadly tedium" in advance of his own show of English and German watercolors that opened in February.[2]

Homebound in his studio, Levitan invited the liberal journalist Victor Goltsev, a friend and colleague of Chekhov's, to visit him and write a profile for the *Russian Gazette*. Goltsev described the studio as a quiet, spacious, well-lit oasis far from the turmoil of the city and its "drab reality." Morozov had spared no expense in appointing the room to impress visitors and potential buyers, decorating it with a bust of Levitan by the sculptor Maria Ris, a piano, a harmonium, and walls covered in gray cloth. Levitan's living quarters on the floor below were far more humble—ascetic furnishings, painted floors, photographs, and unmounted sketches tacked to the walls.[3]

Levitan showed Goltsev five paintings that he was working on, and, given his natural inclination toward liberal politics and positivist art, Goltsev was surprised how "deeply humbled" he was by the landscapes he saw: "Is this not a contradiction? No, no, a thousand times no. With his clouds, waves, and storm gusts, the artist cannot *prove* anything, but he *interprets* nature for us. Such paintings can only be made by a person who deeply, poetically, loves his native land [. . .]. Levitan cannot be thanked enough for this conscious love, for this spiritualization of nature."[4]

When he read the article, Levitan was ecstatic and immediately wrote to Goltsev, thanking him profusely for reacting so sympathetically to his paintings: "It means you were very much touched by the work. For you, who stand on the side of progressive art and possibly, if you will forgive me, tendentious art, to be excited by lyrical painting is an indication that the work is indeed sufficiently strong." Throughout his life Levitan struggled against a sense of inferiority, assuming that critics, the public, and many painters considered landscapes a lesser subject for art. His closest artist friends worked on motifs with much more obvious narrative power. Just as Tolstoy had stated, the landscapes in the paintings of Polenov, Nesterov, and Vasnetsov served as backgrounds for portrayals of biblical and Russian historical and religious figures, often on a grand scale. It came as a pleasant surprise that a liberal critic like Goltsev had the ability to see the world the way a landscape painter does, especially given that the current pieces in Levitan's studio, particularly *Stormy Day*, revealed an unmistakable shift once again toward impressionism. Levitan quoted to Goltsev from memory a stanza from a poem by Baratynsky (although he mistakenly thought it was Lermontov) that he felt captured the essence of the "sensibilities of a landscape painter":

> From nature alone he breathed with life,
> He comprehended the babbling of streams.
> He understood the speech of the leaves on the trees
> And heard the greening of the grass.

"This is the ideal of the landscape painter," explained Levitan, "—to train his psyche so that it can hear the 'greening of the grass.' What a great joy this is! Am I not right?"

By now Levitan was sufficiently worried about the precarious state of his health that he told Chekhov he was thinking of organizing a consultation among several doctors headed by Professor Alexei Ostroumov. He asked Chekhov to come by and give him advice on how to set this up. "Several days ago," he told Chekhov, "I almost croaked [. . .]. Are you listening, you viper?" Feeling vulnerable, he signed his letter with an endearment formed from the diminutive for "Samuel" in Yiddish: "Your Shmulik." Chekhov was listening. During the day on February 15, on the eve of Lent, Chekhov and Goltsev were eating *blini* at the home of Soldatenkov.[5] Chekhov was impressed by Soldatenkov's collection of paintings—the Old Believer merchant had been buying art since the 1840s—although he felt that "almost all of them are poorly hung." Afterward Chekhov and Goltsev decided to go see Levitan, from whom Soldatenkov had recently purchased *Spring. High Waters* and two sketches for

1,100 rubles. While at Levitan's, Chekhov met Polenov for the first time. To Chekhov, Levitan looked very sick and frightened. In the evening, Chekhov visited Ostroumov, who told him that Levitan "cannot escape death."[6] The next day, Ostroumov came to see Levitan and found his condition improved, but the doctor urged him to go abroad for treatment.

Levitan tried to reassure his sister, who had become alarmed by his condition, that it was not as bad as she imagined. "It's serious," he told her, "but with reasonable prudence, it's possible to live a long time. Ostroumov, an authority who is held in higher esteem than Zakharin [a Moscow University therapeutist], says to me that I have gotten significantly better. He advises that I go south."[7] But Tereza's expression of concern was, as usual, mixed with another of her constant requests for money. Levitan had just sold three sketches from the last Itinerant exhibition for 400 rubles, and Tretyakov paid 500 rubles for *Remains of the Past. Twilight (Finland)*, on display in the current exhibition. But he told Tereza that because of the cost of his medical expenses and the planned trip abroad, he would be unable to send any more money to her husband, Pyotr, who had written asking to borrow another 100 rubles.

On March 1, Chekhov wrote Suvorin that all the news he had was "either uninteresting or sad." There was talk of plague and war, of the Orthodox Church's Holy Synod and the reactionary tsar's Ministry of Education merging, and Levitan "apparently will die soon. He has a dilation of the aorta." And to further depress Chekhov, he was being told that his story "Peasants" could not get past the censor without significant changes.

The next day Levitan let Chekhov know that he had had a visit from Tretyakov, who told him that he had commissioned Osip Braz to paint a portrait of Chekhov for the following year's Itinerant exhibition. Tretyakov had asked Levitan to contact Chekhov to arrange for the sittings, preferably in St. Petersburg, where Braz lived. Chekhov visited Levitan on March 4 to check on his friend's heart and discuss the particulars of the sitting. He told Levitan that he could go to St. Petersburg toward the end of Lent or sometime during the second half of May, and Levitan passed this message on to Tretyakov. Chekhov did not know Braz, was understandably irritated at not having been consulted so far in this matter, and made it clear that he wanted to deal with Braz directly. He wrote to Shekhtel hoping that he could tell him something about Braz: "[Levitan] told me that P. M. Tretyakov has already come to an arrangement with the artist Braz regarding my portrait and that now I'm holding things up [. . .]. Do you know him or can you find out from someone where he lives, what his first name and patronymic are, and so forth?" Chekhov also updated Shekhtel on their friend's health: "I listened to Levitan's heart: it's bad. His heart doesn't beat, it whooshes. Instead of a 'took-took' sound, you hear a 'pff-took.' In medicine this is called a 'systolic murmur.'" Shekhtel responded:

> Judging by the portrait shown at the last exhibition of the Moscow Society of Art Lovers, Braz must be a Jew. I feel sorry for Levitan; it's a good thing that he's not completely informed about his condition.[8]

Chekhov and the other consulting physicians were not being open with Levitan about the cause of his illness.

Chekhov wrote Braz that he was planning to be in St. Petersburg around March 28 or 29. But in Moscow on March 22, already en route to the capital, Chekhov began to spit up blood as he was sitting down to dinner with Suvorin at the Hermitage Restaurant. He first decided to go to Suvorin's room at the Slavyansky Bazaar, but then he went back to his room at the Great Moscow Hotel. On March 25 he coughed up blood again and agreed to be admitted to Professor Ostroumov's clinic, near Novodevichy Cemetery. The sole activity the clinic doctors allowed was letter writing in a supine position.[9] Chekhov wrote Tretyakov that he had contacted Braz: "I was heading for St. Petersburg, but a bout of spitting up blood has unexpectedly kept me in Moscow and I'm now staying in Ostroumov's clinic and it's not clear when they will discharge me from here." In telling Braz what happened, Chekhov tried to make light of his condition: "I had set off to come to you, but along the way I had an unpleasant thing happen: the doctors have arrested me and placed me in a clinic. I have been spitting up blood. Now it's better, but the situation is uncertain and it's unclear when they will set me free."

Meanwhile Levitan was making final preparations to leave for Europe. He wrote to Maria on April 3 unaware of what had happened to her brother. Two days later, while Chekhov was still confined to Ostroumov's clinic, Levitan left for Vienna and Nervi, a resort near Portofino in northern Italy popular with tuberculosis patients.

Considering that he had not yet even met Braz, Chekhov was unusually frank in writing to the painter: "The doctors have determined that I have active upper pulmonary tuberculosis. There's no more bleeding. I'm able to walk freely and on the 10th of April will go home to Lopasnya. But my future is uncertain. It's possible that in the second half of May they will send me for koumiss [mare's milk] treatment, and then somewhere south for the fall." His doctors ordered Chekhov from now on to plan on living in the south from September to May. On April 4 Chekhov described Levitan's condition to Braz with a level of detail not shared in writing with any of their mutual friends: "The landscape painter Levitan is seriously ill. He has a dilated aorta. The dilation of the aorta is right where it comes from the heart, so that it results in valvular insufficiency. He has a passionate thirst for life, a passionate thirst to work, but his physical condition is worse than that of an invalid." Braz was shocked: "How awful, how awful about Levitan! Such a huge and likeable talent!"

Based on this and previous descriptions of Levitan's illnesses, and Chekhov's assertion on several occasions that Levitan's promiscuity was to blame for his declining health, tertiary syphilis was a plausible cause of his condition. This may have been the reason why his doctors did not share their diagnosis with him. Gouloushev remained mystified by Levitan's condition, concluding that it was a "strange heart ailment, [. . .] most likely from some sort of infection that no one paid any attention to."[10]

Syphilitic aortitis begins with an inflammation of the outer tissues of the vessels that supply the aorta with blood. The walls of the aorta thicken, weaken, and scar, eventually leading to an aneurysm or dilation of the aorta. Syphilitic aortitis typically affected men around the age of forty and usually occurred ten to thirty years after the initial infection. Levitan's attack of (possibly syphilitic) periostitis, as described by Pereplyotchikov, occurred eleven years earlier in 1886. Before the discovery of penicillin, tertiary syphilis infection was the most common cause of an aortic aneurysm. When the aneurysm occurs in the aortic arch near the heart, as in Levitan's case, it can cause the aortic valve to regurgitate, resulting in the "pff-took" sound that Chekhov heard. In fact, a "rough" systolic murmur was often the first physical sign of the disease.[11] It is, however, possible that Levitan's heart condition resulted from a congenital defect, since this too would present many of the same symptoms.

Levitan arrived in Nervi on April 8 feeling extremely tired. He wrote Elena Karzinkina that he would, as promised, visit her relatives, including her sister Sophia, who was suffering from tuberculosis. Just as he had in Finland, Levitan openly wrote to Karzinkina about his depression: "I've only just arrived and I'm already feeling drawn back! Can you understand this? I feel bad anywhere, but in a strange place it's even worse than in Russia. I only do stupid things! The sun never rises for a broken-down psyche!" It also was apparent that their relationship had deepened. She had written something cryptic to him about marriage. He replied: "The twelfth point of your last letter—get married? Yes? Let's talk about this. Right now I can't—I don't have the head for it, and I want some air." He used the male (and also reciprocal) form of "get married." But whether the "twelfth point" had to do with Levitan marrying her or someone else is unknowable. In any event, the letters they exchanged contradicted what Karzinkina wrote many years later in her memoirs about his reticence. She did, however, admit that "he was very interested in the relationships people had with each other" and was not above teasing those in love with him or others.[12]

Levitan complained to Chekhov about his stay in Nervi in a more jocular vein; news of Chekhov's condition had still not reached him: "Dear Antonio! God damn all doctors, excluding you, of course! They've sent me to some sort of hole and God knows why. It would be better if they learned how to cure melancholia, but instead they send you south, saying that the air and the regimen will restore everything. They don't understand a thing!" Levitan asked whether he had started posing for Braz, sent his best to Lika, and asked Chekhov to tell Maria "that she must work a lot [at her painting], or else I will come and put her in the corner."

To Nikolai Kasatkin, his old classmate from the School of Painting, Levitan unburdened his feelings of homesickness. He felt that Europe had nothing to offer him, either as a painter or as an invalid seeking a cure:

> Why do they exile Russians here who, like me for example, so love their country, its nature? Is it really possible that the air in the south can indeed restore an organism, a body that is so unbreakably tied to our spirit, to our essence!? And our essence, our spirit, can only be at peace at home, on our soil, among our people, who, I allow, can be unpleasant at times, difficult, but without whom it's even worse. With what joy would I be transported to Moscow! But I have to sit here, according to my doctors (may they be swallowed by wolves!). Although, if I get any more depressed, I'll go and return, even if it kills me!

Levitan also mentioned to Kasatkin that on the way to Italy he stopped in Vienna, where his paintings were on display in the Secession exhibition. Above all, he was overwhelmed by "the mass of paintings," wondering what they were all for and "how will it end?" Regarding his own work back in Russia, Levitan asked Kasatkin to ensure that his paintings were "decently hung" in the right rooms for the Itinerant exhibition "so that they can endure the torture" of being in St. Petersburg. He need not have worried. During the exhibition, one of the Morozov brothers bought Levitan's *Blossoming Apple Trees*, and Tretyakov added another Levitan sketch to his collection.[13]

In Nervi the pall of mortality hung over everything. What Levitan knew, but could not bring himself to say, was that he was slowly dying. He saw it as a bad sign that he was starting to dwell on the past. He told Kasatkin about a man with tuberculosis who was staying at the same hotel. He was dying, but whenever someone asked about his health, "he answers that it's very good, wonderful ... And possibly tomorrow, he will die [...]. I understand it mentally, but something revolts inside me and I can't understand ... 'The skull rattles' from all this, to use Hamlet's words." He wished Kasatkin to "be well, like the fattest Nile crocodile."

In mid-April, Levitan left Nervi for nearby Portofino, which he found, at least initially, to be more to his liking, both pretty and quiet. But he was lonely. He wrote Karzinkina again, telling her that he was depressed and feeling very strong chest pains: "If all this continues, I will return if only to die at home. I don't have the strength to drag on with a sick soul and body!" He longed to be back at his studio where "what will be will be." Levitan stayed two weeks in Portofino, painting "a few awful sketches" but spending most of his time reading French novels. He enjoyed *Amitié amoureuse*, an epistolary novel by Hermine Oudinot Lecomte du Nouy that was rumored to be comprised of thinly disguised real letters between Guy de Maupassant and Lecomte du Nouy, a close friend of his. Levitan wrote Karzinkina: "How strikingly the people are depicted! You recognize yourself and others in it a lot." On the other hand, Levitan found Paul Margueritte's stories boring. Karzinkina told Levitan that she was rereading Maupassant's *Fort comme la mort*. He responded that "it's a wonderful piece."

Much of the plot of the novel paralleled the recent melodrama in Levitan's own life. Olivier Bertain is a well-established Parisian painter who has been carrying on a long affair with the Countess Antoinette de Guilleroy while maintaining a friendly relationship with her husband. Now middle-aged, the countess despairs as she notices Bertain's growing infatuation with her daughter, whose beauty matches hers at the time that Bertain first fell in love with her. The painter is tormented by his love for both the mother and daughter, and while roaming the streets in a daze, he falls under an omnibus, possibly intentionally. In *Fort comme la mort*, Bertain on his deathbed asks the Countess to take all their love letters out of a drawer and burn them in the fireplace in his presence. Tearfully she complies, in a scene that would be repeated three years later when Levitan, near death, watched as his brother Adolph carried out his request to burn all his letters.

Karzinkina told Levitan that the novel affirmed that women are more constant in their love than men. The Countess continued to love Bertain deeply, even as they aged, while Bertain, with a painter's eye for ideal beauty, could not resist transferring his affections from the mother to the daughter. Levitan felt that it was unfair to generalize from the exceptional case of the Countess:

> Maupassant depicted a woman in a long novel who knows and feels that her love is a last love (she is not very young!), and that's why she hangs on to it with all her being. You recall, she looks for signs of growing old—she doesn't want to appear that way more than her beloved … she's terrified and indeed it is terrifying! When the meaning of life is based on love, then the approach of old age is like death! Old age and fading beauty are unwanted. It's tragic, but it's true.

In this exchange about the novel, Levitan and Karzinkina were engaged in a dance about their own relationship and unresolved feelings for each other. She had written to him again about the mysterious "twelfth point" and marriage. Which one of them was being evasive? He told her: "With regard to the twelfth point, I completely don't understand anything now after your letter. It's possible to more or less guess, but half of it, I confess, I don't understand! When we meet, please explain it to me." He told her again how lonely he felt: "I want to be in Moscow, to go to the Karzinkin home, find you there and babble to my heart's content. I feel very light and easy with you. You are nice, very nice, but why do you hate me? No, that's nonsense. That's not the case, but . . . silence, silence as Gogol's Poprishchin says," referring to the word the insane civil servant in "Diary of a Madman" uses when he dares not speak of his love for his director's daughter.

In early May, Levitan decided to make his way inland from Portofino on the Ligurian Sea and farther north to Courmayeur in the Italian Alps on the French border at the foot of Mount Blanc. Chekhov finally wrote him about his own medical crisis. The news made Levitan "damn anxious." Sitting by a window in his room that looked out onto Mont Blanc, he wrote back:

> What's going on? Do you really indeed have a lung disease? Have the docs not made a mistake? They all lie, even to you. How do you yourself feel, or is it difficult to diagnose yourself? Do everything possible. Come drink mare's milk. In the summer it's wonderful in Russia, but in the winter let's go south. Even in Nervi together we won't be bored. Do you need some money? I'm sure that if you spend the summer and winter well, it will all pass, and the doctors won't have anything to crow about.

To Levitan, fate had been cruel in choosing to strike down Chekhov: "Oh, why are you sick? For whom is this necessary? Thousands of idle, vile people enjoy magnificent health! It doesn't make sense." He made his affection clear to Chekhov: "God preserve you, my sweet, dear Anton. I embrace you. Your sincerely devoted Shmuel." He told Karzinkina of the "unpleasant news from Chekhov," that his lungs had started to hurt and his doctors had ordered him to go south. "How distressing it was for me to learn this," he wrote her. "I love him."

Levitan continued to complain to everyone of chest pains and the terrible state of his soul. But at Courmayeur he could not fail to be inspired by the magnificence of Mont Blanc and the mountain range that stood before him: "It's tremendous to the point of awe. From its summit you just need to make a small effort to stretch out your hand to God (if you are worthy!)." For the first time on this European journey, he had a strong urge to sketch and paint, although as usual he was initially dissatisfied with his work. He told Chekhov: "I would like to get legally married to my muse, but she, nasty lady, doesn't want to! I would like very much to give birth to Mont Blanc on just a small scrap of canvas, but without my muse nothing comes out. Seriously, I tried to paint it several times—not a damn thing!" He expressed the same frustration, but more broadly, to Benois. His illness had prevented him both from participating in Benois's watercolor exhibition and from completing all the paintings he wanted to include in the latest Itinerant exhibition: "An awful sickness snuck up on me unnoticed which I have been suffering from since autumn and which will be the end of me. I have no reason to be fooling myself. It turned out that I have heart trouble and a dilation of the aorta." He told Benois he "would be more at peace if the disease, robbing me of the pleasures of life, would at least leave the ability to work, since it's painful to put away my weapon so early."

But in reality, more than a dozen sketches and paintings resulted from his week-long stay in Courmayeur. He wrote his brother-in-law Lev Berchansky that the place was "pretty" and he had "made a few sketches."[14] To Karzinkina he was more unequivocally enthusiastic, saying that he was "shaking from rapture." In his excitement to go out on a glacier, he confessed that he "did something stupid," hiking up high on the mountain, which he feared had done more damage to his heart. Even several weeks later while recuperating in Germany, Levitan could not get the snow and glaciers out of his head. "These are amazing subjects! It's no accident that the Greeks populated the snowy peaks of Olympus with gods. Only immortality and silent peace could possibly inhabit it." He talked of spending an entire summer in the Alps if his health would allow. Never before had he found a landscape in Europe that so sparked his creativity.

Levitan now wrote a third letter to Karzinkina without having received a reply. "This will be the last," he told her. He was desperate to hear something from her: "What are you doing, you heartless creature? At least send me a book! Any kind?!" He was worried that her silence meant that someone else was courting her: "Possibly you have retreated 'from the scene.' I congratulate you. That would be the last straw [. . .]. For now I am devoted to you, but if you don't answer—I will hate you."

The next day he left via Paris for the salt springs at Bad Nauheim near Frankfurt. Since the late 1830s Bad Nauheim had been a renowned spa, its natural and carbonated salt waters prescribed for their purported healing powers for those suffering from cardiovascular and neurological ailments. Treatment consisted of indoor brine baths, outdoor inhalation therapy, and a regimen of gymnastics. On May 12, the day after he arrived, Levitan wrote

Chekhov that he was already dutifully taking his prescribed baths. He found it pleasant but was not convinced that it would do any good, and the spa did nothing to improve his mood. "I feel melancholy to the point of stupefaction." He continued to spend a lot of his time reading, especially books banned in Russia, such as the diaries of Catherine the Great.

Although he had told Karzinkina that he would not write to her again without word from her, he sent off yet another letter, angered by her silence: "What are we to do with you! I will put aside my wrath for mercy and will write, but only for the last time if you don't answer me." He was pleading for some sign of affection from her:

> As you can see, I'm already at the spa. Here they specifically treat the heart with baths. What nonsense! The heart can only be treated with the heart! Isn't that true? Nevertheless I have started to take the baths. Such is the contradiction of human nature! The baths are pleasant enough, but it doesn't mean I'll be taking them for long. I'm bored senseless. I don't like Germans, who are swarming around here like mosquitoes in May.

After once again calling her a heartless creature, Levitan wrote something sufficiently intimate that someone literally cut out several lines from the original letter. He told her that there was something he wanted to tell her in secret and to know "what and how you at least occasionally think about Levitan? If not, don't let me catch sight of you again!" He ended the letter: "God be with you. You are splendid just the same, and I love you very much."

A week later, Levitan finally heard from Karzinkina, who was in Paris with her ailing sister Sophia. Her letter dispelled his depression, and he replied to her with great affection and playful humor. He was tempted to go see her. Paris was only twelve hours away and together they could visit the city's art salons. But she told him that Paris was "hot and cold and smells like a kitchen, and the exhibitions are nothing special!" He thought she was just dallying with him: "I know what sort of egoist you are and why you don't want me to come to Paris." He blamed it on her "knowing that if I will be in Paris, then I will certainly stay with you. Oh, you're terrible! How antipathetic I am to you! Well, don't get angry at my stupidity. I'll stop, but I truly do want to see you." In the end he realized it would be impossible—his course of treatment was not yet finished, and by the time it was, she would already have returned to Russia. Levitan proposed another option. His patron Morozov had just invited him to stay at his grand estate at Uspenskoe for the summer. Karzinkina's family estate was nearby, and they could spend time together painting, which he knew would give her great pleasure. "I told Morozov that I would go," he wrote to Karzinkina. "Have I really in my old age fallen in love, and so hopelessly since you are such a horrible person! Congratulations. Just the same, don't you dare go anywhere this summer, do you hear? I ____ you," this time hesitating to spell out the word.

Levitan wrote to Chekhov on the same day, obviously still in an impish mood. He admitted that the salt baths were doing some good—"my heart is getting better, calmer"—but was at a loss to explain why: "God only knows what's in them. After all, water's just water." Why was it not possible to offer the same treatment in Russia? "The Germans are indeed a sly people and, if you will, have invented the monkey," while Russians had to admit they lacked the same gift. Still he had doubts about the treatment regimen: "I'm doing gymnastics with the idea that exercising the muscles must help the heart work more strongly and dilate, but it turns out to be the opposite. It's something I don't understand. Occasionally I'm having sex (with my muse, of course), and it's a good thing—it seems that she's pregnant. What will be born?"

He also told his friend a very Chekhovian anecdote: several days previously he had met some young Russian ladies who had heard a rumor that Chekhov had just arrived at the spa. Someone pointed him out and the ladies ran up to the man only to find out that he was "not Chekhov, and not even a writer, but some civil servant." The young ladies, knowing that Levitan was a friend of Chekhov's, asked him what kind of person the writer was: "I, as is my usual habit with all my acquaintances, create the kind of portrait that apparently squelches any desire for someone to personally get to know you." Even in asking about Chekhov's lungs, Levitan reverted to the good-humored, salacious tone they had used in the past: "How's your health? Have you started to gain weight? Is there no more bleeding? Don't copulate so often. It would be good for you to teach yourself to do without women. It's more satisfying to just dream about them (I'm not talking about wet dreams) [. . .] and if Lika is visiting you, kiss her sugary lips, but by no means anything more."[15]

On June 7, Levitan returned "to dear old Rus. It's an uncultured country," he told Chekhov, "but I love her, the louse!" While Levitan was abroad, the relationship between the two men had warmed again, their mutual concern about each other's health strengthening their bond. Three days after returning to Moscow, Levitan wrote Chekhov in Melikhovo wondering how he was feeling and whether he could visit him. Levitan's weakened condition made living in the city during the summer intolerable. He told Chekhov he would be spending the next few months at Morozov's country estate, and Chekhov decided to come to Moscow and accompany him there. On June 13, Levitan wrote "most wise Anthony" that he could not wait any longer. He confessed that his sex life was giving him no pleasure: "I have sinned here, and once again don't feel very well. It's apparent that I need to refrain completely from sex and only watch my friends copulate! It's so sad it makes me want to cry!"[16] Levitan was leaving for Morozov's in the afternoon, and he instructed Chekhov to come to his studio immediately upon arriving in Moscow. His servant Afanasy would be there at his service and could telephone the estate to let them know that he was coming. Horses would be sent to the train platform near Uspenskoe to bring him to the estate.

Meantime, Lika was just as desperate to see Chekhov as Levitan was. Chekhov told her that he was coming to Moscow midday on June 16 and then immediately setting off to see Levitan at Morozov's. He planned to be back in Moscow after several days and would pick her up to go together back to Melikhovo. She raced over to Levitan's studio to find no one there. "Do I have to keep looking for you," she wrote Chekhov. "If you want, I can come and see you this evening at Levitan's. I was there this morning. Afanasy told me that you would be there at 8 pm."[17]

The weather at Uspenskoe provided no relief to Levitan. "The heat is terrible," he told Karzinkina soon after he arrived. "I have come to hate the sun." Because of the humidity and Chekhov's impending visit, he was putting off seeing her. She asked him how the work was progressing on his Mont Blanc sketches. "What happened to my glaciers?" he responded. "They're frozen—I can't work. What I will do in the fall, I also don't know." He feared he would have no new paintings ready for the next Itinerant exhibition and suffered from a "grinding depression" and a growing sense that he was stuck creatively. He felt the urge to move his art in a new direction. But, influenced by his reading of Schopenhauer, he was paralyzed by the fear that the effort would be pointless. He told Karzinkina:

> A dissatisfaction with an old form, so to speak, an old artistic understanding of things (I'm talking about painting), the absence of new points of departure is causing me to suffer terribly. I should write a lot about this, which at present I'm in no condition to do, and somehow given the opportunity I will explain to you what I think. I'm reading a lot, but in the end it makes me miserable because of the variety of interpretations of life and views of it! Are you too not struck by the conditional nature and futility of attempts to understand what's around us? We're given nothing besides the opportunity to question, question, and question [. . .]. How awful!

Chekhov arrived at Morozov's castle at Uspenskoe on June 17. The imposing house with its turret and steep gables had been constructed in a kitschy Victorian neo-Gothic style to mimic the manor of an English baron. Levitan painted a picture of it: *Dusk. Castle* (1898). Chekhov, with his aversion to the lifestyle and tastes of rich Moscow merchants, was appalled by the place. He left after two days. He told Suvorin: "The house is like the Vatican, the footmen wear white pique jackets with gold chains across their stomach, tasteless furniture, French wines from Levet. The owner has an expressionless face—so I ran away." Levitan's friendly relations with and dependence on Morozov and other patrons grated on Chekhov, whose only patron, Suvorin, was a self-made man, like him, from a peasant family. Chekhov returned to Moscow, picked up Lika as promised, and went home, where he sat down to write to Braz, giving him detailed instructions on how to get to Melikhovo. He was ready to have his portrait painted.

At Uspenskoe, Levitan painted a bit, received word that he had been selected as a member of the Munich Secession Society of Artists, and spent much of his time continuing to read French writers for practice, without much pleasure. For the most part he found them vulgar, although he admitted that Victor Hugo's poems were beautiful and interesting, "but also not lacking in pomposity." On the other hand, he was in awe when he finished reading Chekhov's "Peasants," an unflinching chronicle of the brutishness of peasant life set against the landscape of rural Russia and nature's seasonal cycle. Levitan found the story to be an "amazing thing" in which Chekhov had "attained a striking artistic compactness."[18]

Once the weather became more tolerable, Levitan, accompanied by Morozov, made a visit to Karzinkina at her dacha down the road from Uspenskoe. Levitan and Karzinkina took long walks in the cool of the evening, and he told her about his visit to Italy and Germany. She recalled that he talked about how he did not like Italy, how he loved the simplicity and beauty of "middle Russia" most of all. Levitan also went off hunting birds with Morozov. Karzinkina reproached him for hunting, given that he was always talking about loving life and every living thing. He admitted that "it was difficult to explain." Morozov just laughed: "What sort of hunter is he? He shoots a bird and then shouts to us: 'Pick it up. I can't stand to watch it suffer.'" Karzinkina, like Kuvshinnikova before her, failed to convince him to quit. She understood "he was attracted to the poetry of getting up early and going out before the sun rose, and the valleys, and fields and the sunsets, precisely everything that he so loved to paint, and without hunting he would not have seen this as much and as often."[19]

He still had strong feelings for her. In an undated note sent to her some time in 1897, Levitan apologized for cancelling a rendezvous, saying that he was so depressed that the slightest agitation would send him off crying like a baby. But he also let her know that if he knew she would be alone, he might change his mind.

That summer Levitan also stayed for a week at Bugry, Troyanovsky's estate. During his stay Levitan gave Troyanovsky one of his Mont Blanc sketches, *Spring in the Alps.* The physician's daughter Anna recalled that Levitan cut his visit short "because he felt the landscape lacked the mood that he was looking for in nature. He was enamored by the wonderful moonlight at Bugry, and he painted sketches of various natural scenes lit up by the moon."[20] From this emerged two striking night scenes that he completed in time for the next Itinerant exhibition: *Moonlit Night. Village* and *Moonlit Night. The Big Road.*

Given Chekhov's abrupt visit to Uspenskoe, Levitan was anxious to spend more time with him. "I terribly want to drop in on you, to see you and your family" he told Chekhov, "but the thought of a journey in such hot weather, especially in a train carriage, simply makes me lose heart. I've always had a hard time enduring heat, but since I've developed heart disease, the heat simply kills me." He was curious about Braz, who had arrived at Melikhovo on July 5 and spent seventeen days there, turning Maria's room into his portrait studio. Levitan also told Chekhov, unaware of his friend's true feelings, that Morozov had returned to his country castle fully expecting to find Chekhov still staying there: "He was very disappointed that your track had gone cold. He considers you (and by the way so do many others) to be the best at the present time." Levitan could not resist pulling Chekhov's leg, saying that this opinion is something "which I cannot and do not want to agree with. In my opinion, the best is Ezhov, then Mikheev, and then you, if you please," naming two mediocre writers very much living in Chekhov's shadow, and in Nikolai Ezhov's case, someone Chekhov found personally annoying.

When Chekhov did not reply, Levitan wrote to Maria, "my pigeon Mari, [...] my dear, blessed girl," wondering whether the rumors were true (they were not) that her brother had already left for Odessa. He repeated to her the same refrains on his poor health and lack of inspiration that he had been complaining to others about all summer:

> I terribly want to see you, but I'm in such a bad way that I'm simply afraid of the journey to your place, and in addition, in such heat. I recovered a little bit abroad, but just the same, I'm awfully weak, and to spend two hours in a train carriage and then go six miles along a bad road—I just don't have the strength for it. Possibly when it gets cooler, I will make up my mind to visit you. I'm not working much—I get tired unbelievably quickly. Yes, I'm finally completely spent, and I have nothing left to live for! It must be that I've finished singing my song.[21]

Watching Braz work on his portrait and enjoying her newfound friendship with the painter Maria Drozdova, Maria Chekhova again considered devoting herself more seriously to her own painting. Levitan was asked to help out, and he wrote Chekhov on August 12 that he planned to be in Moscow soon and would "drop into the School of Painting regarding Maria Pavlovna." He told Chekhov that her skills were strong enough that "they will accept her without a doubt," but in fact she was not admitted.[22] Levitan also wondered if Braz had left his incomplete portrait with Chekhov and what he thought of it. Levitan himself, because of his health, was reading more and painting less. He asked Chekhov to buy him the complete collected works of Dostoevsky, Turgenev, Gogol, and, in translation, the works of Shakespeare.

With the coming of a spell of milder summer weather, Levitan finally made the journey to Melikhovo on August 19, arriving at 9:30 in the evening accompanied by Lika. On August 20, Pavel Chekhov noted in his diary that "today we have two female artists and one male artist Levitan having lunch with us."[23] Chekhov gave Levitan a copy of *Motley Stories*, his early collection of stories. He inscribed the book "To the famous Levitan from the magnanimous author."[24] The next day Levitan and Lika left for Moscow together.

Chekhov let everyone know how worried he was about the expense of spending the fall and winter abroad. Nevertheless, following his doctors' orders, he left Moscow on September 1 for Biarritz in the south of France. Levitan, behind Chekhov's back, talked to Morozov about the possibility of loaning Chekhov enough money to cover the cost of his medical treatment. Morozov agreed to send 2,000 rubles. With the best of intentions, but oblivious to whether Chekhov would in fact welcome a loan from someone he obviously disliked, on September 20 Levitan sent a telegram to "Biarritz, Antoine Tschekoff" requesting that he telegraph Moscow immediately indicating the exact address to which to send the 2,000 rubles. After Chekhov telegraphed Levitan back the next day, Levitan followed up with a letter of explanation: "I told Sergei Timofeevich Morozov that you needed some money now and that if he could, he should loan you 2,000 rubles. He eagerly agreed. Of course, he said not a word about a promissory note, but I think it would be nice if you sent him some sort of document." Levitan's tone was very solicitous, but also emphatic, almost to the point of condescension: "My sweet, dear one, I strongly urge you not to be concerned about money matters—everything will be taken care of, and you can sit in the south and take care of your health. Dear one, if you don't want to, don't work at all, don't exhaust yourself." Chekhov had mentioned that he was thinking of going to Algiers, and Levitan responded that "everyone agrees that the climate in Algiers works wonders for those with lung diseases. Go there and don't worry about anything. Stay there until summer, or if you like, even longer." He told Chekhov that he himself might drop in on him there: "Together I think we won't be bored." The money and Levitan's letter were sent to Biarritz, but by then Chekhov had left for Nice, and the whole awkward affair lay dormant for several weeks.

On September 26, Levitan found out that his beloved teacher and mentor Alexei Savrasov had died that day in the pauper's ward of the Moscow City Hospital. Since being dismissed for alcoholism from the School of Painting in 1882, Savrasov had sunk into desperate poverty. His wife and daughters had already left him. He intermittently lived with other women, the last of whom bore him two children, which resulted in bringing them all to the brink of starvation. He survived by making copies of his most famous paintings for dealers who exploited him, paying little for his work. For the most part Savrasov was forgotten, although from time to time his former students and, most notably, his patron Tretyakov tried to help. Savrasov would show up in tatters to stay with the painter Sergei Gribkov, who opened up his home and studio to impoverished artists without charging them anything. Young art students living there took Savrasov to the bathhouse near Krimsky Bridge, from where he would return groomed and dressed in Gribkov's clean clothes. Savrasov would sober up but then after a month or two would disappear again, staying in flop houses, making drawings for bartenders in return for vodka and something to eat.[25]

Only a small group of people, mostly young art students, gathered on a dark, rainy fall day to accompany Savrasov's body from the courtyard of the hospital to the service in a small church nearby. One of the young artists, Pyotr Sizov, noticed that Levitan was among the last to arrive:

> He was sad, his genuine sorrow was sharply displayed among the circle of lively artists. After his first greetings, he went off to the side away from everyone, attracted to the distant panorama of the Vorobyov Hills, the melancholy ravines, the beauty of the noisy city with its factory chimneys, and the ribbon of the Moscow River creating a wondrous landscape.[26]

As Savrasov's closest and most prominent disciple, Levitan was asked to write an article about him for the *Russian Gazette*. It was the only time in Levitan's life that he published anything. He felt that it was important to reassert the significance of Savrasov to the development of Russian landscape painting: "He has not appeared in exhibitions for the past fifteen to twenty years, and it's as if he has been forgotten. This isn't the place to look into the reasons why he left the arena of painting. I will just say one thing: his life for the past fifteen to twenty years was dark and tragic." Levitan reminded the Russian public that before Savrasov, landscape painters were "completely without national roots: they looked outside of Russia, their native country, for motifs in their paintings." Savrasov's approach was radically different. In describing his teacher's attitude toward landscapes, Levitan was in effect describing his own: Savrasov's innovation was in "not selecting exclusively beautiful locations for the subjects of his paintings, but rather, on the contrary, attempting to search out in the most simple and ordinary things those intimate, deeply affecting, often sad features that are so strongly felt in our native landscape and so irresistibly affect the soul." Visual poetry was to be found in simplicity, in the old church, slanted fence, and melting snow of *The Rooks Have Come*; in the lonely cross in the distance and a single birch with falling leaves in *The Grave on the Volga*. Levitan suggested it was time to organize a posthumous exhibition so that "it would then be clear to everyone what a talented and original artist we have lost."[27] It was not to be. The first solo exhibition of Savrasov's work would not take place until long after his death—in 1948 at the Tretyakov Gallery.[28]

In early October, Chekhov told Levitan that he wanted to return Morozov's 2,000 rubles, possibly when Morozov came to Nice in January, and was thinking about returning to Moscow briefly. Reading this, Levitan frantically shot a reply to "Anton the Wise!":

> What got into you to think you could send the money back?!! God knows what the hell this is! You have to keep the money without fail, keep it without fail. Morozov is in no hurry. Why go to Russia for a week?!! Forgive me, but this is just crazy! Even the smallest cold, which it's so easy to catch here in the winter, would destroy all the gains you've made in the south! For God's sake, don't do this! It's horrible here, really horrible. Any thought like this isn't worth an empty eggshell. Stay in the south and take care of your health. Everything else is nonsense, all nonsense. Don't get angry at me, my dear one, but I'm really frightened.

He urged Chekhov to go ahead and spend the money instead of holding it until January. But for Chekhov this unasked for beneficence had become a major irritant. He wrote Lika about the 2,000 rubles he received from "Levitan's Morozov":

> I didn't ask for this money. I don't want it and I asked Levitan to allow me to return it in such a way, of course, that no one would get offended. Levitan doesn't want this, but just the same I'm sending it back. I'll wait another two weeks or a month and return it in a letter expressing my thanks. I have money. All this, I repeat, should remain just between us.

In contrast to haranguing Chekhov about his health and Morozov's money, Levitan struck an unusually cheerful tone in talking about himself. He mentioned he saw Maria occasionally; in fact, she and Lika were gathering at his place that day to go off to see "the psychopath Kundasova." He was enjoying his work: "My muse is again giving herself to me, and I'm feeling generally great." He had enjoyed reading the article "A. P. Chekhov's Dramatic Works" that had appeared in the *Russian Gazette* on October 3, and told Chekhov about his own article on Savrasov that was published in the same newspaper the next day. He still planned to go abroad and join Chekhov, but when that happened depended on when he finished preparing for the upcoming annual exhibitions.

Not surprisingly, Chekhov remained silent rather than respond to Levitan's insistent demands. It finally dawned on Levitan that he may have offended Chekhov. He wrote to him on November 22, asking why he had not heard a thing from him; he had not seen Maria since she had come over on October 17. "So I know nothing about you. Are you angry about something? I've given in to all sorts of guesses. Scribble at least a word."

His failing health notwithstanding, Levitan, as usual, plunged into the fall and winter social whirl of the Moscow art world, especially events organized by the Moscow Society of Art Lovers. In November he showed two drawings in the society's exhibition of watercolors, pastels, and sketches. In December he was tied up with the society's commission that awarded annual prizes and attended three of the society's Saturday salons, where he enjoyed the company of fellow artists Surikov and Serov, among others, and the actress Maria Ermolova, whom he had known from the days she attended Kuvshinnikova's salons. The Twenty-Fifth Itinerant Exhibition had traveled in late November to Odessa, where eight of his studies had sold for 500 rubles, and in December Tretyakov bought *Mont Blanc Range* for 300 rubles.[29]

Toward the end of December, Levitan told Karzinkina's brother Alexander that he "had another attack and felt very bad. Now I again feel better and have started to hope that I will live a bit more." He joked with Ostroukhov that they both should "try to stay alive (just to irritate the doctors!)." Poor health was also the reason Levitan gave Chekhov for being slow to respond after finally getting a letter from "dear Anthony" explaining the disposition of the 2,000 rubles. When he did write Chekhov on December 28, Levitan seemed resigned to the awkward outcome. But he was still unable to understand why Chekhov and Morozov had failed to form the acquaintanceship he so desired:

> That you sent the money back to Morozov—what can I say? That's your affair. But it's too bad that you sent it when you could personally give it to him (I was sure that you would meet), since he's been in Nice already for two weeks (Hotel

Bristol). It's a pity, a real pity that it happened this way. I would have thought that he would drop in on you, but apparently, out of an excess of delicacy, he didn't do it. It's a pity, sad.

Levitan remained convinced that developing a relationship with Morozov would be of immeasurable benefit to Chekhov's career and his finances.

11 1898

PROFESSOR OF PAINTING

ON JANUARY 12, CHEKHOV told his brother Ivan that "Levitan's Morozov" had arrived in Nice. He let Levitan know that he had finally met his benefactor and liked him. Levitan was relieved. "He's a good man," he wrote Chekhov, "just too rich, and for him especially that's bad." Yet he still resented that Chekhov had rejected Morozov's generosity, and he disguised his anger by exaggerating his sense of outrage:

> Oh, you striped hyena, you damned crocodile, you spineless wood demon with one nostril, you utter Quasimodo, I don't know how else to curse you! I'm suffering from worms in my heart!!! Oh, you foul Beelzebub! You yourself are suffering as a result of this, not I, and you will forever suffer from this until the end of your days! Don't cherish the hope that you will see me. I don't want to see you. You are repulsive to me.
>
> If I do go to Nice, I hope to avoid seeing you. Morozov and I will no longer allow ourselves to see you. Otherwise we will be infected by the worms in your heart. Better that you suffer alone!
>
> Really, aren't you just repaying my kindness with your wrath?! Whatever has come between us, I forgive you. Remember my magnanimity in this matter.

Levitan then shifted gears from mock fury to solicitude: "Be well, and let's try to stay alive so that we can irritate our enemies." He shared his thoughts on what he had been reading. Drawn to European modernism, he found Gabriele D'Annunzio, the decadent Italian novelist and poet, to be "a marvelous writer" and added, "Reading his work, I gulp it down." He asked Chekhov whether he had read Tolstoy's *What Is Art*, which even though first published heavily censored was nevertheless, he reported, "causing a big stir" in Moscow art circles. Levitan found it "both brilliant and crazy at the same time." Tolstoy started thinking about the subject when his daughter Tania entered the School of Painting in 1881.[1] His argument that art at its core was a medium for transferring a feeling experienced by the artist was consistent with the expressiveness that Levitan hoped his landscapes achieved. But, like many of his fellow artists, Levitan found Tolstoy's rejection of Greek tragedy, Michelangelo, Shakespeare, and Beethoven for their lack of simple Christian virtues to be wrongheaded. Chekhov dismissed Tolstoy's treatise. "It's all old stuff," he wrote Suvorin. "To say that art has become decrepit, that it's come to a dead end, that it's not what it should be and so on and so forth—that's just what you say when you've grown tired of eating and drinking and it's no longer what you think it should be." He was sure that people would "still eat regardless of what nonsense philosophers and angry old men talk."

Diaghilev was motivated by a desire to display works that flew in the face of Tolstoy's reactionary aesthetics. His exhibition of Russian and Finnish painters opened at the ornate, neo-Renaissance Stieglitz Museum in St. Petersburg on January 16. Among the pictures were six of Levitan's paintings and watercolors, including *Above Eternal Rest*. Diaghilev planned the exhibition as part of his strategy to launch the World of Art movement within the next year. He invited the younger generation of Russian artists to submit their works, promising them that his exhibition would travel from St. Petersburg to Moscow and then on to the annual Munich Secession showcase. The Itinerant critic Stasov considered the exhibition to be "decadent rubbish," and he and Diaghilev engaged in a fierce polemic over it.[2]

Diaghilev's intent was to break the stranglehold that the Itinerant Association had on the selection and exhibition of major Russian painters. Levitan, however much he was sympathetic to Diaghilev's avant-garde movement, still had not turned his back on the Itinerants. When the Twenty-Sixth Itinerant Exhibition opened in Petersburg on February 21, ten Levitan paintings were on display. His popularity among the conservative aristocracy continued to grow, including the highest ranks of the imperial court. During the exhibition, Empress Maria Fyodorovna, the widow of Alexander III, acquired his *Punka-Khariu. Finland* and Grand Prince Georgy Mikhailovich bought *Road. Fall.* However, the tsar himself was not among his devotees. A story was told, possibly apocryphal, that Nicholas II stopped in front of Levitan's paintings and commented to the artist that it looked like he was starting to exhibit unfinished work. Levitan audaciously, but not surprisingly given his well-known reluctance to show a work before he felt it was ready, assured the tsar that his paintings were indeed completely finished works of art.[3] Cementing Levitan's ascendency, on February 23 three members of the St. Petersburg Academy of Arts formally requested that Levitan be inducted into their ranks.

Levitan's precarious health may have played a role in the timing of the recommendation. Word spread that he had become seriously ill with typhus. His brother Adolph briefly stepped in to handle his business affairs, seeing to the sale to Princess Tenisheva of one of the paintings from Diaghilev's exhibition and collecting 500 rubles for the painting purchased by the grand prince. By the time the Academy voted to accept Levitan as a member on March 23, he had recovered. Karzinkina went to visit him and saw him sitting in a warm coat on a bench in front of Morozov's large courtyard. She sat next to him and asked about his illness. "It was awful," he said. "I became more and more ill, and could have died. This is so awful! Death—it's an awful thing!"[4] Maria Chekhova wrote to her brother that the danger had passed for the "poor devil."[5] Chekhov had learned of the honor bestowed on Levitan and joked to Maria that this probably meant he would no longer be able to address his academician friend using the informal "you."

Levitan told Diaghilev that while the typhus had almost killed him, "I'm now filled with joy for having recovered." His doctor insisted that he return to Nauheim for treatment, even though he hated the thought of going. Levitan wrote his sister Tereza about his illness and recovery. He also gave her the good news of his induction into the Academy: "According to the current codex, this designation is the highest rank that an artist can attain." But he must have known that this would only increase Tereza's family's constant appeals for financial help. As it was, her husband, Pyotr, was asking Levitan to convince Sergei Morozov to commit to a business deal to buy certain goods exclusively from him. Levitan accused Pyotr of being naïve: "According to him, all I have to do is say a few words to Morozov, and he will throw his previous buyers out on their ears and take him. That's crazy! Just the same, I'll give it a try."[6]

Having made plans to be in Europe for treatment during May and June, Levitan scrambled to tie up loose ends. He saw Elena Karzinkina and her father off for a stay in the Crimea, noticing that she looked exhausted. Searching for a dacha to move into for the summer after he returned, he found a place on the Olenin estate at Podsolnichny on the outskirts of Moscow. His paintings continued to command ever-increasing prices: Tretyakov paid 500 rubles for a sketch of *Above Eternal Rest*, and Levitan told Khruslov to set the asking price of *Moonlit Night. The Big Road* in the range of 860 to 1,000 rubles.

Chekhov returned home from France on May 5. His mother failed to see any improvement in his health.[7] On the other hand, mutual friends told Levitan that Chekhov's stay in the south had done a lot of good. By mid-May, Levitan left Russia for the fourth time, first stopping in Munich to see his paintings and those of other Russians displayed as part of Diaghilev's section of the International Secession Exhibition. He told Diaghilev that he was "very pleased with the look of our Russian products." Levitan felt that a Russian artist did not necessarily need to be exhibited in Europe to be a success, but just the same, he was grateful that Diaghilev was making the push to expose Europeans to Russian art. Stasov complained to his brother that the "decadents" (he meant Diaghilev's cousin, the art critic Dmitri Filosofov) wrongly claimed that the Munich exhibition had been an overwhelming success, when in fact the Europeans had limited their praise to the works of Serov and Levitan: "and they aren't really decadents (although Vladimir Makovsky considers Levitan to have now moved in the direction of the decadents)."[8]

Returning to the baths at Nauheim at the end of May, Levitan wrote a chatty letter to Karzinkina. He reported that Dr. Schott had promised to completely restore his heart: "I think he's lying, the damn German!" As usual, he was depressed and lonely. Even reading books banned in Russia gave him no pleasure. He wanted to know what Karzinkina thought of the paintings in the latest Itinerant exhibition, and he looked forward to getting back to Russia and settling in at Podsolnichny. Levitan wrote to Chekhov complaining that he had not heard from him since their unfortunate squabble over Morozov's rejected loan. On several occasions Levitan had mentioned joining Chekhov during his recuperation in the south of Europe, but their travel schedules conflicted. "Are you angry about something?" Levitan asked. "Or do you simply not feel like writing? That I can understand." He told Chekhov that he was taking his baths, doing gymnastics, feeling better, despite being surrounded by Englishmen who were at the spa in "endless numbers like flies in the summer." As he had already said to Karzinkina, he told Chekhov that he missed Russia terribly: "It's a wild country, but I love her."

As soon as he returned to Moscow via Paris in early June, Levitan wrote again to Karzinkina. He was still pursuing her: "There's a lot I want to ask you about, but you're right, it can't be cleared up in a letter, so until we meet, I remain your devoted Levitan." Her aloofness had an obvious explanation— she was about to marry the writer Nikolai Teleshov. Karzinkina and Teleshov had much in common—they were close in age, both from prominent Moscow merchant families, and good friends with many of the city's prominent writers and painters. As a result of his connections, Teleshov's "Wednesdays" had become one of the focal points of Moscow intellectual life. He was strongly influenced by Chekhov, who had encouraged him to travel east and write about the peasants who had migrated to the Urals and Siberia.

By late June, Levitan was staying at the Olenin estate near Lake Senezh. The German salt baths had done nothing to improve his health. He begged

Chekhov to come visit him and bring his fishing pole: "I'm living in a marvelous place: on the shore of a very deep, large lake. Around me are forests, and the lake is swarming with fish. There are even crocodiles (I think this would be tempting for you?!)." He promised Chekhov "all the comforts, even a water closet." Levitan had earlier considered making a visit to Melikhovo but concluded his heart was still too weak to endure the horseback ride from the Lopasnya train station along the deeply rutted road to Chekhov's house. Chekhov remained noncommittal, implying that there was still an unspoken friction between them. "What's going on?" Levitan asked. "God knows I love you, even though you're a viper! If you don't want to come and it's hardly possible for me to visit you, then write me sensibly about what's the matter and what you're hinting at." Levitan was offended that Chekhov was planning to go visit friends in Tver two hundred miles away: "Since you intend to be at the home of some princes Nesvirsky, perhaps after the princes you will deign to drop in on a mere mortal. What the hell's going on: it's obvious you're swimming in shallow water with your ass sticking up in the air! You can visit the princes, but not me! You're a real swine."[9] Levitan couldn't resist taunting his friend "Antonio" about their respective reputations: "Praise for me is beginning to overshadow yours. What do you think about that?" He signed his letter "Academician."

Karzinkina was still on Levitan's mind. He wrote her that only the heat and his heart were preventing him from paying her a visit at her estate at Odintsevo: "I very much want to see you, to find out how you're living, to look at you, to see what new things you've painted; in general, I want to be with you." He described his idyllic life by the lake but confessed that the silence was beginning to get to him:

> For now, I'm not working much. As is usual at this time of summer, I have some kind of apathy. For most of the day, I'm in the woods, on the shore of the lake, with a book. If I get tired of reading, I look at the lake, and there is almost always something interesting to look at. If I get tired of the water, then it's the book, and so it goes for the whole day. The older you get, the less necessary socializing becomes, although at times one does want to see people. Being alone is both a blessing and a curse.

He said much the same thing to Diaghilev, mentioning that the estate was delightful but he wasn't getting much work done: "I lie in the woods all day and read Schopenhauer. You would be surprised. As a result, do you think my landscapes would, so to speak, be suffused with pessimism? Don't worry, I love nature too much." Levitan had given Diaghilev permission to make reproductions of several of the paintings in Tretyakov's collection to be included in the first issue of the *World of Art*, set to be published by the end of the year.

Levitan was not having nearly as unproductive a year as he made it sound to his friends. With nine new paintings ready for the upcoming Itinerant exhibition, his output of displayed works had reached the same number as in the previous year. If anything his paintings were becoming more masterful and powerfully expressive as he moved away from his earlier more finished technique to a more impressionistic style. Paintings as dissimilar in subject matter as *Early Spring*, a muted landscape of melting snow, bare trees, and leaden sky, and *Sunny Day. Village*, with its bright skies and high contrast, both share the use of a limited palette and an economy of brush strokes to achieve their effects.

Responding to Levitan's petulance, Chekhov dropped by to see him on August 4 on his way back to Moscow from Tver. One topic on their minds was the endless wrangling over Braz's portrait of Chekhov. In February, Tretyakov told Braz that he was sending him 200 rubles in travel expenses to go to Nice to repaint the portrait and would pay him an additional 400 rubles for the completed painting. At the same time Tretyakov made it clear to Braz how unhappy he was with the original piece: "I heard from I. I. Levitan that Anton Pavlovich is very lively and animated, and in your painting he looks very serious. Is that the reason why the resemblance isn't satisfactory?" In Nice, Chekhov posed for Braz, facing him directly while sitting in an armchair with a green velvet back. He confided to the painter Alexandra Khotyaintseva that he still didn't very much like the portrait, which, he claimed, made him look like he had just inhaled a lot of horseradish.

In mid-August back in Russia, Braz sent the revised portrait to Tretyakov, as requested, so that it could be part of the following year's Itinerant exhibitions in Moscow and St. Petersburg. After several weeks of silence, Tretyakov responded that the portrait had arrived safely. Braz wrote Chekhov that Tretyakov told him he liked the portrait, "although he couldn't make a judgment about its resemblance." Tretyakov also let Braz know that he felt that he shouldn't have to pay the remaining 400 rubles until after the exhibitions closed. Braz took offense at this, pointing out that Tretyakov was familiar with his humble living conditions and knew that he needed the money. For his part, Braz was afraid that he might have offended Tretyakov by asking for the money immediately. He wrote to Chekhov for help: "If you want to, describe my situation to Levitan. He apparently knows Tretyakov well and perhaps, thanks to him, it would be possible to smooth things out."[10]

Levitan told Chekhov that he himself had experienced the same problem with Tretyakov holding back on his payments. At first he recommended that

Chekhov himself contact Tretyakov, but once he saw the painting, Levitan agreed to step in, reassure Tretyakov, and try to settle the conflict. "I find it to be a good likeness," he told Tretyakov. "I thought it important to say this to you, since I know Chekhov very well." Meanwhile, Chekhov tried to ease Braz's financial situation by arranging a commission from Varvara Morozova, the Tver manufacturing millionaire he had visited in the summer.[11] She had married into the same merchant family that Levitan's patron was part of, but when her husband died, she took up with Vasily Sobolevsky, the liberal editor of *The Russian Gazette*.

Surely the most gratifying result of being named to the Academy of Arts came in late July, when Levitan received an invitation from the Moscow School of Painting to revive the advanced landscape painting studio course, which had not been taught since Polenov's departure in 1895. In 1884 the school had humiliated Levitan by granting him a second-class degree that deemed him unqualified to teach painting, and now they had asked him to assume the same position held by his mentors Savrasov and Polenov. Vasnetsov urged Levitan not to accept the professorship, insisting that it would interfere with his own painting. But Levitan saw it as his calling. He remembered an occasion at the Academy when some of the professors expressed doubt that it was even possible to teach landscape painting, but Levitan dismissed the notion, even though he had hardly any teaching experience himself. He returned to Moscow at the end of August to begin preparing for the academic year. On his instructions, following a practice introduced by Savrasov, Levitan had half the studio's space decorated with live plants for student sketching, filling that part of the room with real trees, moss, firs, and ferns. This would enable his students to create landscape scenes without having to go outside.

Levitan taught at the School of Painting for less than two years. Several of his students wrote memoirs that recall what Levitan said in class; these constitute the only detailed accounts we have of Levitan's aesthetics and painting techniques.

Levitan did not see his role as that of a teacher of fundamentals. He was not known to have touched his students' canvases. He treated the studio as a forum for instilling the sensibilities and intellectual approach that he felt were required to succeed as an artist. Levitan repeatedly underscored that great landscape paintings had simplicity and expressiveness. "Don't get wrapped up in trivialities and details," he told his students. "Search for a general tone."[12] Sky, water, and earth existed in nature as separate elements. In a landscape, the painter must find a way to create a visual and emotional relationship among these elements. He advised his students to paint with fewer colors and avoid putting any colors on their palette that they didn't intend to use. He told them to avoid large-scale sketches, which only introduced "a lot of nonsense."[13] A small study was the best way to capture the essence of what a painter saw. He used as an example the sketches he made for *Vladimirka*. The fact that they were small in no way prevented him from creating the final painting on a large scale. Sometimes he would not even make sketches, relying on his acute visual memory: "You see a complete painting in a dream and you try, not always successfully, to reproduce it while awake. At other times, while listening to music or poetry, at first you have a vague image, you draw it many times until it becomes formed. It haunts you like a persistent idea, and then of course, you draw it."[14]

But Levitan's visual memory also allowed him to refine a motif by constantly discarding sketches and starting over. Two of his students, while visiting his studio, were startled to see Levitan using a piece of vitreous paper to vigorously wipe away the sky in a landscape they were admiring. Noticing their bewilderment, Levitan continued to wipe the painting furiously, saying: "You see, sometimes you have to forget what you've painted so that you can once again see it anew. And it will immediately become apparent how much is yet to be done, how persistently you still need to work on the picture. Right now, I'm removing the superfluous elements in the picture that are precisely what's making it scream."[15]

It was not unusual for Levitan to bring up music and literature when teaching students about landscapes. At Plyos, Kuvshinnikova often played the piano while he painted. He once criticized a student's painting technique by asking him: "Where is your hearing, your sense of pitch?"[16] Simplicity was, in fact, the key to achieving expressiveness in a painting, to visually distilling the essence of a landscape. He spoke admiringly to his students about a fresco of angels in white and a Madonna he had seen in one of the Kremlin churches— they were powerful yet simple images made with only a few colors.[17]

A still life, he felt, was dead until the painter emotionally brought it to life. He harangued one of his students, who struggled with painting some flowers: "What are your flowers made of? What is this? Paper? Rags? No! You need to feel that they are alive, filled with juice, leaning towards the light. They must smell like flowers, not like paint."[18] Many of his students, not surprisingly, imitated impressionist techniques—short strokes and raw colors. Sometimes they struck Levitan as patently false. "What the hell is this," he screamed at another student. "You've cheapened nature. You're going for cheap external effects . . . This cannot happen in a genuine painting. There needs to be only truth . . . Where are your flowers?! What have you done to nature? [. . .] No, my brother, work hard to make that which is there in nature. Look, in life it's so pretty and simple. Paint simply. This is the hardest thing to do in nature."[19]

When another student defended his use of violet tones by saying he had seen them in French impressionist paintings, Levitan replied: "But why? Are you French? Paint like a Russian as you see things. Why copy someone else? Search for your own way."[20] Levitan was not hostile to French impressionism. He was just encouraging his students, as Savrasov had done in his classes, to be original and true to themselves. An imitation did nothing but "arouse a physiological feeling of nausea." From the mid-1890s, the student exhibitions at the School of Painting had increasingly reflected what the journal *Artist* called "the influence of far from the best side of French painting." In its review of the Sixteenth Student Exhibition of 1892–1893, the journal reiterated the common critique of impressionism as cheap and facile: "Nature and life demand love and diligent study, a serious relationship with artistic methods, and genuine internal abilities." But in these student impressionists "not much taste and a bold hand easily supplant talent, which possibly the artist has, but it's lazy; it sleeps because its services aren't needed."[21]

In September, Diaghilev and Filosofov came to Moscow to encourage support and finalize participation for the upcoming *World of Art* publication and exhibition. They organized a meeting in Polenov's studio of a group of younger Moscow artists that included Levitan, Serov, Nesterov, and Korovin. The group welcomed the enthusiasm of the Petersburg art lovers and promised to support their efforts. Levitan had already agreed to appear in the publication and exhibit his paintings without necessarily abandoning his loyalty to the Itinerant Association, which, according to one of his students, he still found "more native and of the people" than the more effete Petersburg aesthetes.[22] Repin, too, at first appeared to be ecstatic about Diaghilev's plans, and Vasnetsov gave his permission for his newly completed *Bogatyrs* to be reproduced in the first issue. Levitan had previously, while in St. Petersburg, been a guest at what Princess Tenisheva had called her "conspiratorial" apartment next to her home where she plotted the publication of the journal with Diaghilev. Tenisheva's second marriage was to a much older, wealthy manufacturer who refused to take seriously her interest in collecting and promoting art. She was frustrated by his condescending treatment of her. But she finally realized that if he thought of her as nothing but a sex object, she could use her femininity to demand what she wanted from him: 12,500 rubles to underwrite the printing of the *World of Art*.[23]

On September 9, Chekhov came to Moscow to attend rehearsals for *The Seagull*. For several years Vladimir Nemirovich-Danchenko had considered reviving the play. The opportunity arose in 1898 when he found patrons, primarily Sergei Morozov's brother Savva, to fund the privately run Moscow Art Theater. At first Chekhov resisted the overture, but eventually he agreed to work with the director Konstantin Stanislavsky on the production. While at the rehearsals, Chekhov found himself smitten by the troupe's lead actress Olga Knipper. A few days later, he left for Yalta, banished again by his doctors after another incident of spitting up blood. On October 12, Chekhov received word from Melikhovo that his father had died suddenly from a ruptured hernia. As had happened with the death of his brother Nikolai, the person whom everyone looked to as the head of the household was absent when tragedy struck the family.

Levitan wrote Chekhov that it would be smart to stay put in Yalta: "You're a crank for wanting to go to Moscow! If you could picture how extremely scummy the weather is here, you would stop wishing for this, and you would be in ecstasy that you are surrounded by sun and warmth. It's really true—what you have, you don't value." In reply to Chekhov's inquiry about his own health, Levitan responded that it was changeable—sometimes he felt good, sometimes he lay about breathing heavily "like a fish out of water." He claimed he felt better when working hard, both at his painting and his teaching. "I have learned to copulate with my muse," he told Chekhov. "It's more difficult than learning to copulate with any old woman."[24] He had taken on a commission to produce together with Korovin and a group of other artists a series of sixty-six illustrations for a new three-volume collected works of Pushkin to be published in 1899 to celebrate the centennial of the poet's birth. When the collection came out, Diaghilev thought it a failure. Levitan and Korovin had contributed the most drawings, but Diaghilev found their work to be "incomprehensible, heavy without any style," not even sketches but more like preliminary drafts.[25]

Levitan's poor health had not slowed down his social life. He mentioned to Chekhov that he had twice been to gatherings at Stanislavsky's: "Talented guys!" He regularly attended the Saturday soirees of the Moscow Society of Art Lovers, spending time with Goloushev, Pereplyotchikov, and Pasternak, who was now a fellow teacher at the School of Painting. On November 10, Levitan attended the funeral of Polenov's sister Elena, an artist closely associated with Mamontov's Abramtsevo circle who was drawn to folk themes, modernism, and applied arts. The previous summer she had been diagnosed with a brain tumor but continued to work. Diaghilev had convinced her to be part of the editorial staff of the *World of Art*, the first two issues of which coincidentally came out simultaneously a full month ahead of schedule on the day of her funeral.

The quality of the publication was impressive—an oversized folio with excellent reproductions of artwork (in black and white), photographs, line drawings, and occasional tipped-in signature pages with glued-on, full-color illustrations. The first issue's lead article was Diaghilev's essay "Difficult Questions," accompanied by reproductions of Vasnetsov's folk-themed paintings, followed by "Old Understandings" by the critic Pyotr Boborykin with eight reproductions of Levitan's work. Now that his supporters finally saw the publication, some of them were put off by the arrogance of Diaghilev's writing and approach. Tretyakov, deathly ill at the time, came back from St. Petersburg and commented that it "looked nice, but was horribly chaotic and stupidly put together."[26] Vasnetsov hated the first issue and announced that he wasn't going to submit anything more to it. Repin also changed his mind about the publication and Diaghilev's movement. For her financial support Tenisheva was called the "mother of decadence."[27] Levitan, however, found Diaghilev's essay to be intriguing. "He's not a stupid man," he told Ostroukhov.

On December 4, Pavel Tretyakov died. Levitan attended his funeral three days later, forming part of a procession consisting of virtually every major Moscow artist, each taking turns carrying the coffin from the gallery on Lavrushinsky Lane to the grave site at the Danilov Monastery.

Levitan considered going to Yalta to visit Chekhov for a week or two at Christmas. He was trying to decide whether he should leave his work behind or take it with him: "I really want to see you," he wrote Chekhov, "but I don't know yet whether I will be able to." He was spending time again with Maria, telling her brother that she "had made tremendous progress in her painting. My, you Chekhovs are talented." He joked about Chekhov's poor health: "That you again coughed up blood—you need to copulate more vigorously. Didn't the lady you already wrote about say something 'filthy' to you? Were you not up for screwing? Too tired out?"[28]

With the death of his father and acceptance of his forced medical exile to the Crimea and southern Europe for half the year, Chekhov concluded that holding on to Melikhovo no longer made any sense. He made a down payment on a piece of property in Yalta on which to build a house. Worried that he lacked the money to provide for his illness and his family after his death, he began to consider selling blanket rights to his complete works.[29] Levitan again offered to help Chekhov with his finances: "Listen, if you need money, won't you let me tell Morozov?" This time Chekhov agreed. He told his sister: "I was tempted by this offer and wrote Levitan that I would be happy to borrow two thousand rubles to be paid back in installments." But then Levitan reconsidered whether it would be best if he should be the one to approach Morozov. After all, the two men had met and, as far as Levitan knew, liked each other: "I've thought and thought, dear Anton Pavlovich, about how best, how honestly to settle this matter with Morozov, and decisively came to the conclusion that you yourself should write him a few lines about your loan. This is absolutely better. You yourself will be convinced of this when you think it over for a while." Chekhov was unwilling to do this. He wrote Maria: "Overall this has turned into an awkward thing. Don't say anything to Levitan. I'm of course not going to take any money either from him or from Morozov, and I hope that he will no longer offer me any more friendly proposals." Having in mind selling his publishing rights, Chekhov concluded: "I'll take evasive action and pay off all debts, except bank loans, before the beginning of the twentieth century."

On December 17 the Moscow Art Theater production of *The Seagull* opened to a full house at the Hermitage Theater with Knipper in the role of Madame Arkadina and Stanislavsky playing Trigorin. Nemirovich-Danchenko had sent Maria four tickets in the loge stalls for the opening night. She invited Levitan, but he was too ill to attend, this time with the flu.[30] Going to Yalta to see Chekhov was out of the question.

12

1899

"I'M YOUNG IN SPIRIT"

NEMIROVICH-DANCHENKO'S production of *The Seagull* was a huge success, causing a "furor," as Maria described it to her brother. Every performance sold out. Maria lived close to the Hermitage Theater, and lying in bed she could still overhear people on the sidewalk below her talking loudly about the play at one in the morning.[1] When he felt well enough, Levitan would go to the theater on Carriage Row just before a performance to see whether he could find someone willing to sell him a ticket. Failing on several occasions, on January 7 he finally was able to buy a seat from a lady who charged him twice the normal price. He wrote to Chekhov the next day telling him that only now after having seen the play did he really understand it: "It wasn't very deep for me when I read it. Here, it was excellently, carefully, lovingly staged, thoroughly rehearsed, and worked through to the smallest detail. It makes a splendid impression." The public was thrilled to find itself "under the spell of a genuine work of art." And the mood of the piece resonated with Levitan's own artistic temperament: "It evokes the same melancholy that life itself gives off when you scrutinize it." He ran into Madame Nemirovich at the theater. She asked him to tell Chekhov that she was watching the play for the fifth time and that her interest in it grew with each viewing. Levitan pointedly mentioned to Chekhov that even Lensky, who had still been refusing to talk to Chekhov almost seven years after the publication of "The Grasshopper," was enraptured by the play and its staging and was finally ready to forgive Chekhov. Later in the year, Lensky approached Maria, shook her hand for a long time, and asked her to tell her brother that he had always loved him and still loved him.[2] Levitan ended his letter wishing Chekhov good health: "God grant you everything but floozies and gonorrhea."[3]

Although his own health had improved, Levitan put off his visit to Chekhov in Yalta now that he was again tied down by his teaching obligations and the annual exhibition season in Moscow and St. Petersburg: "School tires me out," he told Chekhov. "Work tires me out, which at the same time I can't quit, since, as your Trigorin says, every artist is a serf." He asked Chekhov whether he had written to Morozov yet about the loan, assuring him that once he asked for the money, Morozov was sure to provide the funds. But Chekhov had no intention of following through. He had signed a contract to sell the rights to all his work, both past and future, to the publisher Marx for 75,000 rubles.[4]

Foremost on Levitan's mind was the opening on January 23 in St. Petersburg of the World of Art International Exhibition, in which he had nine paintings. When he arrived at his hotel in St. Petersburg, Levitan dropped his luggage on the floor of his room and immediately went to the exhibition. "As usual, even at mediocre exhibitions, if they include my works, I feel awful," he wrote to Anna Turchaninova, "but what I saw at the International Exhibition exceeded my expectations. Imagine seeing Europe's best artists and best examples of their work!" Diaghilev had selected forty-two Western artists to participate, including Whistler, Puvis de Chavannes, Degas, Renoir, Monet, and Bonnard. "I was staggered," Levitan wrote. "My own things—I never like them at exhibitions—this time struck me as childish prattle, and I suffered monstrously. Two days went by, in which I didn't go to the exhibition, and I finally started to feel very good. They created a separate section for the Russian artists at the exhibition, and to their benefit, to their great benefit." Although physically weak, Levitan was confident that his artistic talent was at its peak. He was ready to move in a new direction. He, Repin, and Serov talked about how there was much to learn from the juxtaposition of their work with that of the European masters. He had seen Russian artists among the Europeans last spring in Munich "but not in such aristocratic company as this: It was very instructive, and now, having lived through it, I feel full of beans. I want to work. I have a lot of artistic ideas in my head. In general, it's great. I may be tired in body, but I'm young in spirit."

Levitan found himself far more receptive to the French impressionists than he had been previously. He bumped into Troyanovsky standing in front of Monet's *Haystacks* at the exhibition. When Troyanovsky started to criticize the painting, Levitan firmly disagreed: "No, don't say that, don't say that. There is something here."[5] Levitan responded with pangs of jealousy when the painter Alexander Sredin wrote him that he had set himself up with a studio in Paris. "To live in Paris is a blessing for an artist," Levitan wrote back. The city so teemed with artistic energy, it was impossible to sleep; your mind raced just

from taking in the works of painters such as Monet, Cézanne, Renard. He
promised to come to Paris later in the year if his health allowed.

Aside from its description of the artistic impact of Diaghilev's exhibition,
Levitan's letter to Turchaninova is significant because it is the only example we
have of the correspondence between them. Their intimacy is obvious; Levitan
addresses Turchaninova as "my dear wifey Anka." Concerned about his health,
she had urged him not to go to St. Petersburg. "I considered it necessary for
myself," he replied after he returned, "and although I'm awfully tired, at the
same time I'm extremely pleased. I will tell you everything in sequence, my
joy, my happiness, my eternally beloved Niunushechka!"

Turchaninova openly admitted that she was unhappy with Levitan's
movement toward the "decadents" and tried to impose her more conservative
tastes on him. This once led to an argument in which Levitan went into a rage
and tore up a picture of a setting sun painted with violent colors.[6] Levitan's
interest in the World of Art disturbed some of his other friends as well. Maria
Ermolova, the actress who played the role of Sappho that inspired Chekhov's
mocking nickname for Kuvshinnikova, wrote to the Itinerant landscape
painter Grigory Yartsev: "Many true artists in order to please fashion, the
damned fashion of decadence, have changed their art and turned themselves
into jokes. Just look at what Levitan has done to himself. He's gone and turned
into a decadent dauber. It's shameful and unworthy."[7] The World of Art
exhibition was so bold that the public did not know what to make of it. The
press disapproved of what they saw and the old guard accused the organizers
of artistic heresy. Bonnard's full-length portrait of the actress Gabrielle Réjane
standing before the footlights was the object of particular ridicule.[8]

Nevertheless, Diaghilev's assault on the Itinerants produced uneasiness
among Levitan and those of his fellow painters who still had feet in both
camps. Repin, who had left the Itinerants in 1891, agreed to participate in
the exhibition. But when articles appeared in Diaghilev's journal attacking
realistic art in general and him in particular, Repin responded by publishing
a letter denouncing the movement in a way that struck Nesterov as more
irritated than convincing. When Nesterov noticed an announcement that
the next issue of *World of Art* would include drawings by Repin and even his
portrait, he was dumbfounded and glad to be going far away from the World
of Art to his own world in the Caucasus, which he saw as a "calmer, more
robust, and comfortable place to make art."[9]

Still vacillating, Levitan nevertheless felt loyal to those Itinerant painters
(who had supported him when he had been threatened with expulsion from
Moscow) and to the Association's exhibitions (upon which he depended for
his livelihood). On the day before the opening of the Twenty-Seventh Itinerant

Exhibition in St. Petersburg on March 7, Levitan took part in a group portrait of nineteen Itinerant artists, choosing to sit beside Emily Shanks, a Moscow-born artist from a prominent English family who was the first woman admitted to the Association. Among the nine Levitan paintings in the exhibition, *Bright Autumn* was sold to Tenisheva, and the Academy decided to buy *Early Spring* for 600 rubles. When the exhibit came to Moscow in April, Nikolai von Meck paid 2,500 rubles for *Storm*. *Rain*, and *Toward Evening* sold for 400 rubles.

Levitan returned to Moscow exhausted. His deteriorating health was visibly noticeable. Polenov stopped by Levitan's studio just prior to leaving for a second extended journey to the Middle East. Sorry to have missed seeing Polenov, Levitan sent him a note: "I had been planning for a long time to visit you, but recently my heart has been conducting itself indecently, and you have a 'decent' staircase!" His doctors had long ago asked him to avoid using stairs, a challenge since his studio was above his living quarters. Karzinkina coyly remarked that Levitan had taken to visiting her often because her apartment was nearby and on the ground floor.

To his students Levitan still tried to exude boundless energy. One bright spring day, he came into his landscape class and noticed his students' festive mood: "I see, ladies and gentlemen, that you don't feel like working today. It used to be that on days like this Savrasov would chase us out of the city to go sketching. So, shouldn't we go somewhere out of the city, at least to Sokolniki? What do you think?" Along the way Levitan told more stories about Savrasov, about the fact that he painted *The Rooks Have Come* over and over again before he succeeded in painting the version that now hangs in the Tretyakov Gallery. "Savrasov taught me to work long and hard over a painting," he said. "Thanks to him, I understood that creativity is hard work and not always rewarding." He added, ironically: "When you're striving, there's often nothing to eat, and when you've attained something, you look up and there is something to eat, but you don't have any teeth left."[10] In the park the students spread out, working far apart from each other. Levitan, leaning on his walking stick, went from one to the other patiently spending time with each of them. The following day in class he reviewed the finished sketches.

To increase the opportunity for *plein air* painting, Levitan arranged for the school to rent a dacha in Kuskovo from Evdokiya Golitsynskaya, one of his students. Many of the students moved into the dacha for the spring, with Levitan coming out to be with them two or three times a week. "Staying in a large, light-filled dacha with walls made from unpainted pine boards smelling of the forest invigorated us after the dark classrooms of the School and the tiny rooms where we spent the winter," recalled Boris Lipkin, one of the students.[11] He remembered that the natural surroundings were not particularly impressive, since they were barely out of the city, surrounded by fences and other dachas. But with fifteen students gathered together, the atmosphere was lively and cheerful. Levitan became very attached to his students, calling them "my children," although many of them were bearded young men. He half-jokingly called their dacha studio "Barbizon" and told his students that they must do what the Barbizon School did—stir things up so all of Europe would know about it. And if they succeeded, Levitan told them conspiratorially, "I'll put away money into Credit Lyonnaise, buy my own studio, and when I become a very old tub or die, you could set it up as a house of landscape painting."

On occasion Levitan could also be severe. Sizov recalled that "in his pronouncements he was cruel, unwavering, merciless. A flaccid, senile painting especially made him cringe [. . .]. He valued the generalization of a mass and the simplification of technique: 'Make beauty, find God, don't give me the documentary truth, give me artistic truth. Down with the documentary. Nature doesn't need any portraits.'"[12] At the same time he demanded a high level of technical competence, which he considered a necessary cornerstone regardless of genre.

The students lived simply, sleeping on benches or on the floor, using their coats as bedding. The women cooked thick buckwheat porridge. Levitan would arrive with buns and sausages. In the evenings, Levitan returned to Moscow with the female students. Those remaining played music, went for walks, talked and argued, and gently teased one another. In recollection, the experience became something magical. "The breath of something divine touched everyone," wrote Sizov. "We were struck by the harmony and beauty of nature. The languid spring twilight enchanted the agitated soul."[13]

One warm evening Levitan stayed longer than usual, eager to show his students a natural phenomenon that had long fascinated him—the springtime mid-air mating dance of the male woodcock. He even used it as a motif for a pastel he completed later in the year. Wearing high boots, a soft black cap, and using a thick walking stick, Levitan walked briskly ahead of his students in spite of his poor heart. They reached the edge of a pine forest near a swamp. He asked the students to lie down under a large tree and to remain quiet, expecting to see a woodcock dart above the tree tops and start his dance. They heard a mysterious sighing and gurgling coming from the swamp, but saw no birds. Still, as Sizov put it, lying there in the stillness they became "drunk with the poetry of the spring twilight." Lipkin recalled that they felt a sense of renewal "as if we had drunk down birch sap by the glass or bathed in the cold water of a forest spring on a hot day." This exalted, meditative state remained all the way back to the train station. Levitan turned to his students and said, "How I envy you your youth! If only we could join together my life's experience and your youth!"

One day Lipkin had a long conversation with Levitan during a train ride from Moscow to the dacha. The student told his teacher that he dreamed of making monumental paintings and frescoes. He was most likely inspired by the commission undertaken by Nesterov and Vasnetsov to paint the interior of the newly completed Cathedral of St. Vladimir in Kiev. Levitan, aware of his friend Nesterov's frustration with the meddling that accompanied the commission, was frank in his advice to Lipkin:

> There's no demand for wall painting. We're not living in the Renaissance. Maybe someday there will be and possibly you'll live to see that day, but I won't. Of course there are churches, but you have to be religious like Nesterov, Vasnetsov. You'll likely need to be able to satisfy priests and their tastes, as the Italians were able to. I saw a contemporary wall painting in Paris: Puvis de Chavannes—it was such crap. My advice is stick to landscapes. They're more reliable. Otherwise you'll have to decorate merchant residences in baroque or renaissance styles, taking into consideration their taste and the architectural layout and who knows what else. Then, say goodbye to creativity, nature, and your own inimitable art. Unless you're just interested in money—that's another matter. Of course, painting in Russia won't buy you a house and you may have to go hungry.[14]

Before the spring weather peaked, Levitan became too ill to continue his visits to the dacha at Kuskovo. On April 22 he wrote his students that he wasn't feeling very well: "I'm unable to come again as I hoped. I suggest you continue to work on your own. I have only one thing to say in farewell: more love, more bowing down to nature and paying attention, endlessly paying attention." He told them he was sure that they would be able to work together again in the fall. Lipkin decided to visit Levitan in his studio. Too weak to get up as Lipkin walked into the room, Levitan sat sadly looking at a group of children playing outside his window. To lighten the mood, Lipkin joked that perhaps Levitan should get married so that he would have a helpful mistress and some little "Levitanchiki" in the house. Levitan laughed, "Women bring their own female rhythm into life, and it's not so simple. It's better this way, alone, am I not right? As for children," he added, growing a little quieter, "these little kids are nice from a distance, but when they shout and eat right in front of you day and night, my head would swell up."[15]

Feeling extraordinarily tired, Levitan wrote to Sredin in Paris that he had again put off traveling to Europe. In response to Sredin's question about "what's happening in artistic Russia," Levitan wrote: "actually very little besides intrigue, spite, and misunderstanding!" He was referring to the controversies surrounding the World of Art movement, which he continued to view sympathetically: "Apparently a new artists' society is being formed from Diaghilev's circle (it's the most comforting thing that's happened recently). Its members will be Serov, Trubetskoy, Korovin, me, and many other people who for now haven't yet completely ossified."

In early May, Levitan left for the summer to go to a place he found in the village of Okulovka near Novgorod. As soon as he settled in, Turchaninova came to visit him for a week. He hoped to resume painting, but by mid-summer his melancholia returned. Pereplyotchikov also came to see him, and while taking a walk together, Levitan grieved that he was no longer able to hunt. "It's obvious that I will die soon," he told Pereplyotchikov and fell to the ground sobbing.[16] On July 13 Levitan wrote to Karzinkina, who was now married to Teleshov: "As you can see, the devil has brought me to Novgorod province. Such depression that you just want to lie down and die. There's no one to say a word to. I'm not working at all and am almost in no condition to read. Wonderful, isn't it?! My health is tolerable. I still don't know whether I'll be going abroad. We worked with students in the spring. I think I was helpful to them." Levitan saw Teleshova (formerly Karzinkina) infrequently. She had heard that he was offended by not being invited to her wedding. She herself was in poor health and had written Levitan with questions about his treatment regimen at Bad Nauheim, where she was considering going.

Levitan's sister Tereza continued to ask for money and favors. On May 7 he had sent her 15 rubles claiming that he could not send more because he was still planning to go abroad. In August she asked him to help someone get permission to legally reside in Moscow. Her presumptuousness irritated him: "You must think of me as all-powerful to be able to set up F. to live in the very same Moscow where seven or eight years ago I was almost forced to leave because of my difficulty in obtaining the right to settle! Even though I was a relatively well-known artist!"

With Chekhov spending most of his time in Yalta, Levitan kept up with him through occasional visits to Maria in her Moscow apartment. In August Chekhov finally sold Melikhovo. When Knipper dropped in after rehearsals on August 27 to see Maria, she was hosting Lika, Levitan, and Maria Malkiel, Maria Chekhova's wealthy new friend who had been Teleshova's schoolmate. A vestige of the old circle of romantic rivals was still intact. Chekhov wrote to Lika asking if she was seeing Levitan. He also wrote a flirtatious letter to Malkiel telling her that he had converted to Islam and joined a Tatar tribe in the village of Autka near Yalta, where his new home was located. Continuing in the same vein, he sent heartfelt greetings to Malkiel and her sister Sophia, hoping "that both of you join the harem of someone famous who is just as handsome as Levitan." According to Teleshova, Sophia was in fact deeply infatuated with Levitan.

True to his promise, Levitan rejoined his students in the fall and rented another dacha to be used as a studio, this time at Novo-Gireevo. He observed and commented as his students sketched the autumn landscape. On the grounds, the leaves had mostly fallen from an alley of lime trees; the flower bed had gone to seed; and sometimes in the mornings patches of melting snow lay on the fences and nearby rooftops. Writing to Sredin in December and again apologizing for never having "flitted off abroad" to visit him in Paris, Levitan confessed that "the school has dragged me down, which I didn't expect." He continued to complain about the current art world. "In Moscow everyone is sleeping," he told Sredin, "or at least it seems that way to me. There was one exhibition of Moscow artists, nothing much, so-so." He was referring to an exhibition of watercolors, pastels, and drawings organized by the Moscow Society of Art Lovers. Levitan displayed four works in the exhibition, including *Twilight*, which belonged to a distant relative of Teleshova's, and *Autumn*, which Shekhtel had purchased. Levitan went on to more roundly criticize the St. Petersburg establishment:

> There was a competitive examination exhibition at the Academy, which I made a special trip to see. My impression is that the new Academy is more conservative than the old one. I'm beginning to think that in the Academy building itself there is a virus of routine and backwardness, and anyone who goes inside gets infected.

Toward the end of the year Levitan decided that he finally had the time and was healthy enough to see Chekhov in Yalta to celebrate Christmas and the dawn of a new century. A few days before his departure, he visited Maria. He had just been to a literary gathering where they had read "Lady with a Lapdog." Maria Drozdova reported to Chekhov that Levitan "talked a lot about you. He kept saying, 'Damn, how well Anthony wrote "Lady with a Lapdog"—just as well as I paint pictures.'"[17] He must have sensed the similarity of Gurov's reverie, as he sat silently on a bench in Oreanda high above Yalta with Anna Sergeevna by his side, to his own epiphanic sobbing when he had looked out for the first time from virtually the same spot in 1886. "Here was eternal beauty," he wrote Chekhov at the time. "Here was where man feels his complete insignificance! But what can words say?" For Levitan, only a picture could express his feelings, but now, reading "Lady with a Lapdog," Levitan understood that for Chekhov the words in his short story said as much as one of his own paintings:

Yalta was barely visible through the morning mist. White clouds hung motionless on the mountain tops. Not a leaf stirred in the trees, the cicadas chirped, and the monotonous, hollow roar of the sea, coming up from below, spoke of rest and the eternal sleep that awaits us all. It had roared like that down below when there was no Yalta or Oreanda, it was roaring now, and it will go on roaring as indifferently and hollowly when we are here no longer. And in this constancy, in this complete indifference to the life and death of each one of us, there is perhaps a hidden assurance of our eternal salvation, of the never-ending movement of life on earth, of its never-ending perfection. Sitting next to a young woman who looked so beautiful at the break of day, soothed and enchanted by the sight of this fairy-land scenery—the sea, the mountains, the clouds, the wide sky—Gurov reflected that, when you came to think of it, everything in this world was really beautiful, everything but our own thoughts and actions when we forget the higher aims of existence and of our own human dignity.

On December 24 Chekhov received the following telegram sent from Baydar near Sevastopol: "Expect the arrival today of the famous academician I. L."

Maria recalled that Christmas day that year in Yalta was warm, almost 60 degrees in the shade. She left the door to the balcony open and, wearing a white kerchief on her head and unbuttoning her coat, went for a walk with Levitan up into the hills above the house to do some sketching. "Passionate Levitan," as she called him, was physically no longer the same man who had long ago proposed to her on the path at Babkino. He quickly lost his breath and could not keep up. He would frequently stop, leaning on his cane, still determined to get to the top: "I so want to get up higher," he told her, "where the air is better and it's easier to breathe." She grabbed one end of his walking stick and pulled him uphill as he hung on to the other end. "Marie!" he called out, "I don't want to die! How my heart hurts and how terrifying it is to die!"[18] He managed to make a few studies—a rushing stream, an orchard in early bloom—both of which he called *Spring in the Crimea*.

In spite of his own serious illness, Levitan took upon himself the duty of enlivening his fellow invalid, who saw life in Yalta as a form of banishment. Maria noticed that when Levitan arrived, "Anton straightened up, got dressed up, and turned himself into an interesting man." For his part, Levitan was genuinely happy to be spending time with his old friend. "He's in a wonderful mood," Chekhov noted, "and drinks four cups of tea at a time." But Chekhov's own spirits would sink back into gloom. "Oh, you're such a misanthrope," Levitan told him.

The two men discussed the possibility of Levitan working on some illustrations for Chekhov's stories, which were being prepared for Marx's printing of his collected works. Levitan also toured Chekhov's newly completed home with its architect Lev Shapovalov. When they walked through Chekhov's study, Levitan saw that the architect had designed a cavity in the fireplace in the room. He enigmatically whispered to Shapovalov, "I'm going to make use of this cavity."[19] One day during his stay, Levitan was sitting on the couch in front of the fireplace while Chekhov paced around the room. Chekhov was telling Levitan how much he missed the landscape of northern Russia, how nature in the Crimea struck him as pretty but off-putting. He had said much the same thing to Lika after he arrived in Yalta in March 1894: "It's warm, light, the leaves are out, the sea looks summer-like, the young women thirst for passion, but still, the north is better than the south of Russia, at least in spring. Our northern nature is sadder, more lyrical, more Levitan-like. Here it's neither here nor there, like poetry that is good, rich-sounding, but cold."[20] Levitan decided to re-create a bit of northern Russia in Chekhov's study. He turned to Maria, who was also in the room, and asked her to bring him some cardboard. He cut a piece out of the board that fit the dimensions of the cavity in the fireplace, then took out his paints and started to draw. Within a half hour he was done and the painting was set in the cavity, where it remains today. Chekhov described the painting in a letter to Knipper: "Above my fireplace he drew a moonlit night during hay gathering. A meadow, hay stacks, a forest in the distance, and the moon reigning above everything." The sketch *Haystacks on a Moonlit Night* was very similar to a painting *Haystacks. Twilight* that he was preparing to submit to the next Itinerant exhibition, its motif a darker, more moody Russian variant of the haystacks Monet had painted in Giverny.

13

1900

"ONLY NOW DO I UNDERSTAND"

BY JANUARY 10, LEVITAN was back in "damn cold and miserable" Moscow. The stay in Yalta, much to his surprise, had renewed his desire to paint. It had also revived his affection for Chekhov, although, as before, he coated his feelings with sarcasm. While he felt inspired by the time spent in the Crimea, he told Chekhov not to take any credit for it: "You were a bad influence and corrupted me." He was now trying to find someone else to illustrate Chekhov's stories, but he had a hard time coming up with a suitable artist: "Pasternak is busy. Vrubel would be too wild for you."

Soon after Maria's return to Moscow, she and Knipper, who by now had become her friend, set about organizing a party celebrating Chekhov's birthday in absentia on January 17. Earlier that evening Maria accompanied Lika to see *The Seagull* again. Lika watched the performance in tears. "Her memories must have unrolled in front of her like a long scroll," Maria told her brother.[1] Afterward, Levitan joined the women at Maria's apartment. They sent a birthday telegram to Chekhov, congratulating him on the recent news that he had been named an honorary academician. It was a title of lesser distinction than the Academy membership awarded to Levitan, who could not resist the opportunity to needle Chekhov about it. When Chekhov wrote Levitan that he wasn't feeling well, Levitan replied: "I'm inclined to think that this fever of yours is the fever of narcissism—your chronic disease!" He attributed Chekhov's agitation to injured vanity, a result of not being considered a "real academician." Levitan relished the irony: "Here's your Achilles' heel—you unmasker of human weaknesses! My brother, how shameful. While I'm a simple academician, nevertheless I condescend to you, honorary academician, and reach out my hand to you. God be with you."

When Chekhov responded, tongue in cheek, that he felt thankful to be still thought of as his friend, Levitan played along: "If the tsars buy my painting now at the Itinerant exhibition, consider me good for ten pounds of caviar, and I'll throw into the bargain ten dozen condoms. You can debauch yourself to your heart's content."[2]

Levitan playfully noted the shared fame they had achieved, ending his February 7 letter with "Well, my dear, I warmly squeeze your hand, which has managed to soil such a heap of paper!" He signed the letter: "The greatest landscape painter in the universe, what do you think?" In his next letter, Levitan mentioned to Chekhov that everyone was talking about his latest story, "In the Ravine," which Levitan had not yet read: "They say that it is something of remarkable quality. Are you really capable of creating such works?" He joked that he had stopped reading the newspapers because he was tired of constantly seeing the name Chekhov: "No matter where you look, A. Chekhov is everywhere. The papers make me sick." Chekhov had his own issues with the Moscow newspapers. He complained that they were always making things up about him, that they reported conversations with people whom he had not even seen, and in one embarrassing incident quoted him referring to "the late Levitan" when he was still alive.[3] True to form, Levitan's goading also encompassed Chekhov's romantic interests. He told Chekhov that he had met the actress Maria Andreeva, Knipper's rival at the Moscow Art Theater: "She is ravishing and hates you. I have fallen madly in love." Levitan feigned that he was chasing Knipper as well: "I was at Masha's a couple of days ago and saw my sweet Knipper. I'm starting to like her more and more, since I've noticed an expected cooling toward the honorary academician."

Levitan was trying to talk Chekhov out of feeling trapped in the Crimea, far from his familiar world in Moscow: "Sweet one, you are miserable in Yalta, but it's also deadly miserable here. Everything is rosy only from a distance." Saying nothing about his own frail condition, he repeatedly asked Chekhov about his health, enclosing in one letter a clipping from a German magazine about treating tuberculosis. Now Levitan was the one lifting his friend out of a dark mood. "I'm thinking of going to Yalta in the spring," Levitan wrote him, "but, of course, I won't stay with that misanthrope Chekhov." He insisted that being miserable was pointless: "Take strength in the delights of mankind."

One of Levitan's recent delights was his growing interest in photography. He had previously used photographs as an aid to painting, relying on black and white images to capture the chiaroscuro of a motif, notably in the painting *March*.[4] Now he was intrigued by an invitation from the physicist Pyotr Lebedev to join him one evening in an auditorium at Moscow University to look at projected slides of landscape photographs taken by the naturalist

Kliment Timiryazev on several trips to the Baltic. Timiryazev had long been interested in landscape painting and especially liked the works of Turner that he had seen in England. Although Levitan showed signs of being visibly tired during the screening, he nevertheless asked to see some of the photographs several times. "He especially liked a picture taken on the shore of the Baltic Sea, toward evening, against the sun at the moment when the sun was obscured by a small, half-transparent cloud," recalled Timiryazev's son Arkady. "Levitan asked to see this picture three or four times, and each time admired the picturesque waves at the very edge of the shore."[5]

After this presentation, Levitan visited Timiryazev several times to talk about photography over evening tea. When the Timiryazev family dropped by Levitan's studio while he was out, they left behind a copy of Timiryazev's article "Photography and a Feeling for Nature," in which he argued that creative photography was a new and extraordinarily democratic art form that gave people who could not paint or draw a tool to express their feelings for nature.[6] Levitan felt bad that he had missed the opportunity to show them his work. He told Timiryazev that he read his article with great interest, that "there are strikingly deep theses in it. Your thought that photography heightens the sum of aesthetic pleasures is absolutely true, and the future of photography in this respect is enormous."

Levitan's embrace of the new was also reflected in his participation in the second World of Art Exhibition in St. Petersburg, which included eight of his paintings and twenty sketches. The press continued to heap abuse on Diaghilev's modernist tastes in art, and Levitan was not spared from this criticism. One Petersburg reviewer commented that in Levitan's paintings "the holy flame of talent has not yet gone out, but in every piece you feel how Mr. Levitan is trying to surrender to the sick tastes of a group of decadents."[7]

The World of Art exhibition was scheduled to close on February 26 with the Twenty-Eighth Itinerant Exhibition set to open the following day. Still straddling both movements, Levitan left for St. Petersburg on February 16. "I'm going to Peter today," Levitan wrote Chekhov. "I'm an agitated son of a bitch—my students are debuting at the Itinerant exhibition. I'm trembling more than I would for myself! Although you should be skeptical of the opinions of the majority, it's still damn awful!" In addition to the works by two of his students, the Itinerant exhibition included five Levitan landscapes, among them *Haystacks. Twilight.*

Nesterov arrived in St. Petersburg from Kiev on February 19. He understood that for Diaghilev the rivalry between the World of Art and the Itinerants was a war in which artists would eventually have to choose which side they were fighting on. Nesterov and Levitan had already agreed that when the time came, they would choose together. They both attended a meeting at the offices of the *World of Art* journal on February 24 to formalize the organizational basis for the following year's exhibition. Led by Diaghilev, the meeting participants, who also included Benois, Vasnetsov, and Serov, formally agreed to five paragraphs of rules governing future exhibitions.[8] The fourth paragraph explicitly dealt with the timing and duration of the 1901 exhibition in relation to the Itinerant exhibition. Nesterov later concluded that this rule forced them to become "turncoats," in effect stipulating "that we are obliged to display all our best work with Diaghilev and only rubbish at the Itinerant exhibition."[9] The same group of "turncoat" Moscow Itinerants attended a noisy luncheon that took place at the Little Yaroslavets Restaurant, a popular bohemian spot housed in a rose-colored building at the end of Bolshaya Morskaya Street by the arch opening out onto Palace Square. Jammed into the room was a mixed crowd of Moscow artists, St. Petersburg disciples of the painter Kuindzhi, World of Art members, and journalists sympathetic to one or another of the painters present.[10] Sitting next to Nesterov and Levitan, who seemed deep in thought as he sketched something in pencil, the landscape painter Arkady Rylov recalled that "our gathering had the appearance of some sort of conspiracy" against Diaghilev.[11] Most likely it was Nesterov, whom Rylov had just met for the first time, who groused to him about Diaghilev's imperious approach to reserving to himself the right to select works for exhibition based on his own taste.

During his stay in St. Petersburg, Levitan also attended a meeting of the Imperial Society for the Encouragement of Arts, which was hosting the Itinerant exhibition. There he met Ivan Lazarevsky, not yet twenty, who through his mother's connections with Grigorovich and Stasov, had just obtained a position as a secretary of the Society. In a recollection of the encounter written fifteen years later, Lazarevsky quoted Levitan extensively as someone now prepared to turn his back on the Itinerants.[12] Lazarevsky recalled hearing the critic Stasov criticize the value and importance of landscape painting, considering "grasses, clouds, and little streams" as of no benefit "aside from the decoration of God's mansion." Levitan told Lazarevsky that Stasov and the genre painters he supported "just barely have patience for me and several of my fellow landscape painter Itinerants." The Itinerant painter Karl Lemokh had commented, when looking at *Above Eternal Rest*, that it was a pity that so much canvas was wasted on a simple landscape.

According to Lazarevsky, Levitan felt passionately that Russian art was at a transitional point, turning away from the old traditions of the Itinerants to something new. He saw great significance in the artists and the educated public who were gathering around Diaghilev and the World of Art. "I am with them and for them with all my soul," he told Lazarevsky. "My sensibilities tell

me there will be much new genuinely Russian art that will come from them."
He could not wait for the end of the "Itinerants with their intentional art,
their unfailing theorizing, positivism, and moral instruction." For this reason,
Diaghilev felt that he could wrest Levitan away from the Itinerants. He wrote
to Ostroukhov, who had taken charge of Tretyakov's gallery after his death,
that Levitan "recently has come much closer to us and if he now still hasn't
left the Itinerants, it's simply a matter of his having delayed his departure for
a year. His bill with the Association has been settled."[13] Ostroukhov and the
Tretyakov's selection committee had just decided to buy Levitan's study *Gray
Day. Swamp*, which had been on display at the World of Art exhibition, for
200 rubles, and to also pay 600 rubles for the painting *Summer Evening*, which
was part of the Itinerant exhibition.

On February 29, Levitan took the overnight train back to Moscow, sharing
the same car with Lazarevsky. Neither one of them slept. They spent the journey
talking in the narrow corridor of the car. Levitan complained about being
at the mercy of patrons who provide support only because it is fashionable,
not because they have any understanding of art. The exception was Savva
Mamontov, who had a "colossal artistic sensitivity, a remarkable ability to
gather around himself virtually everyone of significance in the world of art,"
and whose fortunes were now collapsing after his arrest for embezzlement
associated with the building of the Yaroslavl railway. "You cannot imagine,"
Levitan told Lazarevsky, "how many people are now standing on firm legs
thanks only to the timely and wise, indeed wise help of the Mamontovs."
Levitan felt that the government, remembering what he had done for Russian
art, should come to the aid of Mamontov and not let him fall into bankruptcy.
The press was ignoring his plight, and Levitan felt too "uneducated" as a writer
to come to his defense. Late in the spring he did sign a joint letter with several
other prominent Moscow artists offering Mamontov encouragement in facing
his legal problems. Mamontov was acquitted of criminal charges; his case was
transferred to a civil court, which declared him bankrupt.

As dawn came and the two men looked out the window to admire the
Moscow countryside, Levitan told Lazarevsky that he had recently bought
a small landscape by Fyodor Vasiliev, who died in Yalta in 1873 at the age of
twenty-three. While in Yalta, Levitan had asked Chekhov to help him negotiate
the purchase of the painting. Levitan spoke warmly of Vasiliev's talent, saying he
was struck by his understanding of the beauty of Russian nature. This prompted
Lazarevsky to remark about how Levitan, "a member of another tribe," that is,
a Jew, could feel and understand Russian nature so well. This observation was
a commonplace in writings about Levitan, used either to confirm that it was
possible for a Jew to be a patriotic Russian expressing deep love for his native

region or more frequently, as was the case in Suvorin's anti-Semitic *New Times*, to bring attention to an inexplicable contradiction.[14] Levitan paused for a moment and replied to Lazarevsky, "You know what I'll tell you. It's possible that some of my landscapes of Russian nature came out successfully because I have had to suffer and endure many terribly difficult things. It seems to me that a cheerful person can't strongly feel Russian nature: in her there is so much melancholia, sad calmness, spiritual loneliness." With the self-consciousness of an assimilated Jew talking to a Russian, Levitan finished his thought, "Oh we Jews—not the ones who sit on gold sacks and, with fingers covered with valuable rings, clutch the throats of the poor—we Jews certainly understand and are close to Russian nature."

The day he returned to Moscow, Levitan wrote to Chekhov. The scuffle between the Itinerants and the World of Art was getting on his nerves. He told Chekhov, "I'm a tired son of a bitch and hate everyone, except you, of course, and the charming Knipper." As a brief respite, Levitan spent a few days near Podolsk at the estate of Nikolai Meshcherin, a factory owner who was an amateur painter and devotee of Levitan. Levitan painted one of his last studies there, a rare snowy landscape titled *The Beginning of March*.

Nesterov was back home in Kiev waiting to hear from Levitan. The Itinerant Association, having learned of the agreement signed by several of its members in Diaghilev's office, sent an inquiry, wanting to know the signatories' intentions with regard to the "affairs of the Association." Nesterov wrote his friend Alexander Turygin: "In short, a point-blank question, and since Levitan and I decided to act jointly, it means that we will have to *jointly leave* the Association." But Levitan telegraphed Nesterov asking him to await a letter from him. "In general," Nesterov told Turygin, "this whole matter has turned into a very awkward situation."[15] By April 7, Nesterov and Levitan finally made up their minds. They had decided to be "prudent." Nesterov wrote: "Having received an inquiry from Diaghilev asking 'How are things?' and his readiness *to do everything* to hold on to us, we decided to write the Association that we will stay with them under their previous conditions." Ostroukhov explained to Diaghilev: Levitan "hasn't come over to you. He is consciously remaining with the Itinerants. We talked for a long time about this. He wavered with great torment and decided what he decided."[16] Vasnetsov joined them in their decision. Nesterov was convinced that their decision would not unduly upset Diaghilev: "It's as if he's at war. For him all means are permissible. Unable to get us to fight against the Itinerants, he'll go on to other things." The next time Nesterov was in Moscow, he visited Levitan and they further discussed their decision: "It was clear we wouldn't fit into either camp. There was much that we didn't like about the Itinerants, and regarding Diaghilev, we were Muscovites and he was a Petersburger. Perhaps it was this, perhaps also something a bit harder to describe. It occurred to us that maybe we should break away from both factions and start one of our own and invite the more gifted of our young artists to join."[17] They had been attracted to the youthful enthusiasm of the World of Art, but in the end they rejected the World of Art group's overly refined Petersburg aesthetics. It was too superficial and soulless, giving off what Nesterov called "a surfeit of excessively successful Russianness, not unlike rosy or blue wigs." He concluded, "It's not what we were looking for in art."[18]

In spite of his poor health, Levitan maintained a consistent but reduced work routine. He usually painted no more than two or three hours in the early morning before eating breakfast. Among the unfinished works in his studio were ten sketches and two canvases for a panoramic motif titled *The Lake (Rus)*. The painting's subtitle, an archaic word for "Russia," implied that he consciously intended for the work to have a symbolic subtext, to be a visual testament of what Russia meant to him. In sketches for the painting he depicted the lake and sky under a variety of atmospheric conditions.[19] But in the larger canvases he settled on a radiant day with brilliant white cumulus clouds floating low over an expansive lake reflecting a deep blue sky and the green reeds in the foreground. On the high bank across the lake two distant clusters of churches and village homes glowed in the sunlight. Levitan, who throughout his life had so often fallen into depression and so often found a way to have nature reflect his melancholy, now near the end was giving expression to a landscape that evoked a feeling of joy. The work synthesized impressionistic intent and a sense of spiritual peace. And yet, the painting was unfinished. He lamented to his housekeeper, Nanny, that if he could only regain his health, he would paint in a totally different way: "Only now, when I have suffered so much, do I understand how to paint."[20] While he had rejected aligning himself exclusively with Diaghilev's World of Art, he was nevertheless becoming more receptive to the modernist aesthetic. When looking at a painting like *The Last Rays of the Sun* (1899), with its flat planes of muted colors moving toward abstraction, we can only imagine what direction Levitan's art would have taken had he lived another twenty years.

After breakfast Levitan typically went for a walk, frequently along Kuznetsky Bridge or to visit friends. His social circle now included the highest ranks of Moscow aristocracy. He attended an evening of drawing at the home of Prince Vladimir Golitsyn, the mayor of Moscow, and subsequently paid a visit to Vladimir von Meck, the art collector and patron, to encourage him to apply for membership in the Moscow Society of Art Lovers. At least once a week he went out to the dacha at Khimka where his students were working. In mid-April, as in previous years, Levitan began his annual search for a place in the country to sketch and paint. Langovoi recommended a dacha, but it involved riding twenty-five miles on horseback to get there, a proposition that scared Levitan. Serov's suggestion that he rent a dacha on the estate of his friend Vladimir Derviz in Tver province was more to his liking.

Early in the spring, Olga Knipper and Maria Chekhova, who were now spending a great deal of time together, went to see Levitan in his studio. For Knipper this first and last visit to the studio made such an indelible impression that in 1956, when she was eighty-eight years old, she chided Maria for not remembering the occasion. Knipper said that she "could not help but recall the stillness and the wonder of those few hours when he showed his paintings and studies." She found Levitan to be "extremely agitated" because of his heart condition, "pale, with burning, beautiful eyes." He showed them one of his *Moonlit Night* paintings and "spoke of the torments he experienced in the course of six years while he was unable to express on canvas a moonlit night in central Russia, its silence, its transparency, delicacy, the distance, the knoll, two or three tender birches."[21] Levitan often frustrated exhibitors with his reluctance to part with a painting that he felt was not ready to be shown. Once when Diaghilev tried to hurry Levitan to submit some paintings, Levitan replied: "To offer paintings for exhibition that I have not agreed to release—besides being no treasure for the exhibition—is a torment for me, especially because my motifs are very dear to me and it would cause me great suffering if I sent them off [prematurely]."[22]

On April 7, Knipper and Maria arrived together in Yalta in advance of the beginning of the Moscow Art Theatre's Crimean tour, which gave Chekhov the opportunity to see his plays without having to travel north. The company performed *The Seagull* and *Uncle Vanya* in repertory with Hauptmann's *Lonely People* and Gorky's *Song of the Hawk*.

In Moscow the weather remained bleak. Korovin bumped into Levitan, who was walking down Tverskaya Street; they had not seen each other for a long time. Korovin was shocked by the way Levitan looked, hunched over a cane: "His cheeks had sunken, and his eyes were lifeless."[23] Levitan still made his weekly visits to his students at Khimka. His rapidly declining health was apparent to them as well. Sizov could not help noticing the sadness in his eyes and how thin he had become. When something agitated Levitan, he drank Valerian out of a flask he carried with him. His visits had the air of a protracted farewell. Although he made it a practice never to touch his students' work, one day he added a bit to the sketch of a female student, and she preserved it as a keepsake. He took each of his students aside, talking with them for a long time and giving them advice, as if offering a final testament. One day he stayed longer than usual, working in the woods into the evening, and caught a cold.

The students talked him into going home. A few days later, Levitan sent his class a note: "I'm not completely well. It's likely that I will no longer be going to the dacha. I wish you all good work. Until fall, Levitan."

With Levitan confined to his bed, Turchaninova came from St. Petersburg to care for him. Warm spring weather returned to the North, and Chekhov's doctors allowed him to return briefly to Moscow. When he arrived, Maria told him about Levitan's illness. He looked in on his friend. It was apparent that Levitan was dying. Turchaninova begged Chekhov to do something to improve his condition, but Chekhov could do nothing. Beginning to feel feverish himself, he made plans to return to Yalta.[24] Before leaving Moscow, Chekhov and Knipper attended the Itinerant exhibition, which was at the end of its stay at the School of Painting. Here they looked at Levitan's *Haystacks. Twilight*, so similar to the picture rapidly sketched in Chekhov's study at Yalta. Some Moscow art critics, whose wrongheaded opinions Levitan so loved to read aloud to his students, mocked his restrained but unmistakable drift toward modernism. One paper said his haystacks "looked like something between the shaggy coiffure of a hairdresser and a bristling porcupine."[25]

As soon as Chekhov returned to Yalta, he wrote on May 20 to Knipper: "How is Levitan? Not knowing anything is tormenting me terribly. If you hear something, write me please." The day before, the Moscow *News of the Day* noted in its regular "Chronicle" column, "We've been told that the famous landscape painter I. I. Levitan is seriously ill." Responding to Chekhov's plea for more news, Turchaninova wrote him: "Anton Pavlovich, since your departure, every day his temperature goes up to 104, yesterday 106, a total decline. We're going completely out of our minds. Another doctor was brought in, who comes in the evenings [. . .]. Today his temperature dropped to 98. We breathed a sigh of relief, but toward evening it again went up. Something will happen. A feeling of terror creeps into my soul, but I refuse to become dejected. I don't believe that I won't find a way out." Maria replied to Turchaninova: "How awful for Levitasha. Antosha says he feels very bad."[26]

Teleshova came to visit Levitan. "He was very afraid of death," she recalled, "and at the same time completely unguarded." No longer able to go upstairs to his studio, he lay in a bed in his downstairs study. A constant stream of friends dropped by. His primary caregivers were Turchaninova and Nanny. According to Teleshova, Sophia Malkiel, still very much in love with Levitan, came every day, bringing him his favorite dish, which she had prepared for him. Teleshova thought about the remarkable connection between the Malkiel women and Levitan. When the youngest Malkiel sister and Teleshova were studying at the same gymnasium, Teleshova made an offhand comment about how poor Levitan was. And one of the older sisters replied, "Yes, mama paid for his school." Their mother was the secret benefactor who had come forward to pay Levitan's tuition in the late 1870s so that he could remain in the School of Painting.[27]

Knowing that he was dying, Levitan instructed his brother Adolph to burn all his correspondence. Rabbis were summoned to bless Levitan. They noticed that he wore a cross on his chest and asked him whether he wanted to be buried in a Jewish or Russian Orthodox cemetery. He answered, "I'm a Jew. Bury me in a Jewish cemetery." He explained that the cross was a gift from "a beloved woman."[28] On July 22 at 8:35 a.m. on a sparkling summer morning, Levitan died. He was thirty-nine years old. Korovin claimed that Levitan's last words were "Close the windows!" He was asked, "Why? The sun is shining." Levitan cried out, "Close them! The sun—it's an illusion!"[29] If Korovin's account is true, then there is heart-breaking pathos in Levitan's final words. He had succumbed to the existential dread so often expressed before in his bouts of melancholia. In his illness, he had come to hate the heat of the sun, and at the end, there was no solace to be found in the light that shone down upon the Russian landscape.

For the next three days his body lay in his studio apartment, where a steady procession of friends paid their respects. Ivan Gorelov, one of his students, sketched Levitan's face as he lay on his deathbed. To one visitor paying his respects it looked as if death had merely frozen his expression, "his peaceful, handsome profile looking as if it were carved from stone."[30] What struck Goloushev, as he looked at the emaciated body lying motionless in the silence of a late summer twilight, was that the room was filled with the scent of lilac, coming from the thick flowering bushes surrounding the house.[31]

Levitan's funeral was held on July 25 in the Jewish section of Dorogomilovskoe Cemetery on the banks of the Moscow River at the western edge of the city. The weather was very warm and only a few dozen people accompanied the body from the studio on Tryokhsviatitelsky Lane. They included his fellow artists Serov, who had come from abroad to attend, Vasnetsov, Korovin, Vrubel, Ostroukhov, Pasternak, and Pereplyotchikov. Also in attendance were students and faculty of the School of Painting. Those who spoke at the graveside included the school's director, Alexei Lvov, and Konstantin Bykovsky, the president of the Moscow Society of Art Lovers.[32] One of Levitan's students recited a poem dedicated to his memory. The last to speak was Samuel Vermel in his capacity as a board member of Moscow's Jewish congregation. His eulogy focused on the significance of Levitan's request to be buried in a Jewish cemetery: "With pride we announce: Isaac Ilich Levitan is ours. In his brief but productive life he devoted himself to Russian art, to the spiritual interests of Russia, but he is a son of our people." To those who expressed surprise that someone who emerged from "the dark alleys of our shtetl towns [. . .] turned out to be an interpreter and poet of Russian nature," Vermel responded, "I will say that in his works one feels that eternal sadness, that sense of longing that the long-suffering Jewish heart has carried within itself for centuries." To those who were dismayed that non-Russian blood flowed in the veins of this Russian artist, Vermel maintained: if Russian blood had flowed in Levitan's veins, he would not have been the kind of Russian artist he was.[33]

The argument over whether it was rightful to claim Levitan as a Jewish painter, a Russian painter, or both, which began while he was alive, continued long after his death. Vermel's belief that "Levitan was a Jew from head to toe, that he loved his people, shared their joys and sorrows," did not sit well with Goloushev, who wrote in his 1913 biography: "This is hardly the case. Levitan never hid his Jewishness, but was quite indifferent to it." Goloushev allowed that a certain Jewish sorrow was reflected in Levitan's works, but it was only a "minor chord" not that dissimilar to the native dolefulness found in Russian landscapes. He insisted that Levitan had become a completely assimilated Russian: "It isn't their fault that Jews have to be reminded so often of their nationality. But those who have grown up surrounded by Russian nature and Russian life are often just as genuinely Russian as the most native Great Russian. One especially sensed this in Levitan."[34]

On Levitan's grave were wreaths from the Itinerant Society, the publishers of the *World of Art*, the School of Painting, and the Moscow Society of Art Lovers. The only relative present was his brother Adolph. Their sister Tereza could not afford to travel to Moscow to attend.[35] Nesterov was abroad attending the Paris International Exhibition. He noticed black crepe draped around one of the four Levitan paintings hanging in a corner of a dark hall where the Russian section was housed. He raced to the exhibition's offices where he found out that they had received a telegram that Levitan had died.

A few months later Diaghilev visited Levitan's apartment to take a look at the unfinished paintings and sketches still standing in the studio. He and his World of Art colleagues were planning a posthumous exhibition. The house was otherwise empty, the windows open. From the silence of the studio he could hear the birches swaying in the wind outside. He soon afterward wrote an appreciation of Levitan in the *World of Art*, lamenting that the painter had died for the most part unrecognized and misunderstood both in Russia and in Europe. He used the occasion to firmly place Levitan in his own camp of Euro-centric artists who had rejected the tired-out realists "with their woodland scenes of bears jumping over logs or phony looking waves crashing in the sea." Setting aside the question of whether Levitan was a Jew or a Russian, for Diaghilev, Levitan was a European painter: "In his outward manner of living, organizing himself, and working, Levitan was not a person in the Russian mold." His focus and concentration, along with his regular work habits, set him apart from most Russian painters.[36] The posthumous exhibition took place in St. Petersburg and Moscow in 1901. On display were 146 works from private collections and those left in his studio, including, for the first time, *The Lake (Rus)*.

Chekhov too felt it was a shame how little people valued Levitan's work. When the writer Mikhail Pervukhin visited Chekhov in Yalta and they stood together in his study looking at Levitan's sketch tucked above the fireplace, Chekhov said to him: "He was such an enormous, unique, and original talent. There is something so fresh and strong that it should have started a revolution. Yes, Levitan died much, much too early."[37]

Diaghilev was convinced that no one was in a better position to write about Levitan than Chekhov. On July 24, he wrote to Chekhov, informing him that he was planning a special issue of the *World of Art* devoted to Levitan and asking him to contribute a recollection: "Say something amicable about him . . . Not much, but it should be something written with love."[38] After additional prodding, Diaghilev was thrilled to receive a letter from Chekhov in the fall of 1900 finally offering to write something. Chekhov promised to send Goloushev, who worked on the staff of the *World of Art*, the beginning of a reminiscence called the "Woodcock Mating Dance." It was to be a description of the hunt by Chekhov and Levitan in the early spring of 1892 in the vicinity of Davydov Monastery near Melikhovo that ended with Levitan begging his friend to put a wounded bird out of its misery. Diaghilev wrote back to Chekhov on October 2 delighted by the offer: "I thank you deeply for your promised article about poor, dear Levitan, memories of whom are still so painful and so precious."[39] Diaghilev even agreed to delay publication of the issue to accommodate Chekhov. But Chekhov continued to put off working on the piece, in spite of other entreaties from Serov and the poet Konstantin Balmont. More than a year later, on December 20, 1901, Chekhov again responded to Diaghilev's repeated requests: "You would like me to say a few words about Levitan, but I don't want to just say a few words, but rather a lot. I'm not rushing because it will never be too late to write about Levitan. I'm not well now. I'm sitting with a compress and have recently been spitting up blood." Filosofov in his review of Vermel's *I. I. Levitan*, published in 1902, said that Chekhov, among several other friends, had an obligation to write his recollections of the artist.

But Chekhov never fulfilled this obligation. We can only guess why. He admired Levitan as an artist and praised his talents without qualification. But can we say, as Diaghilev did, that Chekhov, in fact, loved Levitan? Those who knew Chekhov well saw in him a man with a disarming, warm sense of humor and an artist with a penetrating, cold heart. Chekhov knew and understood Levitan's psychological problems. He disapproved of Levitan's sexual excesses, openly discussed how they had worn him down, and may have known that they ultimately caused his death. In the end, in being true to himself as an artist whose métier was the sometimes comic, sometimes tragic inability of humans to overcome their failings, perhaps Chekhov felt incapable of painting a portrait of Levitan that would be acceptable to those who were looking for an unalloyed eulogy. His health failing, Chekhov stopped responding to Diaghilev's requests. Two years later, in July 1904, Chekhov died in Badenweiler, a spa in Germany less than 200 miles from the salt baths at Nauheim, where Levitan had tried twice without success to find a cure for his worn-out heart.

EPILOGUE

BURNED LETTERS

TATIANA SHCHEPKINA-KUPERNIK, whose reputation as a writer and poet continued to grow in the early 1900s,[1] noted with some sympathy that Sophia Kuvshinnikova's social life never recovered its frisson after Levitan left her in 1894. In 1907 Sergei Goloushev published Kuvshinnikova's memoirs of Levitan, in which she portrayed herself as his devoted student, implicitly making it obvious that she traveled with him as his mistress, but refraining from expressing any bitterness about the end of their affair.

She died suddenly in August of that year. The *Russian Word* newspaper reported, "Her death was unexpected for everyone around her: the deceased was staying with friends on an estate on the Moscow-Kazan train line, became ill with dysentery, from which she died."[2] She became infected while caring for a woman painter who had come down with typhus. Embarrassed to be suffering from acute diarrhea while confined to a room next to that of several men, she refused to take the remedy prescribed by her doctor and soon died.[3] For those who knew her and the background to Chekhov's "The Grasshopper," her death was sadly ironic. For those who could never forgive Chekhov for caricaturing her in the story, the circumstances of her death strongly rebuked Chekhov for his unflattering portrait. She died performing an act of kindness that had more in common with the heroic death of Dymov, infected when treating a child with diphtheria, than with the fickle life of his wife, Olga Ivanovna.

When Anna Turchaninova moved to Paris in the 1920s to live with her daughters, she brought with her more than 200 letters from Levitan. Pavel Smelov, a visiting Leningrad artist, seeing that she intended to burn them, convinced her to give them to him to take back to the Soviet Union.[4] In the late 1930s Smelov decided to donate the letters to the manuscript division of the Russian Museum. But first he gave the letters to a woman acquaintance to be transcribed so that he would be able to retain for himself copies of everything. Before the typist was able to complete the task, she was arrested in the great purge of 1937 and disappeared into the gulag. In the early 1980s, the journalist Evgraf Konchin, assuming that the letters had been swept up by the NKVD together with the typist's other compromising papers, managed through his newspaper to submit a query to the KGB regarding whether they had a record of the seized letters. Konchin was summoned to a meeting at the KGB headquarters at the Lubyanka. After lengthy questioning about why he was interested in such letters, he was told that none were found in their archives.[5]

∾

In 1902, Adolph Levitan put up a headstone on his brother's grave at Dorogomilovskoe Cemetery with an inscription in Hebrew on one side and in Russian on the other side: "Here lie the remains of our dear brother Isaac Ilich Levitan. Born 18 August 1860. Died 22 July 1900. Peace be unto your remains." As executor, Adolph gathered together his brother's unfinished pieces and began selling them off. Some in Moscow art circles, with a whiff of anti-Semitism, accused Adolph of acting like a shopkeeper disposing of his brother's goods.[6] He had decided to expunge his celebrated brother from his life. Vladimir Von Meck, Morozov, and Troyanovsky agreed to submit Levitan works they owned to Diaghilev's posthumous exhibition, but on the condition that 20 percent of the money from the entrance fees would be set aside for his sister Tereza. Serov fretted to Diaghilev over how they should tell Adolph about this: "Should I or you write him. Apparently, this Adolph isn't the most pleasant fellow."[7]

During the war years and the revolution, Adolph disappeared from view, eventually moving to Yalta sometime in 1919 without taking a single painting by Isaac with him. For a while he headed a drawing school, and when that closed in 1927, he lived on a pension of forty rubles a month that just barely staved off starvation. He died in 1933, still refusing to talk to anyone about his brother and their family. When Maria Chekhova sent out a request to all of her brother's correspondents for letters to include in his first complete collected works, she received a curt response from Adolph, reminding her that she already knew he had none. He was deeply offended by what he perceived as malicious gossip about his motives in destroying his brother's letters: "The burning of the letters, as I already earlier related to you, was done by me while he was still alive by his order and before his eyes. It was done by me gladly, since I completely agreed with his decision and would have done the same again even now."[8]

Occasionally in the spring, Nesterov and his wife visited Levitan's grave, "a forgotten, modest black headstone." Together they removed the litter that had gathered at the site and put the grave back in order. Nesterov had accommodated himself to Soviet life, suppressing the religiosity of his art if not his Orthodox beliefs, turning quite successfully to portraiture. In his memoirs, published in 1941, he argued that it was time to move Levitan's remains to Novodevichy Cemetery to join those of Chekhov.[9] Nesterov may have already known about the plans to "liquidate" Dorogomilovskoe, both the Orthodox and the Jewish sections, as part a major reconstruction of Moscow that had started in 1935. Only the graves of well-known figures would be moved to other cemeteries. On April 22, 1941, Levitan's remains and headstone were moved to Novodevichy to a spot three rows away from Chekhov's grave. Nearby lies Elena Karzinkina (Teleshova) and her husband. Right next to Levitan is the grave of Tatiana Shchepkina-Kupernik, forever resting between the painter and Chekhov.

Maria Chekhova devoted the rest of her long life to meticulously preserving, enshrining, and sometimes censoring the work and personal effects of her brother. In June 1953 preparations were under way in Yalta for the celebration of Maria's ninetieth birthday. Evgeny Vorontsov, the director of the city's historical museum, came to see Maria at the "White Dacha," which in 1921 had been turned into a museum under her direction. He was collecting material to be included in a commemorative publication. It was a warm night and they sat down at a table on the second-floor balcony of the house. Pinot gris and chocolate were served. On the table lay two "treasured folders" of letters, including a pack from Levitan. She started telling Vorontsov about the time that Levitan proposed to her at the edge of the forest at Babkino, about how it had frightened and confused her. "Maria Pavlovna suddenly stopped," recalled Vorontsov. "There were tears glittering in her eyes . . . She had unexpectedly cut off her story, gathered herself, played with a medallion engraved with a flying seagull in her fingers, clinked glasses with me, and drank the remains of her pinot gris to the bottom." She gathered up Levitan's letters in a pile and tied them up with a blue ribbon. As they said goodbye, she kissed Vorontsov on the forehead, as was her custom, and said to him in a half whisper: "My dear

Evgeny Andreevich, don't even think of writing about this in your brochure. You are the first to hear me tell about this. I've shown Levitanushka's letters only to you . . . Don't tell anyone about it. When I die after the jubilee, you can carry on however you want." After she died four years later, only three letters from Levitan were found among her papers. She had destroyed the rest.[10]

NOTES

Notes to Introduction

1. A. A. Fedorov-Davydov, *Isaak Il'ich Levitan: Zhizn' i tvorchestvo, 1860–1900*, suppl. (Moscow: Iskusstvo, 1976), 7.

2. Stanislavskii to Chekhov, November 19, 1903. See K. S. Stanislavskii, *Sobranie sochinenii v vos'mi tomakh*, vol. 7, *Pis'ma: 1886–1917* (Moscow: Iskusstvo, 1960).

3. See Robert J. Niess, *Zola, Cézanne, and Manet: A Study of* L'Oeuvre (Ann Arbor: University of Michigan Press, 1968).

4. Iu. A. Koroleva, *Soprikosnovenie sudeb: A. P. Chekhov i I. I. Levitan* (Moscow: Gilios ARV, 2011), 7–8.

Notes to Chapter 1

1. A. P. Chekhov, *Polnoe sobranie sochinenii i pisem v tridtsati tomakh* [hereafter PSS Letters or PSS Works], ed. N. F. Belchikov et al., vol. 1, *Letters* (Moscow: Nauka, 1974–1983), 151–154. All quotes from Chekhov's letters are from this edition unless otherwise noted.

2. Isaak Levitan, *Pis'ma, dokumenty, vospominaniia* (Moscow: Iskusstvo, 1956), 156.

3. Ibid., 137–143.

4. See Benjamin Nathans, *Beyond the Pale: The Jewish Encounter with Late Imperial Russia* (Berkeley: University of California Press, 2002), 183; Leland Fetzer and Ita Sheres, "The Jewish Predicament of Isaak Levitan," *East European Jewish Affairs* 11, no. 1 (1981): 53–63.

5. Richard Stites, *Serfdom, Society, and the Arts: The Pleasure and the Power* (New Haven: Yale University Press, 2008), 326–327. See also Rosalind P. Blakesley, "Academic Foot Soldier or Nationalist Warhorse? The Moscow School of Painting and Sculpture, 1843–1861," in *From Realism to the Silver Age: New Studies in Russian Artistic Culture*, ed. Rosalind P. Blakesley and Margaret Samu (DeKalb, IL: NIU Press, 2014), 13–25.

6. N. A. Ezerskaia, *Peredvizhniki i natsional'nye khudozhestvennye shkoly narodov Rossii* (Moscow: Izobrazitel'noe iskusstvo, 1987), 24.

7. Elizabeth Valkenier, *Russian Realist Art, the State, and Society: The Peredvizhniki and Their Tradition* (Ann Arbor: Ardis, 1977), 33–40.

8. N. Dmitrieva, *Moskovskoe Uchilishche Zhivopisi, Vaianiia i Zodchestva* (Moscow: Iskusstvo, 1951), 95.

9. Levitan, *Pis'ma*, 302.

10. Ibid., 122.

11. Ibid.

12. A. P. Kuzicheva, *Chekhovy: Biografiia semi'i* (Moscow: Artist, rezhisser, teatr, 2004), 160.

13. See Valkenier, *Russian Realist Art*, 64–65; and Alfred J. Rieber, *Merchants & Entrepreneurs in Imperial Russia* (Chapel Hill: University of North Carolina Press, 1982), 168.

14. Levitan, *Pis'ma*, 122.

15. Ibid., 149.

16. RGALI, f. 791, Rukopis' Z. E. Pichugina, "I. I. Levitan (Iz moikh vospominanii)," 1940.

17. Konstantin Korovin, *Vospominaniia* (Minsk: Sovremennyi literator, 1999), 122.

18. Levitan, *Pis'ma*, 123.

19. Ibid., 147.

20. Ibid., 144.

21. Kuzicheva, *Chekhovy*, 157, 164.

22. Levitan, *Pis'ma*, 140.

23. Ibid., 156; and Evgeniia Sakharova, ed., *Vokrug Chekhova* (Moscow: Pravda, 1990), 323. Levitan's speech mannerisms were common to Russian Jewish households. Chekhov describes Susanna Moiseyevna in "Mire" (1886) as having "a mellow feminine voice with a guttural *r* which was not without charm."

24. Vladimir Giliarovskii, *Moskva i moskvichi* (Moscow: Astrel,' 2010), 170.

25. A. P. Chekhov, *Polnoe sobranie povestei, rasskazov i iumoresok v dvukh tomakh* (Moscow: Al'fa-Kniga, 2010), 1:127. All excerpts from Chekhov's short stories are translated from this edition unless otherwise noted.

26. PSS Works, 16:53–54.

27. Levitan, *Pis'ma*, 123.

28. M. V. Nesterov, *Davnie dni* (Ufa: Bashkirskoe knizhnoe izdatel'stvo, 1986), 414.

29. Christopher Ely, *This Meager Nature: Landscape and National Identity in Imperial Russia* (DeKalb, IL: NIU Press, 2009), 174–175.

30. Korovin, *Vospominaniia*, 89, 108, 135.

31. Ibid., 77.

32. Ibid., 77, 79–82.

33. See Fedorov-Davydov, *Isaak Il'ich Levitan*, 18.

34. Korovin, *Vospominaniia*, 191–197.

35. Rosamund Bartlett, *Chekhov: Scenes from a Life* (London: Free Press, 2005), 148.

36. Korovin, *Vospominaniia*, 86.

37. Konstantin Korovin, *Konstantin Korovin vospominaet* (Moscow: Izobrazitel'noe iskusstvo, 1990), 113.

38. Koroleva, *Soprikosnovenie sudeb*, 32.

39. Fedorov-Davydov, *Isaak Il'ich Levitan*, 18.

40. Korovin, *Konstantin Korovin vospominaet*, 377; and Konstantin Paustovskii, *Sobranie sochinenii v 9-ikh tomakh*, vol. 1, *Isaak Levitan* (Moscow: Khudozhestvennaia literatura), 535.

41. Korovin, *Vospominaniia*, 124.

42. In January of the following year Chekhov mentioned to Leikin that he had just treated Levitan's brother Adolph for a "mild psychosis," which he felt had in part been responsible for what Leikin considered the artist's "capricious" decision to leave *Fragments* for another publication. During the period that Chekhov wrote for *Fragments*, he worked more closely with Adolph, a regular contributor to the newspaper, than with Isaac. Chekhov praised Adolph's work to Leikin and pleaded his cause when Leikin was reluctant to give the artist a modest advance.

43. Chekhov had come to know the Kiselyovs through his brother Ivan, who taught school in Voskresensk, the town nearest Babkino. The Chekhov family started to spend their summers in Ivan's home, and when the lodger living in the Babkino dacha died in November 1884, Kiselyov offered it to Anton for the summer.

Notes to Chapter 2

1. For a detailed description of the Babkino estate, see N. V. Golubeva, "Vospominaniia ob A. P. Chekhove," *Literaturnoe nasledstvo* 68 (1960): 557–574.

2. Golubeva, "Vospominaniia," 558.

3. See Mikhail Chekhov, *Anton Chekhov: A Brother's Memoir*, trans. Eugene Alper (New York: Macmillan, 2010), 104; and M. P. Chekhova, *Iz dalekogo proshlogo* (Moscow: Gos izd-vo khudozhestvennoi literatury, 1960), 41.

4. Levitan, *Pis'ma*, 157.

5. Kay Redfield Jamison, *Touched with Fire: Manic-Depressive Illness and the Artistic Temperament* (New York: Free Press, 1993). See Jamison's descriptions of cyclothymia, 105, 129, 264.

6. Mikhail Chekhov, *A Brother's Memoir*, 111.

7. Levitan, *Pis'ma*, 157–158.

8. According to Donald Rayfield, Chekhov took Markova's virginity. *Anton Chekhov: A Life* (New York: Henry Holt and Company, 1998), 107.

9. Korovin, *Vospominaniia*, 91–92.

10. Levitan, *Pis'ma*, 154.

11. V. A. Simov, in *A. P. Chekhov v vospominaniiakh sovremennikov* (Moscow: Gos. izd-vo khudozhestvennoi literatury, 1947), 100–102.

12. PSS Works, 17:146.

13. Ibid., 177.

14. Korovin, *Vospominaniia*, 77.

15. Fedorov-Davydov, *Isaak Il'ich Levitan*, 56.

16. As Deborah Hayden has written, when making a retrospective diagnosis of syphilis "the zeal for accumulating clues must be balanced by caution," since syphilis and other conditions often shared the same symptoms. In Levitan's case, the circumstantial evidence is compelling, particularly his cause of death, but not definitive. See Deborah Hayden, *Pox: Genius, Madness and the Mysteries of Syphilis* (New York: Basic Books, 2003), especially the chapter "Detective Zeal: The Fragile Art of Retrospective Diagnosis," 60–68.

17. A portion of this letter, published in *Levitan*, p. 25, was censored. Quoted from the original in RGALI, 549-1-302. Levitan goes on to say, apparently in response to something that Chekhov said or wrote to him, that it's a bald lie that his dog Vesta had been "fucking around," and that it was just "philistinism" to use such a vulgar expression.

18. PSS Letters, 2:242.

19. The difference in the two writers' narrative techniques is evident when comparing "The Huntsman" with Turgenev's sketch "Meeting," which has a virtually identical plot: the peasant girl Akulina has a meeting in the forest with Victor, a dandified valet who is about to leave for Europe with his master. She's in love with him and desperately seeking some sign of affection; he's content to dally with her while making it clear that he, given his presumed superior status, could not possibly marry her.

20. Levitan, *Pis'ma*, 158.

Notes to Chapter 3

1. A. M. Turkov, *Levitan* (Moscow: TERRA, 2001), 79.

2. S. S. Goloushev [Glagol' i Grabar'], *Levitan, zhizn' i tvorchestvo* (Moscow: Izda-tel'stvo I. Knebel', 1913), 41.

3. Levitan, *Dokumenty, materialy, bibliografiia* (Moscow: Iskusstvo, 1966), 32. Al-exander Stepanovich Prugavin is mistakenly identified as D. I. Prugavin.

4. Rosamund Bartlett, *Tolstoy: A Russian Life* (New York: Houghton Mifflin Har-court, 2011), 290.

5. Tretyakov Archives: 73-222, "Tolstoi i Levitan," typescript, August 9, 1911.

6. Goloushev, *Zhizn' i tvorchestvo*, 41.

7. Levitan, *Pis'ma*, 124.

8. Rayfield, *Chekhov*, 121.

9. Dunya Efros later married the lawyer and publisher Efim Konovitser, left Russia after the 1917 revolution, lived in Paris, was taken from a nursing home by the Nazis, and died at the Treblinka concentration camp in 1943.

10. Levitan, *Pis'ma*, 255.

11. Rayfield, *Chekhov*, 129–130.

12. Manuscript Division of the Russian State Library (hereafter cited as RGB), 331-63-25a.

13. Ibid.

14. RGB, 331-49-24a.

15. PSS Letters, 1:447.

16. M. P. Chekhova, *Iz dalekogo proshlogo*, 40; Mikhail Chekhov, *A Brother's Memoir*, 108.

17. Goloushev, *Zhizn' i tvorchestvo*, 35.

18. Levitan, *Pis'ma*, 124.

19. Ibid., 255.

20. Koroleva, *Soprikosnovenie sudeb*, 362.

21. See PSS Works, 5:648. The references are to the landscape painters Ivan Shish-kin and Arkhip Kuindzhi, the genre painter Vladimir Makovsky, and his brother Konstan-tin Makovsky who had recently had an exhibition in which some of the portraits were of his rather beautiful wife. Ilya Repin's realism was sometimes criticized as excessive.

22. Sakharova, *Vokrug Chekhova*, 324.

23. Mikhail Chekhov, *A Brother's Memoir*, 109.

24. Kuzicheva, *Chekhovy*, 345.

25. Sakharova, *Vokrug Chekhova*, 324–325.

26. Different parts of this letter are quoted in Leo Iakovlev, *Anton Chekhov: Roman s evreiami* (Kharkov: RA-Karavella, 2000), 25; Helena Tolstoy, "From Susanna to Sarra: Chek-hov in 1886–1887," *Slavic Review* 50, no. 3 (Fall 1991): 593; and PSS Letters, 1:521–522.

27. PSS Letters, 1:523.

28. See Iakovlev, *Anton Chekhov*, ch. 2, *Tina dnei*, 18–31; and Tolstoy, "From Su-sanna to Sarra," 590–600.

29. Chekhov again uses the slur about garlic in his play "Ivanov," written a year lat-er. In the first version of the play, Ivanov's anti-Semitic uncle Nikolai Shabelsky complains about how Anna Petrovna plays the piano: "A Semitic guttural touch, you can smell the gar-lic in it a mile off." Chekhov deleted this in the final version, but in Act II of that version he

keeps what the old woman Avdotya Nazarovna says about Ivanov and his wife: "sometimes he locks her up in the cellar with 'Eat your garlic, you so-and-so . . .' She eats it and eats it until she starts to stink from the inside out."

30. Tolstoy, "From Susanna to Sarra," 594.

31. Chekhov, *Literaturnoe nasledstvo*, 275–276.

Notes to Chapter 4

1. Levitan, *Pis'ma*, 164.

2. Christopher Ely, "The Origins of Russian Scenery: Volga River Tourism and Russian Landscape Aesthetics," *Slavic Review*, 62, no. 4 (Winter 2003): 666–668.

3. Levitan, *Pis'ma*, 30.

4. Evgraf Konchin, *Zagadochnyi Levitan: Izbrannye stat'i, poiski, nakhodki, gipotezy, problemy* (Moscow: Mediastudiia Respekt, 2010), 36.

5. Levitan, *Pis'ma*, 163.

6. Ibid., 29–30.

7. Golubeva, "Vospominaniia," 562.

8. Ibid., 566.

9. T. L. Shchepkina-Kupernik, *Vospominaniia* (Moscow: Zakharov, 2005), 179.

10. Mikhail Chekhov, *A Brother's Memoir*, 115.

11. Ibid.

12. Konchin, *Zagadochnyi Levitan*, 104.

13. Levitan, *Pis'ma*, 176.

14. Shchepkina-Kupernik, *Vospominaniia*, 178.

15. Kuzicheva, *Chekhovy*, 185.

16. RGALI, 1949-1-302.

17. Levitan, *Pis'ma*, 166.

18. Ibid., 167.

19. Ibid.

20. Ibid.

21. Ibid., 168.

22. Goloushev, *Zhizn' i tvorchestvo*, 52.

23. Ibid., 53

24. Korovin, *Vospominaniia*, 139.

25. Levitan, *Pis'ma*, 260.

26. Ibid., 168.

27. Quoted from Carolina de Maegd-Soep, *Chekhov and Women: Women in the Life and Work of Chekhov* (Columbus: Slavica Publishers, 1987), 111.

28. RGB, 331-48-72; letter dated 15 [February] 1889.

29. Levitan, *Pis'ma*, 145.

30. Ibid., 169.

31. Ibid., 170.

32. Chekhov, *Literaturnoe nasledstvo*, 581.

33. V. D. Polenov, *Pis'ma, dnevniki, vospominaniia* (Moscow-Leningrad: Iskusstvo, 1950), 236.

34. Ibid., 263.

Notes to Chapter 5

1. From the memoirs of N. M. Ezhov in *Letopis' zhizni i tvorchestva A. P. Chekhova 1889-aprel' 1891* (Moscow: Nasledie, 2004), 2:357.

2. See Giliarovskii, *Moskva i moskvichi*, 159–161.

3. Levitan, *Pis'ma*, 193.

4. Elizabeth Kridl Valkenier, "Opening Up to Europe: The Peredvizhniki and the Miriskusniki Respond to the West," in *Russian Art and the West: A Century of Dialogue in Painting, Architecture, and the Decorative Arts*, ed. Rosalind P. Blakesley and Susan E. Reid (DeKalb, IL: NIU Press, 2007), 50.

5. Alison Hilton, "The Impressionist Vision in Russia and Eastern Europe," in *World Impressionism: The International Movement, 1860–1920*, ed. Norma Broude (New York: H. N. Abrams, 1990), 399.

6. See Fedorov-Davydov, *Isaak Il'ich Levitan*, 116.

7. RGB, 331-49-25.

8. Quoted in Koroleva, *Soprikosnovenie sudeb*, 188.

9. Fedorov-Davydov, *Isaak Il'ich Levitan*, 120.

10. Koroleva says that Levitan refused to join Chekhov because he wanted to work on his Italian sketches and lacked the money to make the journey. See Koroleva, *Soprikosnovenie sudeb*, 104.

11. See Rayfield, *Chekhov*, 215.

12. Shchepkina-Kupernik, *Vospominaniia*, 180.

13. Mikhail Chekhov, *A Brother's Memoir*, 151.

14. Anton Chekhov, *Sakhalin Island*, trans. Brian Reeve (London: Oneworld Classics, 2007), 121.

15. From the memoirs of N. M. Ezhov, *Letopis'*, 2:491.

16. *Perepiska A. P. Chekhova v trekh tomakh*, (Moscow: Nasledie, 1996), 2:280. All quotations from Mizinova's letters are from this volume unless otherwise indicated.

17. See Douglas Smith, *Former People: The Final Days of the Russian Aristocracy* (New York: Farrar, Straus and Giroux, 2012), 36, 44–45.

18. Fedorov-Davydov, *Isaak Il'ich Levitan*, 127.

19. P. Muratov, "Peizazh v russkoi zhivopisi," *Apollon*, no. 4 (1910): 13; see Valkenier, *Russian Realist Art*, 79.

20. Chekhov, *Chekhov v vospominaniiakh sovremennikov* (Moscow: Gelios ARV, 2005), 136.

21. Mikhail Chekhov, *A Brother's Memoir*, 171–172.

22. RGB, 331-48-72.

23. Levitan, *Pis'ma*, 171.

24. Mizinova's June 17, 1891, reply to Chekhov is not included in her published correspondence. Quoted in Rayfield, *Chekhov*, 250; Koroleva, *Soprikosnovenie sudeb*, 136; and *Letopis'*, 3:27–28.

25. Levitan, *Pis'ma*, 172.

Notes to Chapter 6

1. In Russian the story's title (*Poprygun'ia*) literally means "flitterer" or "fidgeter." Chekhov's readers would have recognized it as a reference to Krylov's fable "The Ant and

the Dragonfly," which begins *"Poprygun'ia strekoza . . ."* ("The flittering dragonfly . . ."). Krylov in turn borrowed the fable from La Fontaine's "The Ant and the Grasshopper." Lev Vygotsky in *Thought and Language* (MIT Press, 1986, pp. 221–222) states that Krylov changed La Fontaine's "grasshopper" to "dragonfly" in Russian to preserve the use of a feminine word to "symbolize a lighthearted, carefree attitude." While the recent Pevear-Volokhonsky translation of the story as "The Fidget" is the most literally accurate, I prefer to continue using "The Grasshopper," both because it has been the most commonly published title and because for English readers it preserves the familiar reference to La Fontaine's and Aesop's fables.

2. Chekhov, *Perepiska A. P. Chekhova*, 2:77.

3. See Hans Rogger, *Russia in the Age of Modernisation and Revolution, 1881–1917* (London and New York: Longman, 1983), 63–64; and Theodore H. Von Laue, *Sergei Witte and the Industrialization of Russia* (New York: Atheneum, 1974), 30–31.

4. Konchin, *Zagadochnyi Levitan*, 87.

5. Levitan, *Pis'ma*, 182–183.

6. M. V. Nesterov, *Iz pisem* (Leningrad: Iskusstvo, 1968), 58–60.

7. Chekhov, *Letopis'*, 3:188.

8. Koroleva, *Soprikosnovenie sudeb*, 240. She is quoting Rayfield ("Zhizn' Antona Chekhova"), who is in turn quoting Maria Chekhova.

9. Iu. A. Bychkov, *Prosto Chekhov* (Moscow: Muzei Cheloveka, 2008), 180.

10. H. Peter Stowall, *Literary Impressionism: James and Chekhov* (Athens: University of Georgia Press, 1980), 9. Stowall calls Levitan "a sort of unconsciously primitive impressionist," 48.

11. Chekhov, *Perepiska A. P. Chekhova*, 2:76.

12. See I. Tverdokhebov, "Darovityi iz dorovitykh . . ." (Zametka tekstologa i kommentatora) *Voprosy literatury*, no. 1 (1985): 174–175.

13. Konchin, *Zagadochnyi Levitan*, 29–30.

14. Levitan, *Pis'ma*, 170–171.

15. Ibid., 181.

16. Konchin, *Zagadochnyi Levitan*, 181.

17. Quoted in Rayfield, *Chekhov*, 277. Original letter is July 2, 1892.

18. Levitan, *Pis'ma*, 174.

19. Goloushev, *Zhizn' i tvorchestvo*, 80.

20. Margarita Lobovskaia, "Putovoditel' po evreiskoi Moskve," *Evrei v Moskve: istoricheskii ocherk*, http://libatriam.net/read/307322.

21. S. S. Vermel', *Moskovskoe izgnanie, 1891–1892 gg.: Vpechatleniia, vospominaniia* (Moscow: Izdanie avtora, 1924), 35.

22. Ibid., 38.

23. Goloushev, *Zhizn' i tvorchestvo*, 80.

24. Vermel', *Moskovskoe izgnanie*, 36.

Notes to Chapter 7

1. Levitan, *Dokumenty, materialy, bibliografiia*, 8–9.

2. D. L. Podushkov, *Chekhov i Levitan na Udomel'skoi zemle* (Tver': SFK-ofis, 2010), 9.

3. Ibid., 11.

4. Levitan, *Pis'ma*, 171.

5. Podushkov, *Chekhov i Levitan*, 13.

6. See Fedorov-Davydov, *Isaak Il'ich Levitan*, 171.

7. Levitan, *Pis'ma*, 185.

8. Chekhov, *Chekhov v vospominaniiakh sovremennikov*, 457.

9. Ibid., 458.

10. RGALI, 1949-1-6.

11. Rayfield, *Chekhov*, 301.

12. RGALI, 571-1-1204.

13. Shchepkina-Kupernik, *Vospominaniia*, 211.

14. Chekhov, *Perepiska A. P. Chekhova*, 2:389.

15. Levitan, *Pis'ma*, 106.

16. Ibid., 175.

17. Ibid., 164.

18. Rayfield, *Chekhov*, 309.

19. Levitan, *Pis'ma*, 184.

20. RGB, 331-95-2.

21. M. G. Litavrina, *Iavorskaia, bezzakonnaia kometa* (Moscow: MIK, 2008), 43–44. Also see Rayfield, *Chekhov*, 314.

22. Rayfield, *Chekhov*, 322.

23. Chekhov's letter to Surovin on June 12, 1894, was excluded from the letters in PSS. It was published in Igor' Sukhikh, *Chekhov v zhizni* (Moscow: Vremia, 2010), 245–246.

24. Shchepkina-Kupernik, *Vospominaniia*, 181.

25. Levitan, *Dokumenty, materialy, bibliografiia*, 50.

26. T. L. Shchepkina-Kupernik, "Starshie," in Podushkov, *Chekhov i Levitan*, 105–119.

27. Shchepkina-Kupernik, *Vospominaniia*, 228.

28. Ibid., 183.

29. Chekhov, *Perepiska A. P. Chekhova*, 2:322.

30. Rayfield, *Chekhov*, 336.

31. Shchepkina-Kupernik, *Vospominaniia*, 227.

Notes to Chapter 8

1. Shchepkina-Kupernik, *Vospominaniia*, 228.

2. Rayfield, *Chekhov*, 337.

3. Ibid., 338.

4. RGB, 331-93-80.

5. Koroleva, *Soprikosnovenie sudeb*, 249.

6. Shchepkina-Kupernik, *Vospominaniia*, 198.

7. Chekhov, *Perepiska A. P. Chekhova*, 2:393.

8. Ibid., 393.

9. P. E. Chekhov, *Melikhovskii letopisets: Dnevnik Pavla Egorovicha Chekhova* (Moscow: Nauka, 1995), 102.

10. Rayfield, *Chekhov*, 331.

11. RGALI, 571-1-1137.

12. Rayfield, *Chekhov*, 343.

13. PSS Letters, 6:389.

14. M. P. Chekhova, *Pis'ma k bratu A. P. Chekhovu* (Moscow: Gos. izd-vo khudozhestvennoi literatury, 1954), 31.

15. Ibid., 30. Maria Chekhova erroneously dates her letter January 9, but her mention of the neighbor's fire at Melikhovo and her father's diary entry confirms that the letter was written February 9.

16. S. Prorokova, *Levitan* (Moscow: Molodaia gvardiia, 1960), 160.

17. Valkenier, *Russian Realist Art,* 131.

18. Podushkov, *Chekhov i Levitan,* 30.

19. Levitan, *Pis'ma,* 261–262.

20. Mikhail Chekhov, *A Brother's Memoir,* 116.

21. M. P. Chekhova, *Iz dalekogo proshlogo,* 44.

22. Koroleva, *Soprikosnovenie sudeb,* 259.

23. Levitan, *Pis'ma,* 262.

24. Leonid Grossman, "Roman Niny Zarechnoi," *Prometei* 2 (1967): 248.

25. Grossman quotes the critic N. E. Efros in "Roman Niny Zarechnoi," 258.

26. PSS Works, 13:357–359.

27. Podushkov, *Chekhov i Levitan,* 38.

28. Chekhov, *Perepiska A. P. Chekhova,* 2:331.

29. PSS Works, 13:361.

30. Chekhov, *Perepiska A. P. Chekhova,* 2:298.

31. Grossman, "Roman Niny Zarechnoi," 241.

32. Podushkov, *Chekhov i Levitan,* 123–124.

33. Levitan, *Pis'ma,* 263.

34. Shchepkina-Kupernik, *Vospominaniia,* 211–212. See also Rayfield, *Chekhov,* 355.

Notes to Chapter 9

1. Konchin, *Zagadochnyi Levitan,* 31.

2. Goloushev, *Zhizn' i tvorchestvo,* 94.

3. V. F. Kruglov, *Isaak Levitan* (St. Petersburg: Zolotoi vek, 2012), 175.

4. Averil King, *Isaak Levitan: Lyrical Landscape* (Suffolk, England: Antique Collectors' Club, 2011), 102.

5. Sjeng Scheijen, *Diaghilev: A Life,* trans. Jane Hedley-Prole and S. J. Leinback (London: Profile, 2009), 66.

6. Ibid., 71.

7. See Janet Kennedy, "Closing the Books on Peredvizhnichestvo: Mir Isskustva's Long Farewell to Russian Realism," in Blakesley and Samu, *From Realism to the Silver Age,* 141–151.

8. Koroleva, *Soprikosnovenie sudeb,* 287.

9. King, *Isaak Levitan,* 118.

10. Alla Gusarova, *Konstantin Korovin* (Moscow: Tret'iakovskaia Galereia, 2012), 25.

11. Tretyakov Gallery Archives, 73–36.

12. Kruglov, *Isaak Levitan,* 183.

13. See http://levitan-world.ru/levitan-letters13.php.

14. A. P. Chekhov, *Perepiska s zhenoi* (Moscow: Zakharov, 2003), 596.

15. Kruglov, *Isaak Levitan,* 176.

16. Ibid.

17. Prorokova, *Levitan,* 180. It's possible to place Levitan's collapse during the first

week in November because his letter to Alexander Lukin dated November 25 mentions that he "has been suffering from an ailing heart for the past three weeks."

18. Nesterov, *Iz pisem*, 114.
19. Rayfield, *Chekhov*, 402
20. Chekhov, *Perepiska A. P. Chekhova*, 2:328–331.
21. Rayfield, *Chekhov*, 409.
22. PSS Works, 17:223.
23. P. E. Chekhov, *Melikhovskii letopisets*, 169.

Notes to Chapter 10

1. Levitan, *Dokumenty, materialy, bibliografiia*, 55.
2. Scheijen, *Diaghilev*, 76–77.
3. Levitan, *Pis'ma*, 221.
4. Ibid., 266–267.
5. Rieber, *Merchants & Entrepreneurs*, 166.
6. PSS Works, 17:224.
7. Levitan, *Dokumenty, materialy, bibliografiia*, 11–12.
8. RGB, 331-63-25g.
9. Rayfield, *Chekhov*, 428.
10. Goloushev, *Zhizn' i tvorchestvo*, 71.
11. The connection between syphilis and aortic aneurysms first began to be recognized in the late 1880s. By the early 1900s, it was well established. See Henry H. Hazen, *Syphilis: A Treatise on Etiology, Pathology, Diagnosis, Prognosis, Prophylaxis, and Treatment* (St. Louis: C.V. Mosby Co., 1919), 211–219; also see Burton Peter Thom, *Syphilis* (Philadelphia and New York: Lea & Febiger, 1922), 383–387. For a current description, see "Syphilitic aneurysm of the ascending aorta," on the National Institutes of Health web site: http://www.ncbi.nlm.nih.gov/pmc/articles/PMC3279976.
12. Tretyakov Gallery Archives, 73-36.
13. Levitan, *Dokumenty, materialy, bibliografiia*, 56.
14. Ibid., 12.
15. RGB, 331-49-25b.
16. RGB, 331-49-25v.
17. PSS Letters, 7:404.
18. Levitan, *Dokumenty, materialy, bibliografiia*, 13.
19. Tretyakov Gallery Archives, 73-36.
20. Levitan, *Pis'ma*, 188.
21. Levitan, *Dokumenty, materialy, bibliografiia*, 13.
22. Rayfield, *Chekhov*, 434.
23. P. E. Chekhov, *Melikhovskii letopisets*, 197.
24. Levitan, *Dokumenty, materialy, bibliografiia*, 57.
25. Giliarovskii, *Moskva i moskvichi*, 166–167.
26. Levitan, *Pis'ma*, 227.
27. Ibid., 108–109.
28. Ibid., 279.
29. Levitan, *Dokumenty, materialy, bibliografiia*, 58.

Notes to Chapter 11

1. Bartlett, *Tolstoy: A Russian Life*, 368.
2. Scheijen, *Diaghilev*, 91.
3. Prorokova, *Levitan*, 208.
4. Tretyakov Gallery Archives, 73-36.
5. M. P. Chekhova, *Pis'ma k bratu A. P. Chekhovu*, 69.
6. Levitan, *Dokumenty, materialy, bibliografiia*, 14.
7. Rayfield, *Chekhov*, 456.
8. Konchin, *Zagadochnyi Levitan*, 294.
9. Portions of the July 5, 1898, letter were excised in PSS; RGB, 331-49-29v.
10. Levitan, *Pis'ma*, 272–273.
11. Koroleva, *Soprikosnovenie sudeb*, 323.
12. Levitan, *Pis'ma*, 207.
13. Ibid., 200.
14. Ibid., 212.
15. Ibid., 201.
16. Ibid., 200.
17. Ibid., 222.
18. Ibid., 208.
19. Ibid., 232.
20. Ibid., 207.
21. N. Dmitrieva, *Moskovskoe Uchilishche Zhivopisi, Vaianiia i Zodchestva* (Moscow: Iskusstvo, 1951), 141–142.
22. Levitan, *Pis'ma*, 219.
23. M. K. Tenisheva, *Vpechatleniia moei zhizni* (Leningrad: Iskusstvo, 1991), 162–163.
24. RGB, 331-49-25v.
25. S. P. Diaghilev and A. N. Benois, eds., *Mir iskusstva*, no. 2 (St. Petersburg: Izd. M. K. Tenishevoi i S. I. Mamontova, 1899), 37.
26. Nina Nenarokomova, *Pavel Tret'iakov i ego galereia* (Moscow: Art-Rodnik, 2011), 222.
27. Tenisheva, *Vpechatleniia*, 165.
28. RGB, 331-49-25v.
29. Rayfield, *Chekhov*, 464.
30. M. P. Chekhova, *Pis'ma k bratu A. P. Chekhovu*, 91.

Notes to Chapter 12

1. M. P. Chekhova, *Pis'ma k bratu A. P. Chekhovu*, 95.
2. Ibid., 136.
3. RGB, 331-49-25g.
4. Rayfield, *Chekhov*, 482.
5. Levitan, *Pis'ma*, 188.
6. Prorokova, *Levitan*, 206.
7. Ibid., 206–207.
8. Tenisheva, *Vpechatleniia*, 165.

9. Nesterov, *Iz pisem*, 138.
10. Levitan, *Pis'ma*, 210.
11. Ibid.
12. Ibid., 212.
13. Ibid., 229.
14. Ibid., 211.
15. Ibid., 211–212.
16. Goloushev, *Zhizn' i tvorchestvo*, 71.
17. PSS Letters, 8:600.
18. Goloushev, *Zhizn' i tvorchestvo*, 74.
19. PSS Letters, 8:610.
20. Chekhov, *Perepiska A. P. Chekhova*, 2:319.

Notes to Chapter 13

1. M. P. Chekhova, *Pis'ma k bratu A. P. Chekhovu*, 145.
2. RGB, 331-49-25g.
3. PSS Letters, 9:330.
4. Levitan, *Pis'ma*, 238.
5. V. A. Prytkov, *Chekhov i Levitan* (Moscow: Izd-vo Gos. Tret'iakovskoi galerei, 1948), 60.
6. Levitan, *Pis'ma*, 276.
7. Kruglov, *Isaak Levitan*, 240.
8. *Mir Iskusstva*, vol. 3, nos. 5–6 (1900): 113.
9. Nesterov, *Iz pisem*, 143.
10. Nesterov, *Davnie dni*, 423.
11. A. A. Rylov, *Vospominaniia* (Leningrad: Khudozhnik, 1960), 117.
12. Tretyakov Archives, 73-221, I. I. Lazarevskii, "Davnie vstrechi s I. I. Levitanym," typescript, July 25, 1925.
13. Prorokova, *Levitan*, 216.
14. S. S. Vermel', *Isaak Il'ich Levitan i ego tvorchestvo* (St. Petersburg: Khudozhest-vennaia literatura, 1902), 7.
15. Nesterov, *Iz pisem*, 143.
16. Prorokova, *Levitan*, 216.
17. Levitan, *Pis'ma*, 128–129.
18. Prorokova, *Levitan*, 213.
19. Kruglov, *Isaak Levitan*, 254.
20. Quoted in Vermel', *Isaak Il'ich Levitan i ego tvorchestvo*, 16.
21. O. L. Knipper-Chekhova, *Vospominaniia i perepiska* (Moscow: Iskusstvo, 1972), 51.
22. Levitan, *Pis'ma*, 106.
23. Korovin, *Vospominaniia*, 289.
24. Koroleva, *Soprikosnovenie sudeb*, 350.
25. Kruglov, *Isaak Levitan*, 243.
26. PSS Letters, 9:347.
27. Tretyakov Gallery Archives, 73-36.
28. RGB Archives, S. G. Kara-Murza, "'Poprygun'ia' A. P. Chekhova i salon S. P. Kuvshinnikovoi," doklad v obshchestve imeni Chekhova 1928 (15 marta v dome uchenykh).

NOTES TO EPILOGUE   235

29. Korovin, *Vospominaniia*, 149.
30. Kruglov, *Isaak Levitan*, 250.
31. Goloushev, *Zhizn' i tvorchestvo*, 74.
32. Vermel', *Isaak Il'ich Levitan i ego tvorchestvo*, 6.
33. S. S. Vermel', *Evrei v Moskve*, http://libatriam.net/read/307322, 54.
34. Goloushev, *Zhizn' i tvorchestvo*, 82–83.
35. Koroleva, *Soprikosnovenie sudeb*, 353.
36. *Mir Iskusstva*, vol. 4 (1900): 29–32.
37. Koroleva, *Soprikosnovenie sudeb*, 353.
38. Quoted in Konchin, *Zagadochnyi Levitan*, 310–311.
39. PSS Letters, 9:556.

Notes to Epilogue

1. Donald Rayfield, "The Forgotten Poetess: Tat'iana L'vovna Shchepkina-Kupernik," *Slavonic and East European Review* 79, no. 4 (October 2001): 601–637.
2. *Russkoe slovo*, September 3 (August 21) 1907.
3. Shchepkina-Kupernik, *Vospominaniia*, 183.
4. Prorokova, *Levitan*, 206.
5. Konchin, *Zagadochnyi Levitan*, 235.
6. Iu. V. Strelnikova, "Nekotorye materialy biografii khudozhnika Adol'fa Il'icha Levitana, brata Isaaka Il'icha Levitana," http://plyos.org/stat/ples-levitan-2009-15.html.
7. Quoted in Konchin, *Zagadochnyi Levitan*, 308.
8. Prorokova, *Levitan*, 9.
9. Nesterov, *Davnie dni*, 413.
10. Prorokova, *Levitan*, 223–224.

BIBLIOGRAPHY

Primary Sources

ARCHIVES:

Manuscript Division of the Russian State Library (RGB)

331-48-72	Kuvshinnikova's letters to Chekhov
331-49-25	Levitan's letters to Chekhov
331-63-25	Shekhtel''s letters to Chekhov
331-93-80	Lidiia Mizinova's letters to Chekhov
331-95-2	Potapenko's letter to Mariia Chekhova, May 31, 1894

LECTURE NOTES:

Kara-Murza, S. G. "'Poprygun'ia' A. P. Chekhova i salon S. P. Kuvshinnikovoi," doklad v obshchestve imeni Chekhova 1928 (15 marta v dome uchenykh).

Moscow State Archive for Literature and Art (RGALI)

1949-1-6	Kuvshinnikova's album and 1883 diary
549-1-302	Levitan's letters to Chekhov brothers, summer 1885
571-1-822	Levitan's letter to Shchepkina-Kupernik, August 23, 1893
571-1-1137	Mariia Chekhova's letter to Shchepkina-Kupernik, January 18, 1895
571-1-1204	Lidiia Iavorskaia's letters to Shchepkina-Kupernik, 1893

TYPESCRIPTS AND PRINTED MATERIALS:

Vermel', S. S. Moskovskoe izgnanie, 1891–1892 gg. Vpechatleniia, vospominaniia. Moscow, 1924.

Pichugin, Z. E. "I. I. Levitan. Iz moikh vospominanii." December 21, 1940.

Tretyakov Gallery Archives

TYPESCRIPTS OF MEMOIRS:

73-219	A. M. Vasnetsov
73-220	I. I. Gorelov
73-221	I. I. Lazarevskii
73-222	D. Prugavin
73-223	A. I. Troianovskaia
73-36	E. A. Teleshova (Karzinkina)

Published Correspondence, Memoirs, Diaries

Chekhov, A. P. *Chekhov v vospominaniiakh sovremennikov*. Moscow: Gos. izd-vo khudo-zhestvennoi literatury, 1947.
———. *Chekhov v vospominaniiakh sovremennikov*. Moscow: Gelios ARV, 2005.
———. *Letopis' zhizni i tvorchestva A. P. Chekhova*. Vols. 1–3. Moscow: Nasledie, 2000–2004.
———. *Literaturnoe nasledstvo*. Vol. 68. Moscow: Nauka, 1960.
———. *Perepiska A. P. Chekhova v trekh tomakh*. 3 vols. Moscow: Nasledie, 1996.
———. *Perepiska s zhenoi*. Moscow: Zakharov, 2003.
———. *Polnoe sobranie povestei, rasskazov i iumoresok v dvukh tomakh*. Moscow: Al'fa-Kniga, 2010.
———. *Polnoe sobranie sochinenii i pisem v tridtsati tomakh* [cited in notes as PSS Works or PSS Letters]. Edited by N. F. Belchikov et al. 30 vols. Moscow: Nauka, 1974–1984.
Chekhov, Mikhail. *Anton Chekhov: A Brother's Memoir*. Translated by Eugene Alper. New York: Macmillan, 2010.
Chekhova, M. P. *Iz dalekogo proshlogo*. Moscow: Gos. izd-vo khudozhestvennoi literatury, 1960.
———. *Pis'ma k bratu A. P. Chekhovu*. Moscow: Gos. izd-vo khudozhestvennoi literatury, 1954.
Chekhov, P. E. *Melikhovskii letopisets: Dnevnik Pavla Egorovicha Chekhova*. Moscow: Nauka, 1995.
Giliarovskii, Vladimir. *Moskva i moskvichi*. Moscow: Astrel', 2010.
Golovin, A. Ia. *Vstrechi i vpechatleniia: Vospominaniia khudozhnika*. Moscow-Leningrad: Iskusstvo, 1940.
Iasinskii, I. I. *Roman moei zhizni*. 2 vols. Moscow: Novoe Literaturnoe Obozrenie, 2010.
Knipper-Chekhova, O. L. *Vospominaniia i perepiska*. Moscow: Iskusstvo, 1972.
Korovin, Konstantin. *Konstantin Korovin vspominaet*. Moscow: Izobrazitel'noe iskusstvo, 1990.
———. *Vospominaniia*. Minsk: Sovremennyi literator, 1999.
Levitan, I. I. *Dokumenty, materialy, bibliografiia*. Edited by A. A. Fedorov-Davydov. Moscow: Iskusstvo 1966.
———. *Pis'ma, dokumenty, vospominaniia*. Edited by A. A. Fedorov-Davydov. Moscow: Iskusstvo, 1956.
Nesterov, M. V. *Davnie dni*. Ufa: Bashkirskoe knizhnoe izd-vo, 1986.
———. *Iz pisem*. Leningrad: Iskusstvo, 1968.
Polenov, V. D. *Pis'ma, dnevniki, vospominaniia*. Moscow-Leningrad: Iskusstvo, 1950.
Rylov, A. A. *Vospominaniia*. Leningrad: Khudozhnik, 1960.
Sakharova, Evgeniia, ed. *Vokrug Chekhova*. Moscow: Pravda, 1990.
Shchepkina-Kupernik, T. L. *Vospominaniia*. Moscow: Zakharov, 2005.
Tenisheva, M. K. *Vpechatleniia moei zhizni*. Leningrad: Iskusstvo, 1991.

Secondary Sources

Bartlett, Rosamund. *Chekhov: Scenes from a Life*. London: Free Press, 2005.
———. *Tolstoy: A Russian Life*. Boston-New York: Houghton Mifflin Harcourt, 2011.

Blakesley, Rosalind P. and Margaret Samu, eds. *From Realism to the Silver Age: New Studies in Russian Artistic Culture*. DeKalb, IL: NIU Press, 2014.

Blakesley, Rosalind P. and Susan E. Reid, eds. *Russian Art and the West: A Century of Dialogue in Painting, Architecture, and the Decorative Arts*. DeKalb, IL: NIU Press, 2007.

Broude, Norma, ed. *World Impressionism: The International Movement, 1860–1920*. New York: H. H. Abrams, 1990.

Bychkov, Iu. A. *Prosto Chekhov*. Moscow: Muzei Cheloveka, 2008.

Diaghilev, S. P., and A. N. Benois, eds. *Mir iskusstva*. St. Petersburg: Izd. M.K. Tenishevoi i S. I. Mamontova, 1899–1904.

Dmitrieva, N. *Moskovskoe Uchilishche Zhivopisi, Vaianiia i Zodchestva*. Moscow: Iskusstvo, 1951.

Domiteeva, V. M. *Konstantin Korovin*. Moscow: TERRA, 2007.

Ely, Christopher. "The Origins of Russian Scenery: Volga River Tourism and Russian Landscape Aesthetics." *Slavic Review* 62, no. 4 (Winter 2003): 666–668.

———. *This Meager Nature: Landscape and National Identity in Imperial Russia*. DeKalb, IL: NIU Press, 2009.

Evdokimov, Ivan. *Levitan i Sof'ia Kuvshinnikova*. Moscow: Algoritm, 2007.

Ezerskaia, N. A. *Peredvizhniki i natsional'nye khudozhestvennye shkoly narodov Rossii*. Moscow: Izobrazitel'noe iskusstvo, 1987.

Fedorov-Davydov, A. A. *Isaak Il'ich Levitan: Zhizn' i tvorchestvo, 1860–1900*. Moscow: Iskusstvo, 1976.

Fetzer, Leland, and Ita Sheres. "The Jewish Predicament of Isaak Levitan." *East European Jewish Affairs* 11, no. 1 (1981): 53–63.

Ginzburg, Izabella. *Levitan*. Leningrad-Moscow: Iskusstvo, 1937.

Goloushev, S. S. [Glagol' i Grabar']. *Levitan: Zhizn' i tvorchestvo*. Moscow: Izdatel'stvo. I. Knebel', 1913.

Golubeva, N. V. "Vospominaniia ob A. P. Chekhove." *Literaturnoe nasledstvo* 68 (1960): 557–574.

Grossman, Leonid. "Roman Niny Zarechnoi." *Prometei* 2. Moscow: Molodaia gvardiia, 1967.

Gusarova, Alla. *Konstantin Korovin*. Moscow: Tret'iakovskaia Galereia, 2012.

Haldey, Olga. *Mamontov's Private Opera: The Search for Modernism in Russian Theater*. Bloomington: Indiana University Press, 2010.

Hayden, Deborah. *Pox: Genius, Madness, and the Mysteries of Syphilis*. New York: Basic Books, 2003.

Hazen, Henry H., MD. *Syphilis: A Treatise on Etiology, Pathology, Diagnosis, Prognosis, Prophylaxis, and Treatment*. St. Louis: C.V. Mosby Co., 1919.

Iakovlev, Leo. *Anton Chekhov: Roman s evreiami*. Kharkov: RA-Karavella, 2000.

Jamison, Kay Redfield. *Touched with Fire: Manic-Depressive Illness and the Artistic Temperament*. New York: Free Press, 1993.

Khlebnova, T. I., editor in chief. *Peredvizhniki: Tovarishchestvo peredvizhnykh khudozhestvennykh vystavok*. Moscow: Art-Rodnik, 2012.

King, Averil. *Isaak Levitan: Lyrical Landscape*. Suffolk: Antique Collectors' Club, 2011.

Konchin, Evgraf. *Zagadochnyi Levitan: Izbrannye stat'i, poiski, nakhodki, gipotezy, problemy*. Moscow: Mediastudiia Respekt, 2010.

Kopshitser, Mark. *Polenov*. Moscow: Molodaiia gvardiia, 2010.

Koroleva, Iu. A. *Soprikosnovenie sudeb: A. P. Chekhov i I. I. Levitan.* Moscow: Gilios ARV, 2011.

Kruglov, V. F. *Isaak Levitan.* St. Petersburg: Zolotoi vek, 2012.

Kuzicheva, A. P. *Chekhovy: Biografiia semi'i.* Moscow: Artist, rezhisser, teatr, 2004.

Litavrina, M. G. *Iavorskaia, bezzakonnaia kometa.* Moscow: MIK, 2008.

Lobanov, Sergei. *Polenov i Levitan.* Moscow: Gos. izd-vo khudozhestvennoi literatury, 1925.

Maegd-Soep, Carolina de. *Chekhov and Women: Women in the Life and Work of Chekhov.* Columbus: Slavica Publishers, 1987.

Maltseva, F. S. *Aleksei Kondratievich Savrasov.* Leningrad: Khudozhnik RSFSR, 1984.

Nathans, Benjamin. *Beyond the Pale: The Jewish Encounter with Late Imperial Russia.* Berkeley: University of California Press, 2002.

Nenarokomova, Nina. *Pavel Tret'iakov i ego galereia.* Moscow: Art-Rodnik, 2011.

Podushkov, D. L. *Chekhov i Levitan na Udomel'skoi zemle.* Tver': SFK-ofis, 2010.

Prorokova, S. *Levitan.* Moscow: Molodaia gvardiia, 1960.

Prytkov, V. A. *Chekhov i Levitan.* Moscow: Izd-vo Gos. Tret'iakovskoi galerei, 1948.

Rayfield, Donald. *Chekhov: A Life.* New York: Henry Holt and Company, 1998.

———. "The Forgotten Poetess: Tat'iana L'vovna Shchepkina-Kupernik." *Slavonic and East European Review* 79, no. 4 (October 2001): 601–637.

———. [Reifild, Donal'd]. *Zhizn' Antona Chekhova.* Moscow: Nezavisimaia gazeta, 2005.

Rieber, Alfred J. *Merchants & Entrepreneurs in Imperial Russia.* Chapel Hill: University of North Carolina Press, 1982.

Rogger, Hans. *Russia in the Age of Modernisation and Revolution, 1881–1917.* London and New York: Longman, 1983.

Rostislavov, A. A. *Levitan.* St. Petersburg: Izdatel'stvo N.I. Butkovskoi, 1911.

Sarab'ianov, D. V. *Istoriia russkogo iskusstva vtoroi poloviny XIX veka.* Moscow: Izdatel'stvo Moskovskogo universiteta, 1989.

———. *Russkaia zhivopis' XIX veka sredi evropeiskikh shkol.* Moscow: Sovetskii khudozhnik, 1980.

Scheijen, Sjeng. *Diaghilev: A Life.* Translated by Jane Hedley-Prole and S. J. Leinback. London: Profile, 2009.

Smith, Douglas. *Former People: The Final Days of the Russian Aristocracy.* New York: Farrar, Straus and Giroux, 2012.

Stanislavskii, K. S. *Pis'ma, 1886–1917.* Edited by M. N. Kedrov. Vol. 7 of *Sobranie sochinenii v vos'mi tomakh.* Moscow: Iskusstvo, 1960.

Stites, Richard. *Serfdom, Society, and the Arts: The Pleasure and the Power.* New Haven: Yale University Press, 2008.

Stowall, H. Peter. *Literary Impressionism: James and Chekhov.* Athens: University of Georgia Press, 1980.

Sukhikh, Igor.' *Chekhov v zhizni.* Moscow: Vremia, 2010.

Thom, Burton Peter, MD. *Syphilis.* Philadelphia and New York: Lea & Febiger, 1922.

Tolstoy, Helena. "From Susanna to Sarra: Chekhov in 1886–1887." *Slavic Review* 50, no. 3 (Fall 1991): 590–600.

Tretyakov Gallery exhibition catalog. *Isaak Levitan: k 150-letiiu so dnia rozhdeniia.* Moscow: Gosudarstvennaia Tret'iakovskaia galereia, 2010.

Turkov, A. M. *Levitan*. Moscow: TERRA, 2001.

Valkenier, Elizabeth. "Opening Up to Europe: The Peredvizhniki and the Miriskusniki Respond to the West." In *Russian Art and the West: A Century of Dialogue in Painting, Architecture, and the Decorative Arts*, ed. Rosalind P. Blakesley and Susan E. Reid. DeKalb, IL: NIU Press, 2007.

———. *Russian Realist Art, the State, and Society: The Peredvizhniki and Their Tradition*. Ann Arbor: Ardis, 1977.

Vermel,' S. S. *Evrei v Moskve*. http://libatriam.net/read/307322, 54.

———. *Isaak Il'ich Levitan i ego tvorchestvo*. St. Petersburg: Khudozhestvennaia literatura, 1902.

Von Laue, Theodore H. *Sergei Witte and the Industrialization of Russia*. New York: Atheneum, 1974.

INDEX